Vision Sensors and Edge Detection

edited by

Francisco J. Gallegos-Funes

Vision Sensors and Edge Detection
Edited by Francisco J. Gallegos-Funes

Republished by InTech
Janeza Trdine 9, 51000 Rijeka, Croatia

Publishing Process Manager Jelena Marusic

Technical Editor Goran Bajac

Cover Designer Martina Sirotic

Additional hard copies can be obtained from orders@intechopen.com

Vision Sensors and Edge Detection, Edited by Francisco J. Gallegos-Funes
p. cm.
ISBN 978-953-307-098-8

For EU product safety concerns:
IN TECH d.o.o., Prolaz Marije Krucifikse Kozulić 3, 51000 Rijeka, Croatia,
info@intechopen.com or visit our website at intechopen.com.

Contents

Preface

Vision sensors are commonly video cameras with integrated signal processing and imaging electronics. They are used in several applications, such as, industrial inspection, quality control, and design and manufacturing diagnostic. Inspection applications include edge and object detection, image direction, alignment, object measurement, object position, optical character recognition, color recognition, etc.

This book reflects this diversity by presenting a selection of recent developments within the area of vision sensors and edge detection. There are two sections in this book. The first section presents vision sensors with applications to panoramic vision sensors, wireless vision sensors, and automated vision sensor inspection. The second one shows image processing techniques, such as, image measurements, image transformations, filtering, and parallel computing.

We sincerely hope this book with plenty of comprehensive topics of vision sensors and edge detection development will benefit readers to bring advanced brainstorming to this field. Finally, the editors would like to thank the authors, who have invested so much effort to the publication of this book.

Editor

Francisco J. Gallegos-Funes
National Polytechnic Institute of Mexico
Mexico

1

Panomorph Based Panoramic Vision Sensors

Simon Thibault
Laval University & ImmerVision
Canada

1. Introduction

During the last few years, innovative vision strategies to generate and control image mapping have been successful in producing high-resolution digital vision system. This success has, in turn, increased the interest in the high-resolution camera and absolute measurement with high-resolution larger and larger field of view. New generation of panoramic vision sensor includes multi-cameras, catadioptric panoramic lenses, panoramic annular lenses, fisheye lenses, anamorphic wide-angle attachments, and panomorph lenses. The increasing trend to use panoramic vision sensors in various applications is driven by the need to have complete information about our surrounding environment. Seeing of what surrounds a vehicle can directly increase our safety, providing hemispheric vision endoscopic functionality can provide a higher patient confort and better surgeon procedure. Indeed, video and vision processing have become a growing technologies deployed in various applications. Increased integration of electronic and optical components and the declining prices of electronics in general are the primary enablers of this trend. This chapter presents the most recent advances in the panomorph vision sensor from the sky lens to the multi-task cameras.

A panomorph lens is a hemispheric wide-angle lens with enhanced resolution in a predefined zone of interest. Because panomorph lenses feature an optimal pixel-per-degree relationship, the resulting vision systems provide ideal area coverage, which in turn reduces and maximizes the processing. For example: a single panomorph sensor on the front of a vehicle could provide all the information necessary for assistance in crash avoidance, lane tracking, early warning alerts, parking aids, road sign and pedestrian detection, as well as various video monitoring views for difficult areas such as blind spots.

2. From the "Sky Lens" to the "Panomorph Lens"

It is well know that adding a large negative meniscus element mounted on the head of a compact positive component will create a system with a long back focal distance and a short focal length, which is namely a reversed telephoto (Kingslake, 1985). These lenses were very popular, since any lens used with a 35 mm camera had to have a back focal length of at least 35-40 mm to clear the rocking mirror on the camera. Consequently, any lens with a focal length of less than approximately 40 mm is a reversed telephoto type. Fortunately, this type is favourable for a wide-angle field of view. Wide-angle lenses are generally considered to be lenses with a field of view greater than 60 degrees.

However, for angles larger than 100 degrees, the barrel distortion becomes difficult to correct. With an extended field of view, the reversed telephoto lens will cover a hemispherical field -- we will call such lens a fisheye lens. This lens is not really an extension of a wide-angle lens. The fisheye lens has inherent large distortion, but this distortion should not be considered an aberration but rather the result of the projection of a hemispheric field on a circle, which is not possible *without* distortion.

The classical example of a fisheye lens "type" of image formation is an actual fish eye under water (Miyamoto, 1964). Robert W. Wood described in his book, *Physical Optics* (1911), a water-filled pinhole camera that was capable of simulating a fish's view of the world (Figure 1A). Bond added a hemispheric lens with a pupil at the centre of the curvature in place of the water (Figure 1B). In 1924, Hill developed his Sky lens by adding a diverging meniscus lens (Figure 1C) before the hemispheric lens to improve the field curvature (thereby reducing the Peztval sum). This lens was a first prototype of the modern fisheye lenses (Figure 1D) which was patented by Schultz (1932) and Merté (1935). Some 40 years later, the now famous afocal wide-angle door viewer was patented (Artonne, 2005).

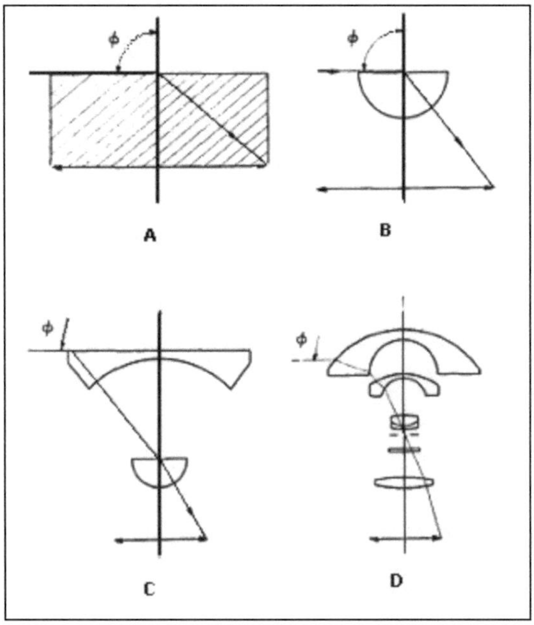

Fig. 1. Development of wide angle views (Miyamoto, 1964)

At that time a severe drawback was encountered when the fisheye was facing up or down, because in these positions the subject of interest might have appeared at the edge (large angle) of the field where the barrel distortion is very large. We will see later in this chapter how the modern high-resolution lens design can now control this distortion, to improve the field coverage of a panoramic lens and solve this historical concern.

Motivated by the need to record a distortion-free panoramic image, the flat cylinder perspective was born (Greguss, 1991). The panoramic feature is different from the fisheye in that there is no longer imaging of a hemispheric field onto a circle, but instead a 360° cylindrical field of view imaged onto a two-dimensional annular format (Figure 2). This kind of image will still suffer from severe image deformation. The annular image produced by such a geometrical transformation will not produce (theoretically) radial distortion (cylinder height); however, the horizontal (circle circumference) direction will suffer from compression, from the edge to the centre of the image plane (see figure 4).

Fig. 2. Flat cylinder image

There are many known panoramic viewing optical arrangements that use this cylinder perspective. In particular, Greguss' patent was one of the most promising approaches (Greguss, 1986). The main disadvantages are the limited dimension of the annular image on the sensor and the blind zones above and below the device.

Another approach to getting a flat cylinder perspective is to rotate a conventional camera around the vertical axis. This technique requires several frames with proper synchronization for the camera to complete a full rotation. This method is useful and widely used today in the production of high-quality panoramic photography. The technique is time consuming because it requires a long time for the image acquisition and extensive image processing to stitch all the images together.

Ideally, the goal in panoramic imaging is to be able to capture the entire scene in a single image from a single camera. This ideal imaging system would allow more than one hemisphere to be visible, similar to some insects' vision system (Horridge, 1977) as figure 3. In reality, this can be achieved by using a multi-lens system with individual consecutive fields-of-view, totally covering a hemisphere. One of the major problems with this concept is the very complex image processing required, particularly on a moving platform.

Reflective optics offers an alternative to panoramic imaging. A standard camera placed below a convex mirror will image a large field-of-view, the properties of which will depend on the shape of the reflective surface (Chahl and Srinivasan, 1997). This approach has been used predominantly for producing panoramic TV displays. The projected images are captured by another equivalent optical arrangement (the reversibility property of light). For such an arrangement, the surface shape is not important as long as the projection mirror and the acquisition mirror are equivalent.

Systems with spherical and conical mirrors have been used to capture wide-angle images for robotics and machine vision devices (omnidirectional vision system). The mirror shape design is important and can provide a global image on the sensor, which presents a polar image with elevation and azimuth linearly distributed to radius and angle respectively.

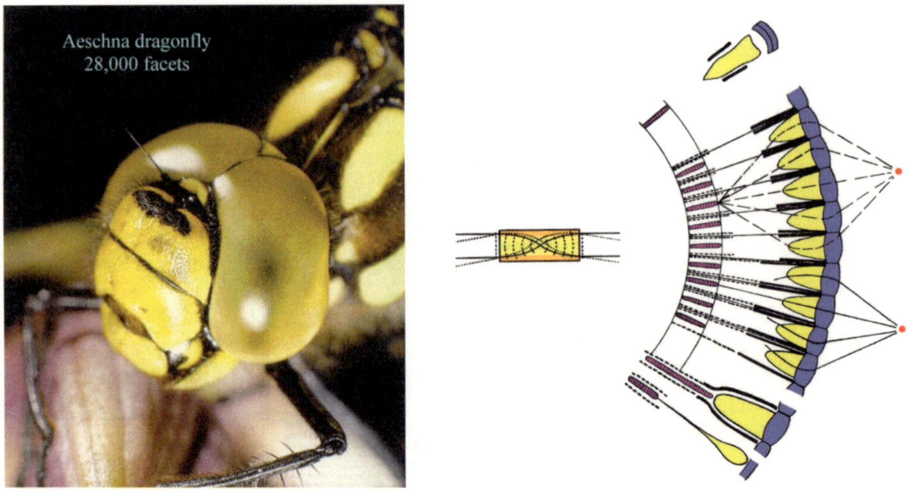

Fig. 3. Compound eye allow light to travel through several facts before striking the light sensitive surface.

These systems are called omnidirection camera. An omnidirectional camera (from omni, meaning all) is a camera with a 360-degree field of view in the horizontal plane (flat cylinder perspective), or with a visual field that covers (approximately) the entire sphere. Omnidirectional cameras are important in areas where large visual field coverage is needed, such as in panoramic photography and robotics. In robotics, omnidirectional cameras are frequently used for visual odometry that can be used for navigation. Visual odometry is the process of determining the position and orientation of a robot or a car by analyzing the associated camera images. It has been used in a wide variety of robotic applications, such as on the Mars Exploration Rovers.

Modern panoramic lenses are now able to add a distortion control which is considered a major enhancement in panoramic vision (Thibault, 2005). The distortion is not anymore a consequence of the panoramic vision that we have to manage but it can be used to increase the sensor performances. Specifically, the panoramic sensor can be designed to increase the number of pixels in the zones of interest (ZOI) using a distortion control approach. By controlling the distortion, we change the effective magnification of the sensor in the ZOI. Consequently, the sensor can be custom-designed to meet real and very specific needs required by a specific application.

The Panomorph lens uses this distortion control approach and an anamorphic image mapping to provide a unique full hemispheric field coverage. In contrast to other types of panoramic imagers that suffer from blind zone (catadioptric cameras), low-image numerical aperture and high distortion, the Panomorph lens uses distortion as a design parameter, in order to provide a high-resolution coverage where it is needed. It also features an anamorphic image mapping of the full hemispheric field, which produces an ellipse image footprint rather than a circle (or annular footprint) as do all other types of panoramic imagers. This feature provides an immediate 30% gain in pixels used on the sensor (the ellipse footprint matches the 4:3 ratio of a standard CCD or CMOS imager). The combination of distortion control and anamorphic design provides an important gain in resolution, and an advantage over all other types of panoramic imagers. The figure 4 shows the panoramic lens evolution over the last 30 years. Each panoramic image falls on the same sensor size from the same scene. The Panomorph lens image (right), clearly covers a larger area on the sensor.

Fig. 4. Panoramic Lens Evolution

3. Panomorph lens theoretical background

Panomorph (from the Greek word **pan** meaning *all*, **horama** meaning *view*, and **morph** meaning *form*) lens is a particular type of panoramic lens. It features two important parameters, the amount and location of the resolution within the panoramic field of view.
The human eye could be the most common panomorph device. Indeed, with its field of view close to 180°, we can classify the human eye as a very wide angle imager. Furthermore, the visual acuity is not linear across the field of view.

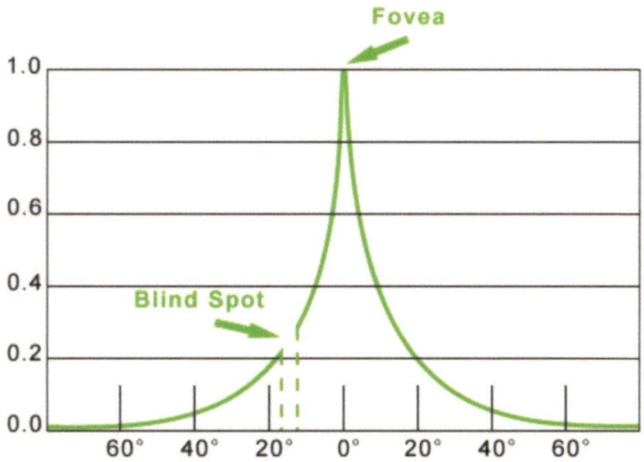

Fig. 5. The relative acuity of the right human eye (horizontal section) in degrees from the fovea

Natural evolution shaped the human eye to provide a higher visual acuity where needed. The fovea located in the center of the macula region of the retina sees only the central two degrees of the visual field but takes up over 50% of the visual cortex. The fovea is an augmented resolution (Ross 2006) area in the middle of the field of view.
As opposed to human eyes, in the case of a panomorph lens, the resolution is directly related to the lens magnification and not the variable sensor pixel size. The magnification variation across the field of view can be described by the distortion function or by the relation between the hemispheric field of view projected into the sensor plane.
The following figure shows different images capture by different panomorph lenses which have various resolution distribution within the field of view. In each case, the original scene is the same, only the location of the augmented resolution is different ranging from the center to the edge of the field of view.

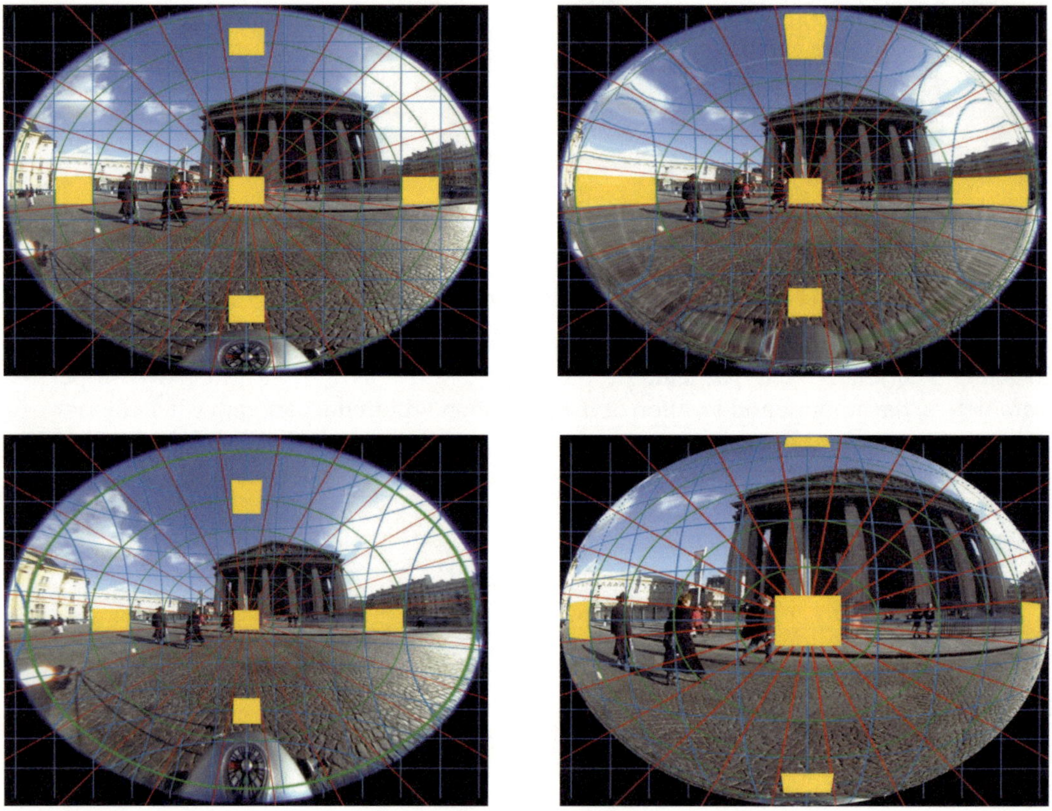

Fig. 6. Resolution zone by zone - Examples

3.1 Hemispheric field of view projected into a plane

A panoramic lens has inherent distortion, however this distortion should not be considered as an aberration but as a result of projection of a hemisphere on a plane. Consider the angle of incidence θ (in radian) of a light coming from an object at a long distances, the coordinates in the image plane of the image will be (u,v). The lens will image the objet has a function of the angle θ. This function can be linear but not necessarily (u=v= constant X θ for an ideal fisheye). In the case of a panomorph lens, the relation between u and v is proportional to the anamorphic ratio but a polynôme within θ. The variation across the field of view (θ) is the main advantageous of the panomorph lens. The derivative of u or v with respect to θ is the lens resolution. For a fisheye, the resolution is constant (ideal fisheye) but for a panomorph lens, the resolution is also a polynomial function with θ.

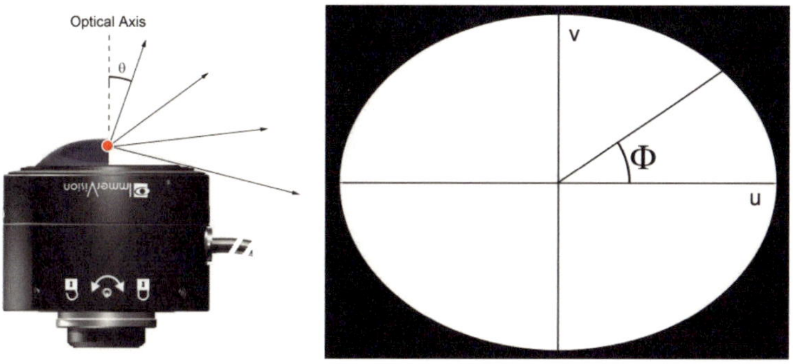

Fig. 7. Image Formation.

3.2 Panomorph image projection model

To be effective, the panoramic video-viewing library corrects image distortion from cameras equipped with a panomorph lens for display and control of one or more standard views, such as a PTZ (Figure 8) in real time. The viewing library allows simultaneous display of as many views as desired from one or more cameras (Figure 9).

Consequently, the viewing process must unwrap the image in real time in order to provide views that reproduce real world proportions and geometrical information. The algorithms can be customized and adapted for each specific application, which is then related to human vision (display) or artificial vision (analytic function).

The viewing process can be decomposed into three main steps:

- the definition of the panomorph geometrical model (PGM) associated to each custom panomorph lens application;
- the projection of the recorded image onto the PGM to provide a discretized mapping based on the recorded pixel position on the sensor;
- finally, the rendering, which uses well-known standard rendering techniques.

Fig. 8. Real-time distortion-free display (left: original image produced by the panomorph lens).

Fig. 9. Four PTZ views (left), and two strips to display a 360° total camera surround in one single view (right).

The image produced by each panomorph lens is unique to its application. The image mapping can be defined by a unique 3D geometrical model (Panomorph Geometrical Model, or PGM), which reproduces the panomorph lens design characteristics.

The PGM is a geometric representation (surface) of the relative magnification of the lens as a function of the angles, expressed in spherical or polar coordinates (R, θ, ϕ). In other words, if the surface is represented by vector R, the length of the vector is proportional to the lens magnification (resolution) in the direction defined by the polar angles. This model depends on lens parameters such as the anamorphic ratio, the field of view, as well as position, size, and the magnification in the zones of interest.

The PGM is a mathematical transformation of the image footprint I(u,v) into a surface S(R, θ, ϕ) representation using spherical coordinates:

$$I(u,v) \rightarrow S(R,\theta,\phi), \tag{1}$$

The anamorphic ratio is used only as a scale factor, which is function of the angle ϕ (Figure 10) This angle defines the azimuth direction of the recorded image taken by the panomorph lens.

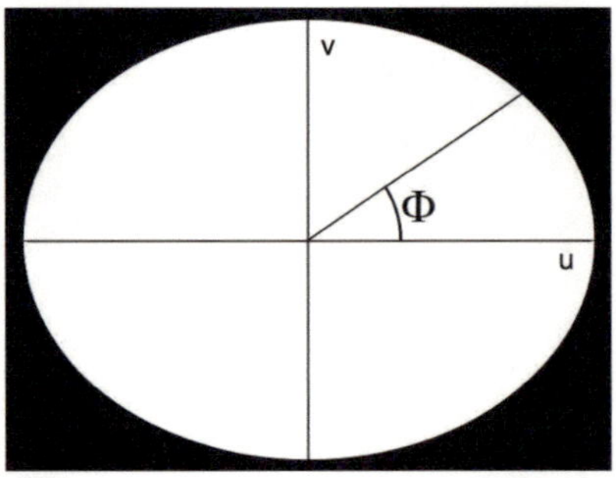

Fig. 10. Panomorph elliptical footprint I(u,v); scaling defined with ϕ angle.

The field of view, or FOV, determines the angular limit (theta) of the PGM. The FOV of the panomorph lens is about 180 degrees and can be more or less, depending on the application. Figure 11 shows two schematic PGMs with 180 degree and 250 degree FOVs respectively.

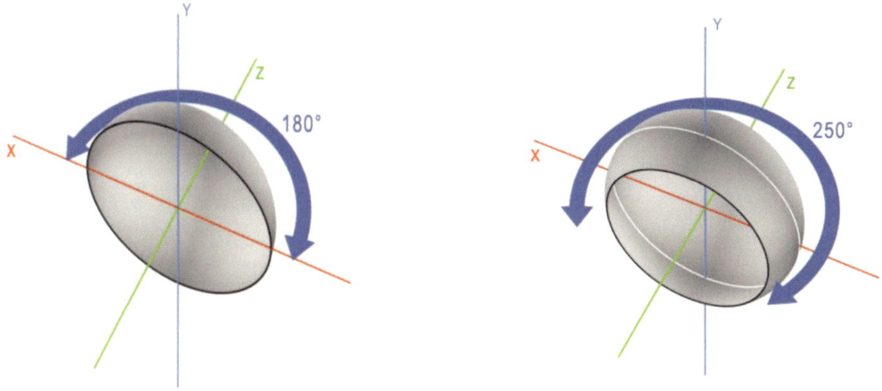

Fig. 11. PGM with 180 and 250 degree FOVs respectively.

The panomorph lens uses distortion or resolution as a design parameter, in order to provide high-resolution coverage in a specific zone of interest. In other words, the FOV can be divided into different zones, each with a defined resolution as discussed in the next section. To illustrate the impact of the distortion profile on the PGM, we will study two examples. In these examples, the FOV is 180 degrees wide, the zone of interest is 30 degrees wide, and the resolution is two times greater in the zone of interest than it is in the rest of the FOV (2:1). From one example to another, only the position of the zone of interest changes.

Example 1:

The first example is based on the design of a front view camera (Figure 12). In this case, the zone of interest is the central part of the image, even though the entire 180-degree FOV is still recorded. A panomorph lens with this feature can be used on a cell phone (for video conferencing) or on an ATM surveillance camera.

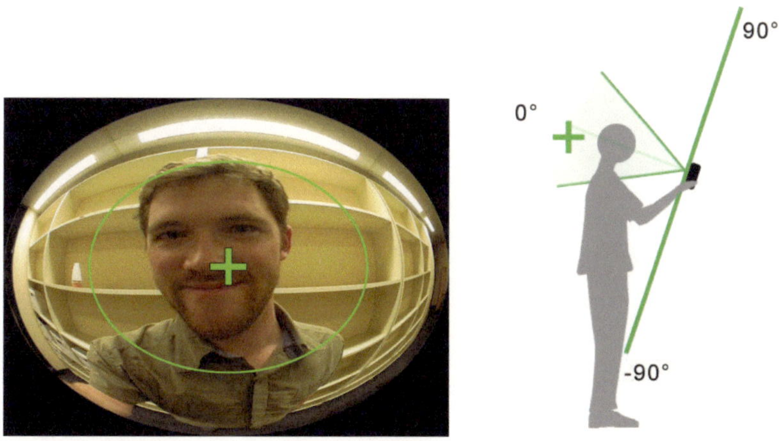

Fig. 12. Panomorph lens for a front-view camera.

The panomorph lens resolution in the central zone is twice that of the resolution in the periphery. Figure 13 shows the image footprint with the proper resolution for each zone. On the left of Figure 13, we have a Cartesian plot of the resolution as a function of the view angle (defined from the centre). We note that a transition zone exists between the central and the periphery areas. Theoretically, this transition can be very small, but as the panomorph lens is a real product, this transition can extend over 10 degrees.

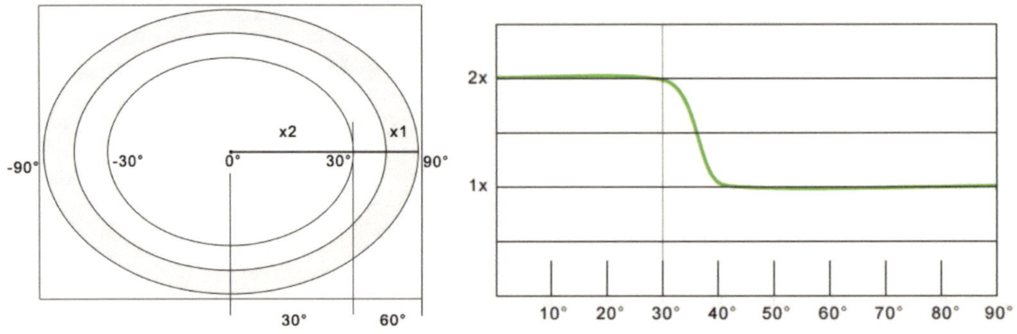

Fig. 13. Image footprint (left) and resolution graph (right) for the front-view panomorph lens.

As defined, the PGM in the polar coordinate space represents the resolution of the panomorph lens, or a surface in space where the spatial resolution is constant in terms of azimuthal (θ) direction. Mathematically, it means that the Cartesian graph (Figure 13, right side) is transposed into the spherical coordinate plane. Figure 14 shows the 3D PGM representation.

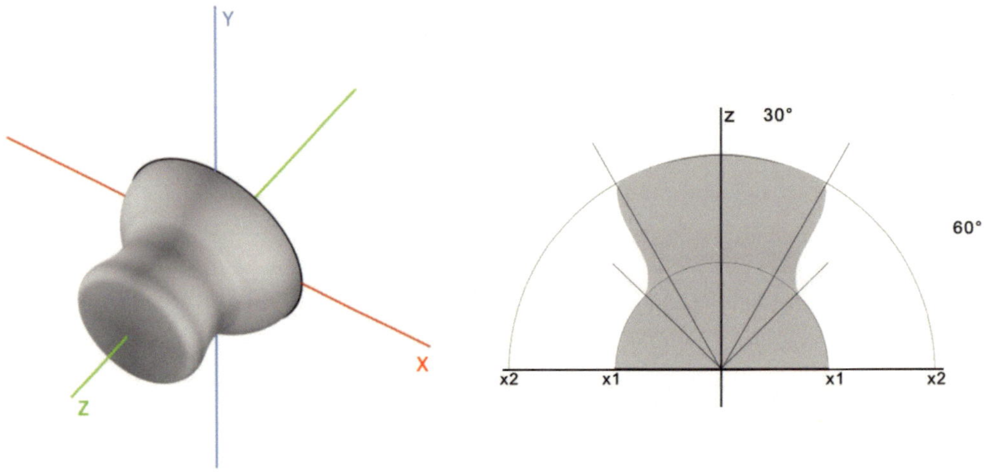

Fig. 14. 3D PGM (left), 2D view in Y-Z plane.

Example 2:

The second example demonstrates a panomorph lens optimized for video conferencing, where the zone of interest is not in the centre but on the edge of the field of view. Figures 15, 16 and 17 show the image footprint, the resolution and the corresponding PGM respectively.

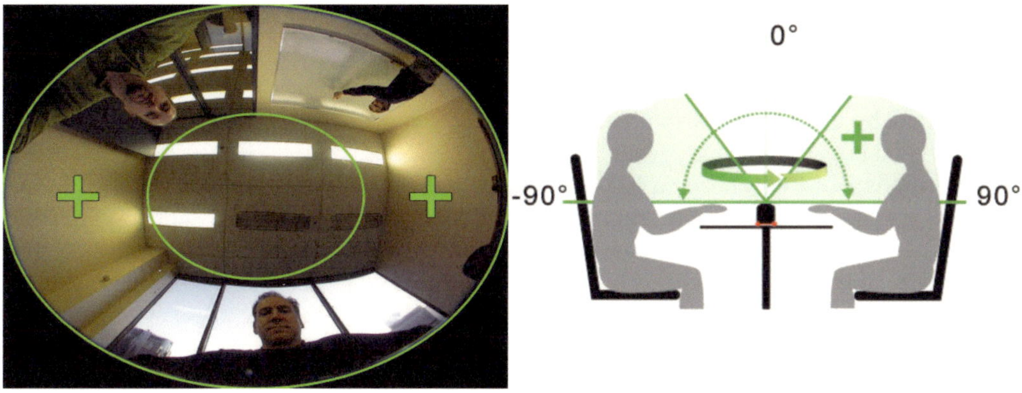

Fig. 15. Panomorph lens for video conferencing.

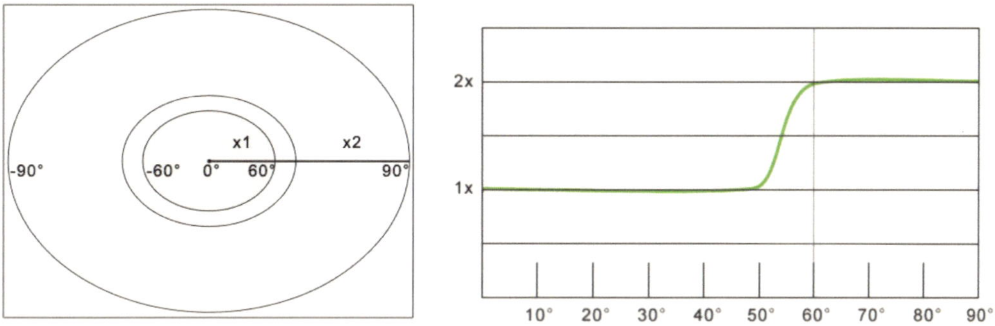

Fig. 16. Image footprint (left) and resolution graph (right) for the video-conferencing panomorph lens.

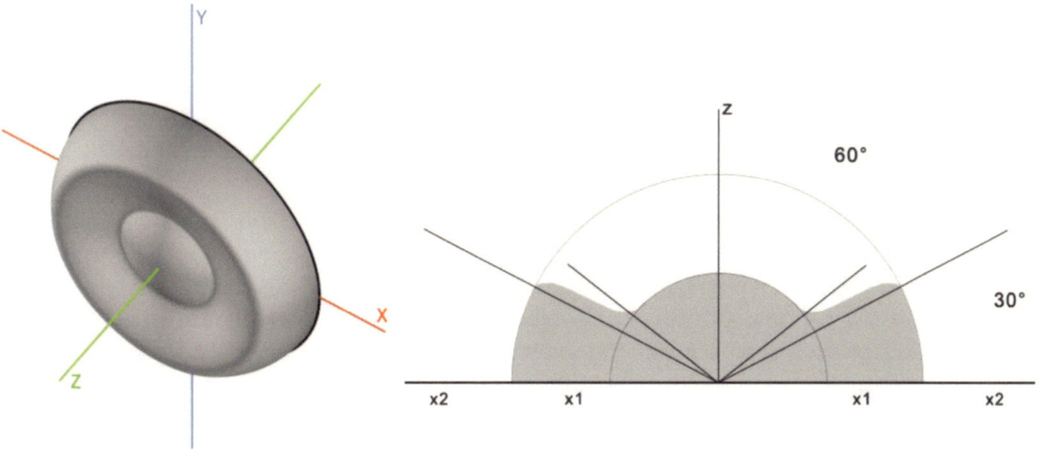

Fig. 17. 3D PGM (left), 2D view in Y-Z plane (right).

The panomorph lens can be used with any sensor format (VGA, XGA, etc.) as long as the lens performance matches the Nyquist frequency of the sensor. The number of pixels will have an impact on the discretization of the model for the PGM. Up until now, the PGM has been defined by a continuous mathematical surface, however, on sensor we have a finite number of pixels.

The continuous PGM will be sampled by the pixels. The number of pixels required to map the entire surface of the PGM is equal to the number of pixels on the sensor. Figure 18 shows a 2D sampling of the PGM using only 22 elements. You should note that the pixel dimension is constant over the entire PGM, and the pixels are always perpendicular to the direction of regard (direction of the vector R). With a higher number of pixels, the discrete PGM will be closer to the continuous PGM, as shown in Figure 19.

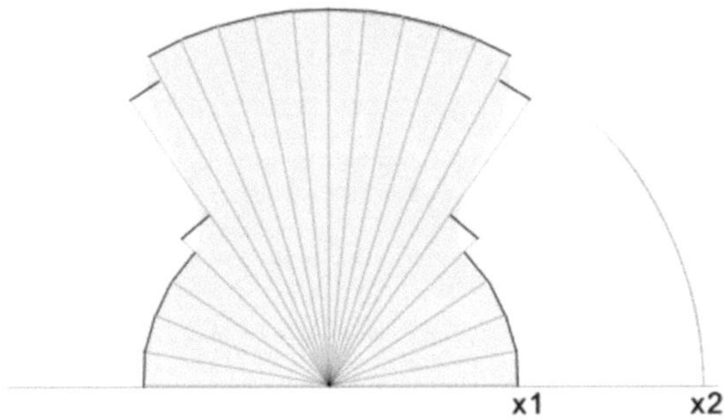

Fig. 18. Discrete PGM with 22-unit (pixels) sample

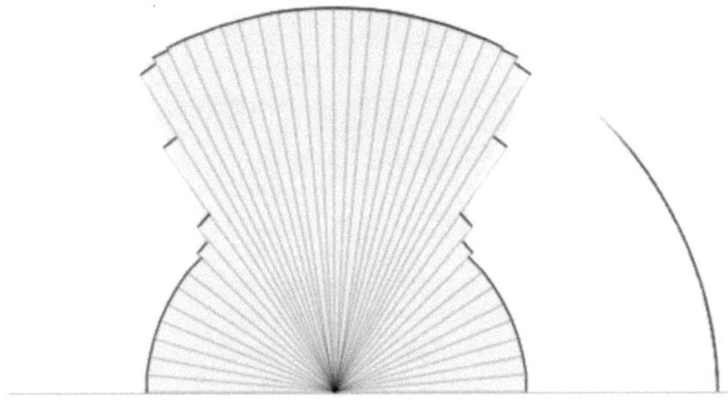

Fig. 19. Discrete PGM with 44-unit (pixels) sample

The image I (u,v) from the panomorph lens is projected onto the PGM, as shown in Figures 18 and 19. The final result is a discrete surface. The PGM is mapped with the panomorph image and can then be viewed using any classical 3D visualization techniques.

Each pixel of the panomorph image is projected onto a discrete element of the PGM. The pixel position in the 3D space (on the surface) represents the real object position in the recorded scene. The projection uses the adapted azimuthal projection technique (see *MathWorld*--A Wolfram Web Resource) with anamorphosis and distortion parameters added.

The final goal is to visualize the recorded scene without distortion. The PGM can be used to achieve this goal using a standard algorithm (Horaud & Monga, 1995). A virtual camera is placed at the central position (0,0,0). Viewing the scene with this virtual camera requires first selecting the angle (θ,ϕ) of viewing direction. Figure 20 shows two cameras pointing in two different directions. The camera pointed at the centre of the PGM will show a total of four elements (1D, 16 elements in 2D). The camera pointed at the edge of the PGM will show only two elements. This is the distortion effect. The resolution is twice in the centre than it is on the edge. A zoom can also be applied to change the Δθ and provide virtual functionalities.

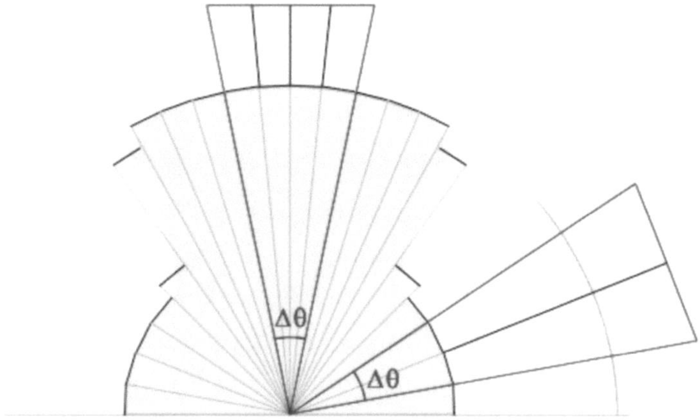

Fig. 20. Virtual camera at the centre of the mapped PGM

The following Figure 21 shows the final projection on a 2D plane of each virtual view. This 2D view can be sent to a display monitor.

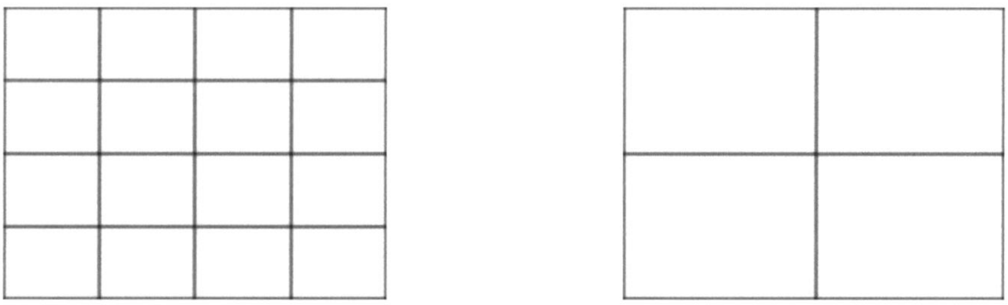

Fig. 21. Viewing pixel as a function of the pointing direction of the virtual camera (left = centre, right =edge).

3.3 Panomorph lens resolutions

As shown in the last section, an efficient panomorph lens, the coverage area is divided into different zones. A specific resolution requirement as well as a particular field of view is defined for each individual zone. Figure 1 shows a typical surveillance scenario.

For this particular scenario, the panoramic coverage area is divided into five adjacent and continuous zones. Zones B and C are symmetrical with the vertical axis. The five adjacent zones, while still providing full hemispheric coverage together, each feature a different resolution requirement, as the most significant objects are in Zone B. (Zone B in a surveillance application enables facial recognition and identification.) An object in Zone B is

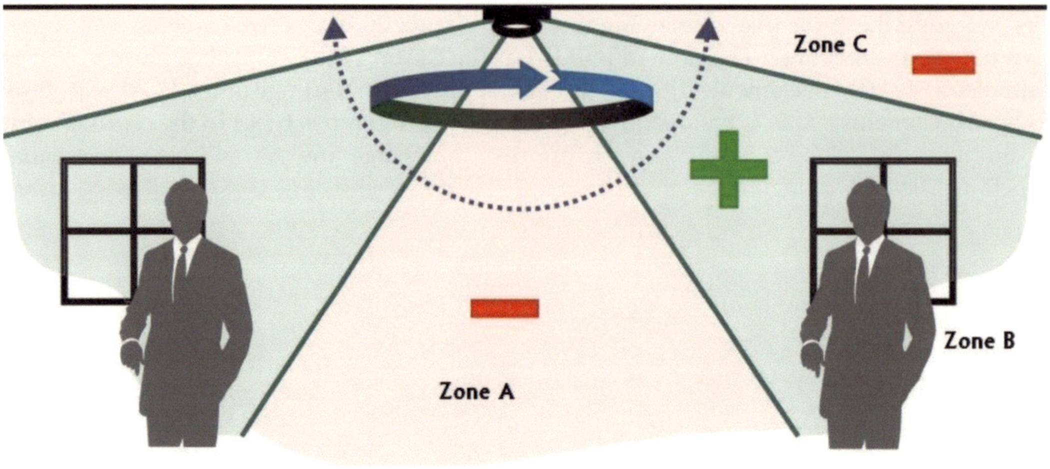

Fig. 22. Specific security zones.

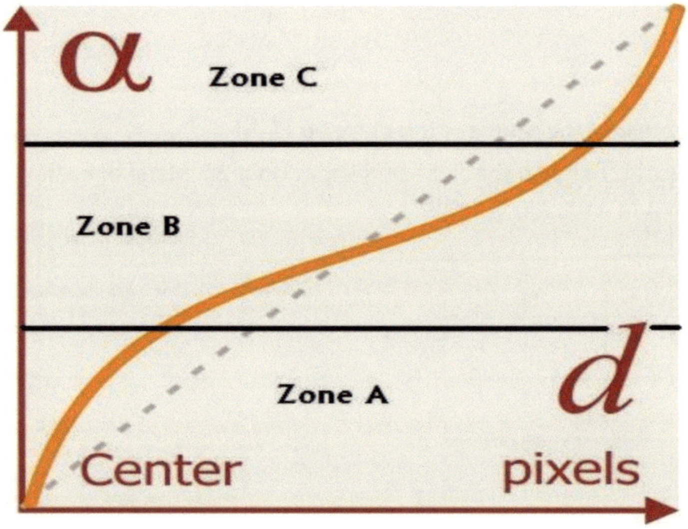

Fig. 23. The ideal FOV (α) vs. the position (d) on the sensor for the scenario presented in Figure 22.

also more distant from the camera than an object in Zone A. This means that the relative angular resolution (pixels/degree) in Zones A and B should be different.

For example: A human face in Zone B (located at 60 degrees from the vertical axis) will subtend an angle by half the amount that it would in Zone A (above the camera). To get the same number of pixels per face in both Zones A and B, the pixels/degree in Zone B must be twice the pixels/degree in Zone A. This means that the number of pixels required on the sensor to image Zone B is twice the number of pixels required to image Zone A.

It is difficult to evaluate the exact resolution as a function of the sensor, because this would depend on the resolution chosen for the zone of interest. However, if we define i zones (1 to

n) where each zone covers an angle (θ_I, up to θ_{max}) with a number of pixels (N_i, #pixels is the number of pixel used on the sensor) we can describe the resolution (R_i) for each zone:

$$R_i = \frac{N_i}{\theta_i} \tag{2}$$

with the following limit conditions:

$$\sum_{i=1}^{n} N_i = \sum_{i=1}^{n} R_i \cdot \theta_i = \#\,pixels \tag{3}$$

and

$$\sum_{i=1}^{n} \theta_i = \theta_{max} \tag{4}$$

showing that if you increase the resolution in the *i* zone, the result is less resolution in the other zones. The figure 24 and 25 show a graphical view of the process. In real system, a transition zone exists to connect but zone A-B and B-C. Consequently, these zones should also be considered within the calculation.

4. Panomorph based vision sensor - examples

As a new technologie, the design of a Panomorph based visual sensor requires particular attention. The following section shows a number of examples that illustrated how the panomorph vision sensor can be used in various applications. These examples can also be considered as starting point to design any custom applications.

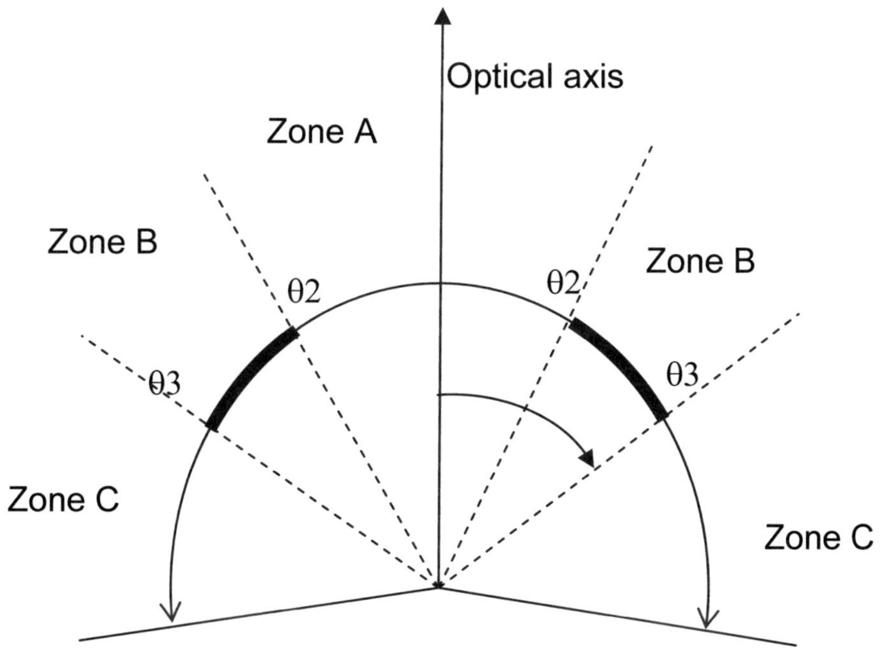

Fig. 24. Zone definition

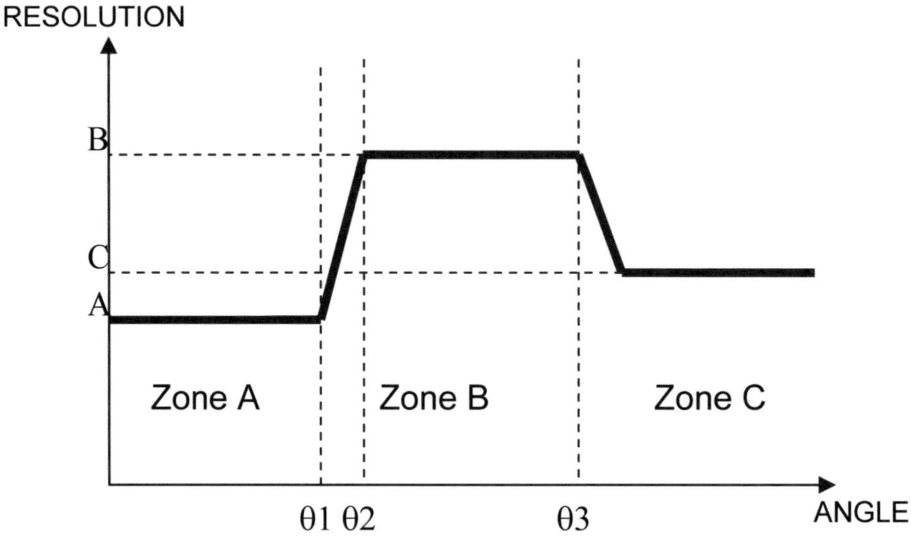

Fig. 25. Resolution graph per zone

4.1 Surveillance & security applications

The security application is probably to most important up to now for the panomorph technology. To illustrate an application, we can base the panomorph lens resolution requirement on the detection range. The detection range is a function of the number of pixels on the target used to recognize, identify or detect. Based on Figure 22, we define the range detection vertically (height of the people). Range detection can also be defined as the number of horizontal pixels on the target (width). This last definition uses the number of pixels on a circumference at a given angle to define, for a given FOV angle, the detection range. Because the number of pixels on the perimeter of an ellipse is larger than on the circumference of a circle, the detection range for horizontal detection is also always larger when using a Panomorph lens.

In order to understand the detection range we will further develop this example. We want to define the distance from which the face of a human body might have at least 30 pixels per dimension. Using simple mathematical expressions we can calculate this distance for each FOV angle. The distances then define a surface that is illustrated in Figure 26 for a 360 KPx CCD sensor (NTSC).

This example shows how a well designed Panomorph lens can provide a facial recognition range as far as 3 meters away from the camera (3 m calculated on the floor for a 30 pixel/face resolution). This means an extended range for detecting, identifying and recognizing a target. This extended range also provides an extended coverage rate for following the target. The red circle marks the detection area, which has a constant pixel to angle function similar to a fisheye lens.

Defining the resolution requirements for surveillance systems is not necessarily a simple task. A rough indication of the practical meaning of resolution can be defined from the following correlation between the resolution criteria and pixels on the sensor (Johnson's criteria) (Johnson, 1958).

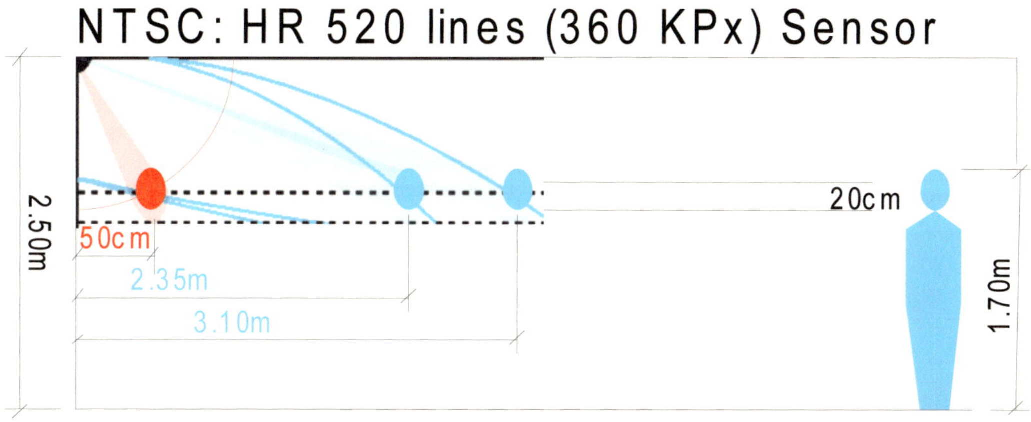

Fig. 26. Detection range (30 pixels/dimension). The red curve (constant) corresponds to a lens with a constant resolution on this sensor. The blue curves correspond to a Panomorph lens axis (two curves for long and short axis).

The criteria usually used are:

Detection	2 pixels per target
Orientation	3 pixels per target
Aim	5 pixels per target
Recognition	8 pixels per target
Identification	12-16 pixels per target
Recognition with 50% accuracy	15 pixels per target
Recognition with 90% accuracy	24 pixels per target

4.2 Automotive

The increasing trend to use vision sensors in transportation is driven both by legislation and consumer demands for higher safety and better driving experiences. Awareness of what surrounds an automotive vehicle can directly affect the safe driving and maneuvering of that vehicle. Consequently, panoramic 360° imaging is becoming an industry prerequisite. However, to obtain a complete view of the area around a vehicle, several sensor systems are necessary. This section presents how panomorph based vision sensor can satisfy the needs of various vision applications with only one sensor or panomorph lens configuration.

Consider the simplified situation of a camera flush-mounted on the front of a vehicle. The goal of this section is to determine the appropriate parameters of the panomorph lens and the projection (un-warping) algorithms which correspond to the application requirements.

Lens and algorithm parameters to be determined:

- Field-of-view (FoV) of the application
- Lens distortion, anamorphosis ratio and resolution
- Lens mathematical model and calibration
- Software projection type, treatment and performance

Applications requirements:

- Lane departure and lane curvature recognition:

  - Large FoV: Larger than 180° to increase the robustness of line tracking
  - Projection algorithms to rectify the image and provide a straight line for recognition
- Collision warning using vehicle detection:
  - Large FoV to detect oncoming vehicles from all sides of a road intersection
  - 2-meter vehicle width must cover 10 to 40 pixels wide
- Road sign detection and recognition:
  - Large FoV to detect road signs at different locations
  - 0.5-meter sign width must cover 12 to 24 pixels wide
- Blind zone avoidance:
  - Large FoV: Larger than 180° to avoid blind zones
  - Projection algorithms to rectify the image and provide a user-friendly view to the driver

A collision warning application needs to have at least 10 pixels to define a two-meter wide object (vehicle). As defined by Thibault (Thibault, 2007), a fisheye lens is 5.04 pixels/degree on the targeted sensor (1280*960) over the entire FoV.

$$\alpha = \frac{Size_p}{Res_{P/\circ}} \tag{5}$$

Where $Size_p$ is the object size on the sensor in pixels, and $Res_{p/o}$ is the resolution of the system lens-sensor in pixels/degree: A 10-pixel object represents a α=1.98° FoV and a 40-pixel object represents a α=7.9 FoV.

$$d = \frac{Size_m}{Tan(\alpha)} \tag{6}$$

Where $Size_m$ is the object size in meters: A 10-pixel object is d=57.8 meters from the car. This means that a two-meter wide object will illuminate 10 pixels or more when the objects are within 57.8 meters.

With a panomorph lens, we can customize the distortion mapping to provide better resolution where required. Based on Figure 27, we define three zones of interest in the horizontal plane. The first area of interest in which we would like to increase resolution is the forward view.

For a collision warning application, there is a need to see farther on both sides when crossing an intersection. One needs also to see farther right in the middle, to detect a vehicle in the same lane. Figure 27 shows the resulting areas of interest over the entire FoV. The resolution of this type of lens is 8.42 pixels/degree on the targeted sensor within the zone of interest (Thibault, 2007). Using formulas (5) and (6), a 10-pixel object would be 97 meters from the car, a 70% increase compared to a theoretical fisheye lens within the same area of interest.

The safe distance between two vehicles is based on the driver's reaction time; some governments have determined that this reaction time is at least the distance travelled during two seconds. We can deduce the following formula:

$$ds_{meter} = 0.56 \times V_{km/h} \tag{7}$$

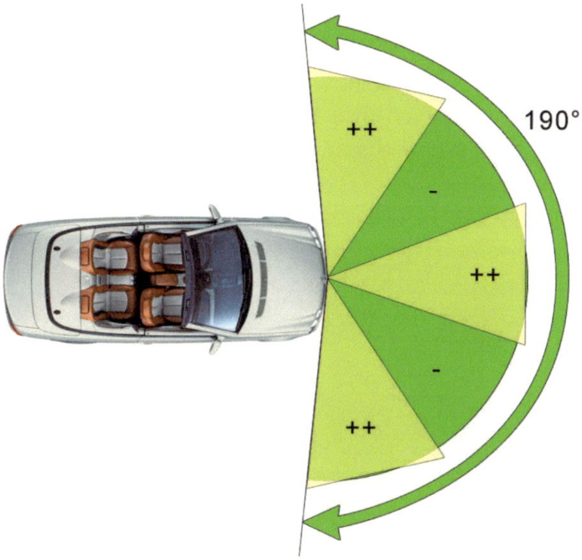

Fig. 27. Augmented-resolution areas of interest for a panomorph front view lens.

Speed	50 km/h	70 km/h	90 km/h	110 km/h	130 km/h
Safe distance	28 m	39 m	50 m	62 m	73 m

Table 1. Safe distance between two vehicles at conventional speed limits

Road sign detection and recognition applications need to have at least 12 pixels to define road signs of widths from one meter up to 1.5 meters.

With a fisheye lens, using formulas (5) and (6):

- For a one-meter wide road sign, a 12-pixel object is 24 meters from the car and a 24-pixel object is 12 meters from the car.
- For a 1.5-meter wide road sign, a 12-pixel object is 36 meters from the car and a 24-pixel object is 18 meters from the car.

With a panomorph lens, using formulas (5) and (6):

- For a one-meter wide road sign, a 12-pixel object is 40 meters from the car and a 24-pixel object is 21 meters from the car.
- For a 1.5-meter wide road sign, a 12-pixel object is 60 meters from the car and a 24-pixel object is 30 meters from the car.

Again, because of the specific panomorph resolution pattern suggested in this case study, panomorph optics will increase the distance in its areas of interest (++ areas on Figure 27) by a factor of 70% compared to a theoretical fisheye lens.

For side views (blind spot monitoring), a higher resolution image will significantly enhance the viewing for long distance objects and vehicles on the periphery.

For example, to avoid a blind zone at a garage entrance created by vehicles parked on the street side.

Using the PGM (section 3.2), different software projection types can be created, depending on OEM requirements. The two following figures show ways to display a view of the intersection to the driver while avoiding the blind zone created by a parked vehicle. This

type of projection is simply a pixel displacement that has been computed during the calibration phase on a production chain. This can be hard coded in a lookup table in the camera module. No special CPU horse power is required.
Figures 29 and 30 show ways to avoid a blind zone. The driver can see everything in the blind zone using his/her on-board display. The panomorph lens design suggested in this

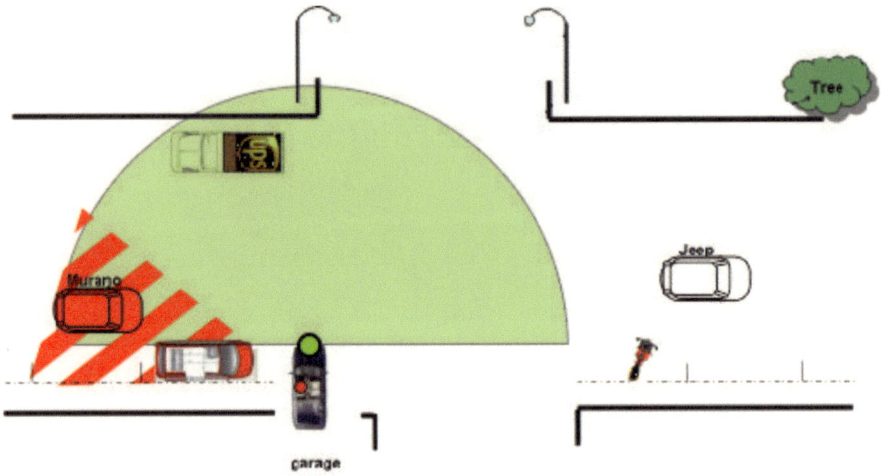

Fig. 28. Panomorph coverage of a blind zone created by a parked vehicle

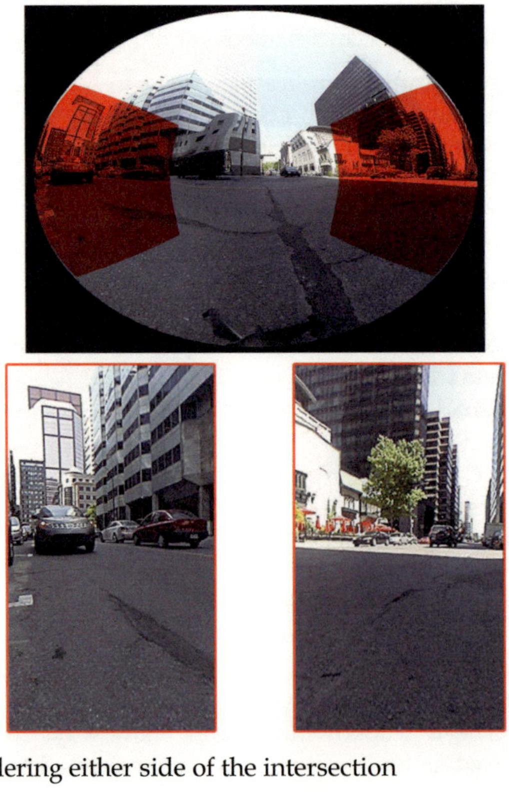

Fig. 29. Two views rendering either side of the intersection

Fig. 30. 190° strip integrating full intersection

example increases the resolution of objects along the border and right in the middle. Where the resolution is higher, the camera is able to see for a longer distance. The panomorph distortion is optimized for this type of application. The driver is able to see far down each side of the street.

The final example for automotive is one could mount four (4) panomorph lenses all around the vehicle to provide a complete view with the added benefits of panomorph technology's augmented resolution (figure 31).

4.3 Endoscopy

The last example of this section is about medical imaging. Researchers and physicians are always looking for the most effective and least invasive techniques to benefit the patient. For example, single-incision laparoscopic surgery - which is a critical advancement in minimally-invasive surgery (MIS), may soon become a preferred method. Minimally invasive surgical procedures or examinations require increasingly sophisticated devices to explore the interior of the patient's body while limiting the impact on the human body.

Recently, optic miniaturization and sensor improvements in size and resolution have led to the development of new smaller and improved videoscopes for medical imaging in various procedures. These modern visual instruments benefit from sensor miniaturization to increase their resolution up to 1.3Megapixel (HD).

Even with such high resolution, the endoscopic vision remains quite different than human vision, especially regarding the field of view and the type of viewing projection. The limited field of view produces poor visualization for the clinician and increases the scope manipulations and procedure time. These drawbacks have driven industry to design

Fig. 31. View of area surrounding vehicle using four (4) panomorph lenses.

endoscopes with a larger field of view. Several optical systems have been developed featuring convex mirrors, prisms or wide angle lenses to meet large field of view requirements. However most of these optical systems suffer from low resolution or poor quality. A particular concern in the optical design of these types of wide angle imager is the uniformity of the image quality and the fact that the more the field of view is enlarged, the more distortion is created on the viewing display.

Recently a new approach that can play a significant role in improving endoscopic procedures based on the use of the Panomorph technology have been proposed (Roulet, 2010).

During an open surgery, the surgeon uses the wide field of view of his eyes to analyse the situation. He has a bird's eye view of the surgery and he always has his tool in his field of view. However in MIS, using a standard endoscope causes a narrow viewing angle (figure 32). With its wide field of view, the panomorph lens increases the coverage of the operating area. Then, the surgeon observes a hemispheric field of view in the front of the endoscope.

By increasing the coverage, this device decreases the number of manipulations and repositioning of tools and endoscope (figure 33). For example, by placing the endoscope near the insertion point, the surgeon has an overview of the whole body cavity. He can well appreciate each tool position in the operating area.

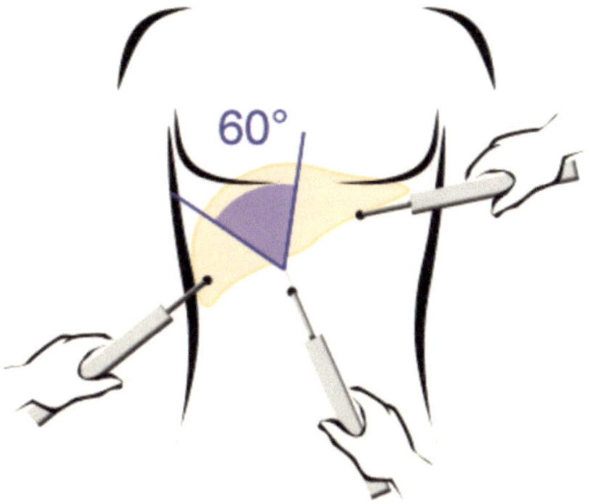

Fig. 32. Cholecystectomy procedure field of view with a classic laparoscope

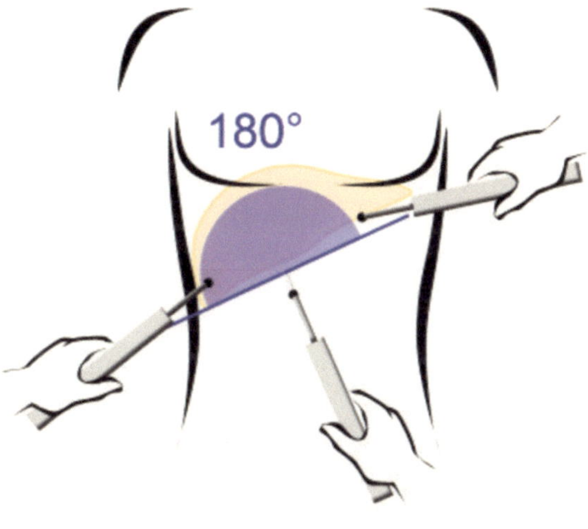

Fig. 33. Cholecystectomy procedure field of view with a panomorph laparoscope

Furthermore, the panomorph endoscope displays more anatomical landmarks which help to localise the dissection plan and increases the perception of depth. Being able to keep an eye on his/her tools all along the procedure is a major improvement for the surgeon, to avoid manipulation mistakes.

For MIS, we could design a laparoscope panomorph lens with augmented resolution in the center. This resolution distribution enhances the operating area (center area) while keeping the large field to survey the whole scene. The following figures (34-35) show the simulated panomorph lens images with increased resolution in the center. This augmentation is close to human eye behaviour. Figure 36 shows the normalised resolution ratio of the lens (pixels ratio/degrees) across the field of view. The resolution along the center is 3 times higher than in the periphery. Consequently the object's magnification in the center is larger and more details can be analysed in this part of the image.

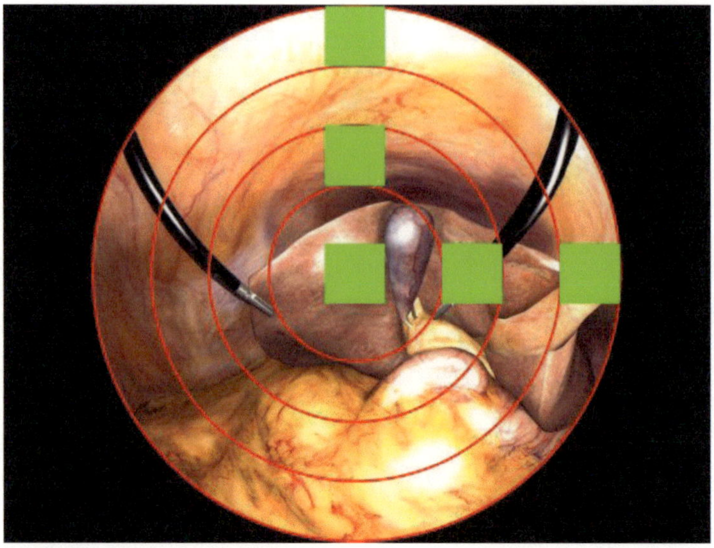

Fig. 34. Linear resolution wide angle lens

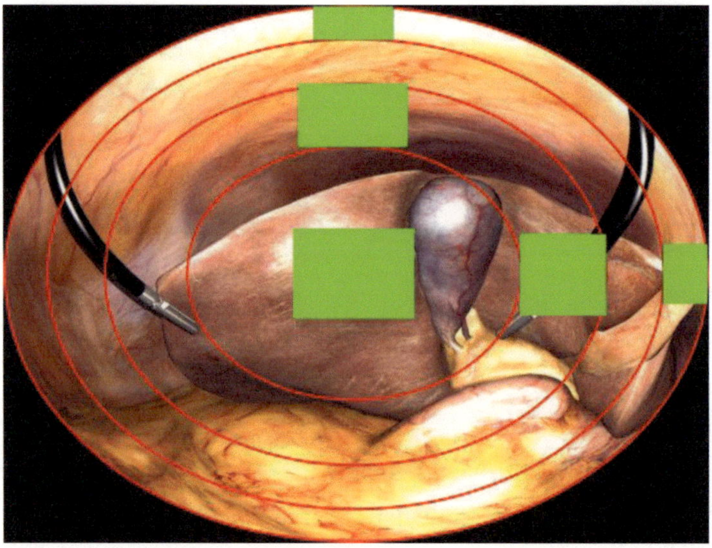

Fig. 35. Panomorph lens with an augmented resolution in the center and 4:3 anamorphic ratio

The image display on the screen for the surgeon is an improved representation of the image captured by the panomorph lens and the sensor. The associated video-viewing algorithms will correct the image distortion to provide a rectilinear view (or a more natural view). These unwarping algorithms project pixels from the endoscope sensor to the display and produce one or more standard virtual views in real time. The viewing algorithms allow simultaneous display of as many views as desired from one endoscope as shown in figure 37.

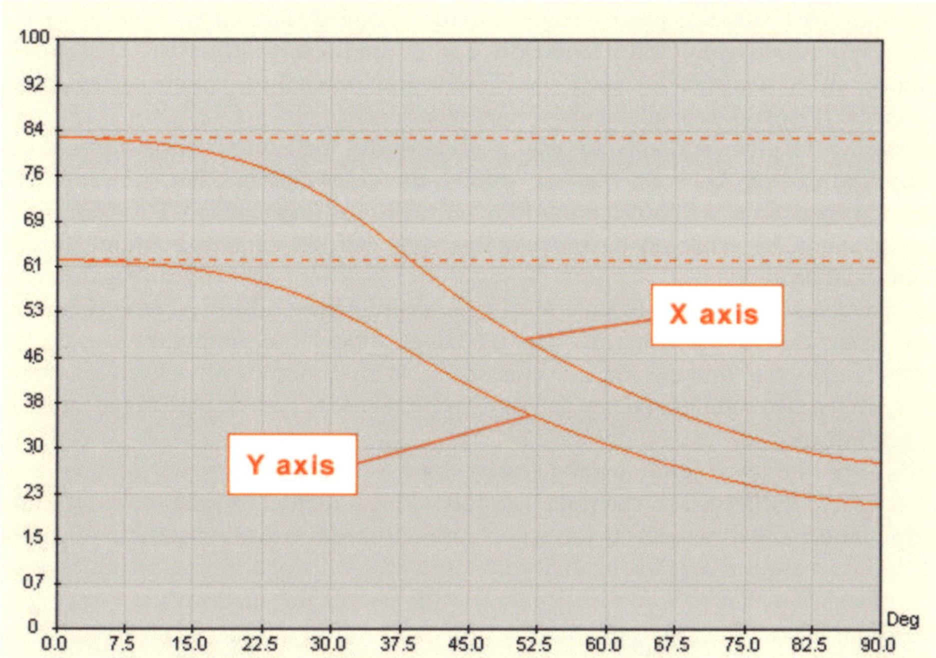

Fig. 36. Normalized resolution across the field of view

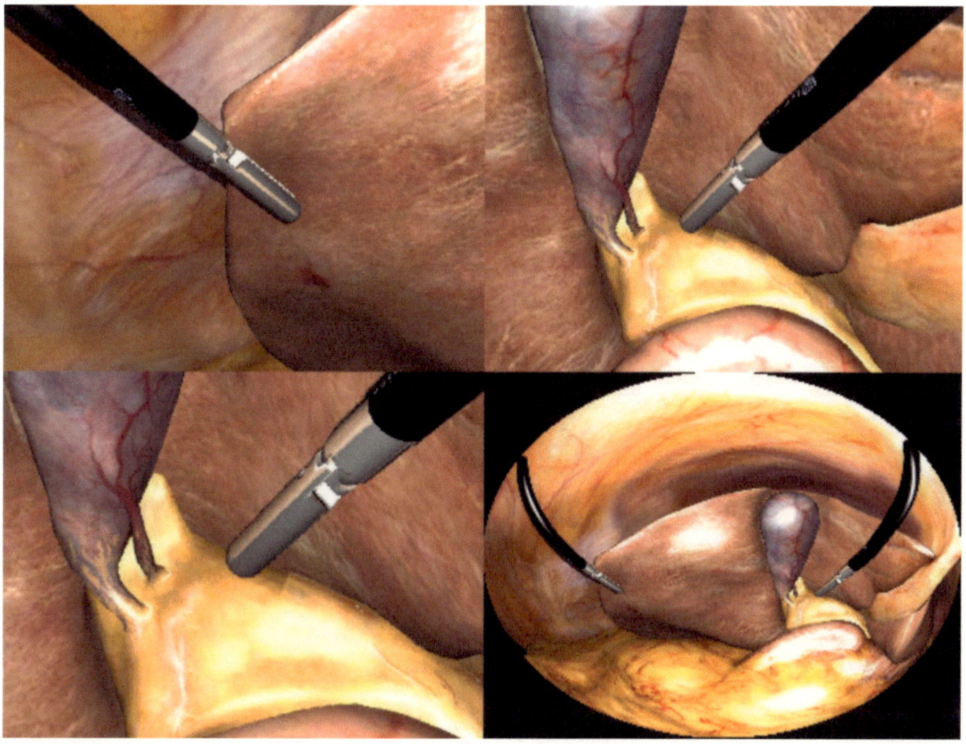

Fig. 37. Different views processed from the same endoscope

Consequently, the viewing process unwarps the image in real time in order to provide views that reproduce real world proportions and geometrical information. These projection algorithms can be adapted for each specific surgical procedure, which is then related to human vision (display) or artificial vision (analytic function).

It is possible for the surgeon to easily choose the best view (projection algorithm configuration) which best fit his/her psycho-motor skills, his/her position and the intervention conditions without having to manipulate the laparoscope. For example, trocar positioning could be achieved by moving the view (virtual camera) without moving the panomorph laparoscope.

Surgeons and assistants have to deal with counter-intuitive endoscope manipulations. For example, in the case of a laparoscope with a 30 degree view, by rotating the laparoscope the assistant changes the viewing angle of the scene. With panomorph technology, views are based on image processing, and virtual camera movements can be performed without any endoscope movement.

Moreover, the surgeon could arrange each view on several screens to have a global overview of the surgery. For example, the following screen configuration well known in flight simulation software respects the aspect ratio, proportion and orientation of each object and would increase the surgeon's perception of depth and surrounding positions. Previous work demonstrates that panoramic visualisation increases the surgeon's accuracy (Naya et al, 2008). In this case the panoramic view consists in different videos calculated from only one laparoscope which provides a surrounding view of the working area in real time. This concept is presented in figure 38.

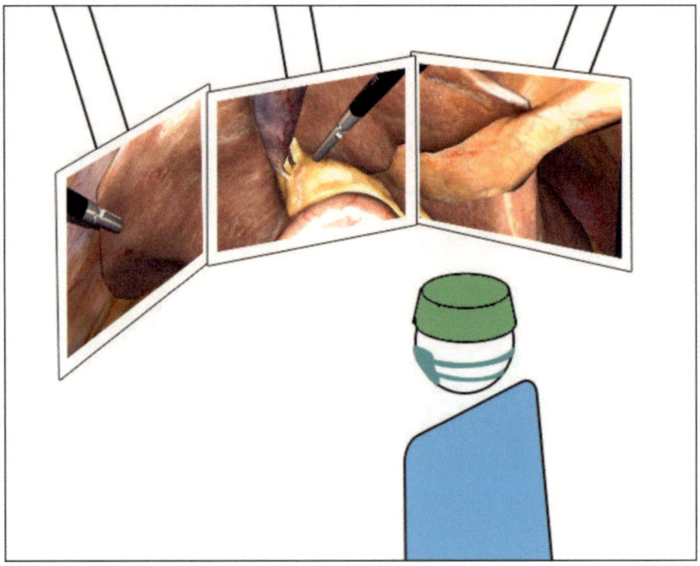

Fig. 38. Immersive screen configuration sample

5. Conclusion

Panomorph lens development has led to new types of panoramic imager that can be customized to enhance any panoramic imager application. The design features full hemispheric coverage, better use of sensor areas and increased resolution in the zone of interest. During the last few years, several research teams have developed custom applications using the Panomorph lens differentiator. This chapter has presented state of the art example of recent development using this technology. Panomorph lens based sensor make application more and more feasible in various application fields. Combines with proper viewing process, the Panomorph sensor can play a significant role in the future of visual sensor.

The viewing process is composed of three steps. The first step is the definition of the panomorph geometrical model (PGM) associated with each custom panomorph lens application. The second step is the projection of the recorded image onto the PGM to provide a discretized mapping based on the recorded pixel position on the sensor. The third is a final rendering based on an azimuthal projection technique. The algorithms developed over the years have been optimized for use on small CPU and memory, enabling embedded processing. The algorithms are available thru a SDK running on Linux and Windows operating systems, and can be ported to many processors and systems.

In conclusion, a panoramic imaging sensor contributes most to our perception of the world. Several sensor systems are necessary to obtain a complete vision of the environment around a vehicle, a robot, an airplane, or a security vehicle; however, a 360° visual sensor using panomorph lenses is probably one of the most promising ways to fuse many sensors into one, and thus reduce risk and cost.

6. References

Artonne, JC. , Moustier, C., Blanc, B., (2005) US Patent 6,844,990. Method for capturing and displaying a variable resolution digital panoramic image, issued, January 18, 2005.

Chahl JS and Srinivasan MV., (1997) Reflective surfaces for panoramic imaging. *Applied Optics* Vol. 36, No. 31, pp. 8275-8285.

Greguss P. (1986), Panoramic imaging block for three-dimensional space. US Patent 4,566,763.

Greguss, Pal. (1991), Panoramic Security. *SPIE* Vol. 1509, pp. 55-66 (1991).

Horaud, R and Monga, O., (1995), Vision par Ordinateur - Outils fondamentaux, ,Ed. Hermès.

Horridge GA., (1977), The compound eye of insects. *Sci Am* Iss. 237, p 108-120.

J. Johnson, (1958), Analysis of image forming systems, in Proc. Image Intensifier Symp., pp. 249-273.

Kingslake R. (1985), Development of the photographic objective. *Proc SPIE* Vol. 0531, pp. 60-67, 1985.

Miyamoto K. (1964), Fish Eye Lens, Letters to the Editor. *JOSA*, Vol. 54, pp. 1060-1061, 1964.

Naya, Y., Nakamura, K., Araki, K., Kawamura, K., Kamijima, S, Imamoto, T.,, Nihei, N, Suzuki, H.,Ichikawa, T.,and Igarashi, T., (2008) "Usefulness of panoramic views for novice surgeons doing retroperitoneal laparoscopic nephrectomy," International Journal of Urology, vol. 16, no2, 177-180.

Roulet, P., Konen, P., Villegas, M., Thibault, S., Garneau, P. Y., (2010), "360° endoscopy using panomorph lens technology" in Endoscopic Microscopy V, edited by Guillermo J. Tearney, Thomas D. Wang, Proceedings of SPIE Vol. 7558 (SPIE, Bellingham, WA 2010) 75580T.

Russ, J.C. (2006), The Image Processing Handbook. CRC Press, Inc. Boca Raton, FL, USA, Fifth Edition.

Thibault S., (2005), Distortion Control Offers Optical System Design a New Degree of Freedom. *Photonics Spectra* May 2005, pp. 80-82.

Thibault, S, (2007), "360 degree vision system: opportunities in transportation". Photonics in the Transportation Industry: Auto to Aerospace. Edited by Kazemi, Alex A.; Baldwin, Christopher S. Proceedings of the SPIE, Volume 6758, pp. 67580H.

2

Design of Stereo Omni-directional Vision Sensors with Full Sphere View and without Dead Angle

Tang Yi-ping, Lin Bei, Chen Min-zhi and Sun Jun
Zhejiang University of Technology
China

1. Introduction

As the sensor technology and image processing technology rapidly developped, more and more scholars have paid attention to the panoramic imaging technology. Panoramic imaging technology can be applied to military, medicine, security, etc. Panoramic imaging technology has became an important research topic in the field of computer vision. There are four current methods to obtain panoramic images which are rotation imaging, multi-camera imaging, fish-eye lens imaging and catadioptric imaging. This chapter explores the existing panoramic imaging technology, proposes improved ideas and methods to the original ODVS, which are average angular resolution and second catadioptric imaging technology, and achieves 360°×360° full sphere panoramic image by integrating two images acquired by two symmetrical ODVSs. Experiments confirm that this method can obtain a sphere view field and has important application value in field of video surveillance.

2. Related research

Herman and other scholars, rotated camera around the fixed axis which was perpendicular to the optical axis to shoot multiple image by rotation imaging technology, then stitched these images together to obtain panoramic image. But this method is time-consuming, and dose not meet the real-time requirement. Multi-camera imaging is shown in Fig. 1, the U.S. IMC company have developed multi-camera imaging device wihich uesd a number of cameras capturing images facing different directions, and stitched these images to get panoramic image. Fig. 1(a) is a hemispherical ODVS composed of multi-camera, and this device can obtain video images within a half-sphere; Fig. 1(b) is a sphere ODVS composed of multi-camera, and this device can obtain video images within the entire sphere. The cost of multi-camera device is high, the stitching algorithm is time-consuming, and the computational cost of the implemention of video data fusion is high. Another way to obtain panoramic image is fish-eye, but this approach requires a very short focus, and the vision of the imaging system can be expanded to half sphere or more. However, this imaging technology introduces image distortion, whose model does not meet the perspective projection requirements and could not get the undistorted perspective projection image by the acquired images. In addition, the resolution of the image is uneven and the fish-eye is expensive. Catadioptric ODVS is composed of a CCD camera and a mirror facing the camera. In the horizontal direction, the viewing angle range is 360°, while in the vertical direction there is a blind angle about 120°. KoyasuH has used a pair of hyperbolic mirrors and a projection lens to compose a panoramic vision system, but there was still inherent dead angle. Zhu Feng the researcher of China's Shenyang Institute of Automation also has carried out pioneering research work in this area, and proposed design method with an ordinary camera to achieve omnidirectional stereo vision. This device is low cost, but one of the panoramic video is vague due to shooting two panoramic video images of catadioptric mirror with different depths only by one video camera, and it is still difficult to obtain full sphere panoramic video image without dead angle.

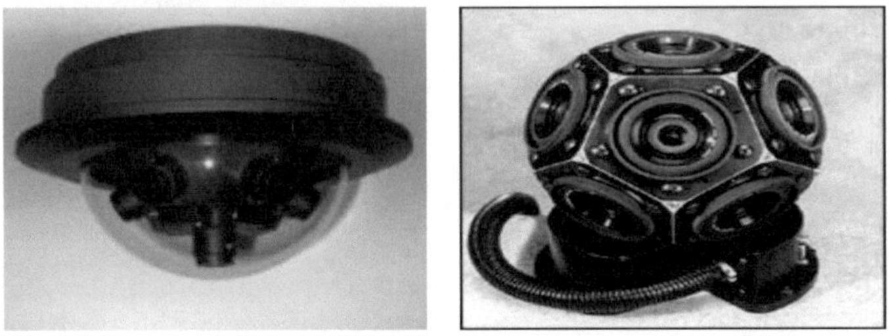

(a) Hemisphere camera device (b) Full sphere camera device

Fig. 1. Multi-camera ODVS device

Viewing deficiencies in the designed system above, this chapter presents a full sphere ODVS structure. It can obtain the sphere panoramic image with the advantages of convenience, real-time processing, novelty, low cost. Work to be done first is to design a kind OVDS with average angular resolution so as to stitching the two ODVS seamlessly later, followed is to analyse the dead angle of the original ODVS in vertical direction to improve the ODVS structure, and then is to stitch 360°×360° video image seamlessly by unwrapping algorithm to achieve a 360°×360° sphere ODVS.

3. Design of the sphere 360°×360°ODVS

3.1 Design of the ODVS structure

The first work is to design ODVS with no dead angle, which can sense all points on hemispherical surface in real-time, and its view scope is the same as the hemisphere device in Fig. 1(a). Omnidirectional vision device is shown in Fig. 2. The second is to configure the camera behind the hyperbolic mirror. The camera's lens fixed at the single view point (SVP) of the catadioptric mirror. There is a small hole at the center of firstly reflection mirror through which camera shoots video information before the firstly reflection mirror; in front of firstly reflection mirror equips a secondary reflection mirror, at the center of which there is also a small hole with a embedded wide-angle lens; omni-directional video information first reflects by firstly reflection mirror, then secondly reflects by secondary reflection mirror, and then through the small hole in firstly reflection mirror images in camera device; in addition, the projects in front of the firstly reflection mirror through the wide-angle lens image between the wide-angle lens and the camera lens, known as the first imaging point, the image point through the small hole in firstly reflection mirror images at the focus of the lens of camera imaging component. This design of ODVS eliminates the dead angle before secondary reflection mirror.

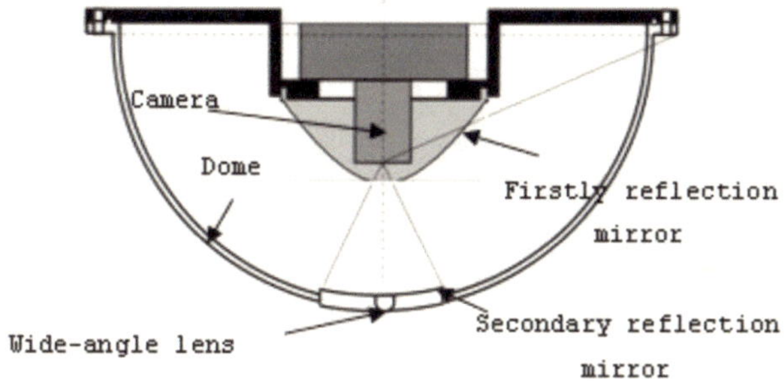

Fig. 2. Structure of ODVS without dead angle

As shown in Fig. 2, we obtain real-time 360°×360° omnidirectional image based on no dead angle ODVS. The following two key issues are to be resolved at least: (1)two devices of no dead angle omnidirectional vision can be combined together as requested, and meet the unshaded requirement in structure design; (2)imaging in the transition zone of the two integrated ODVSs is continuous, and can meet certain image laws so as to fusing the video information.

3.2 Design of catadioptric mirror

In order to make imaging in the transition zone of the two integrated ODVSs continuous, this chapter adopts average angular resolution to design ODVS. There is a certain linear relationship between the point on the imaging plane and the incidence angle. The average angular resolution design method is following.

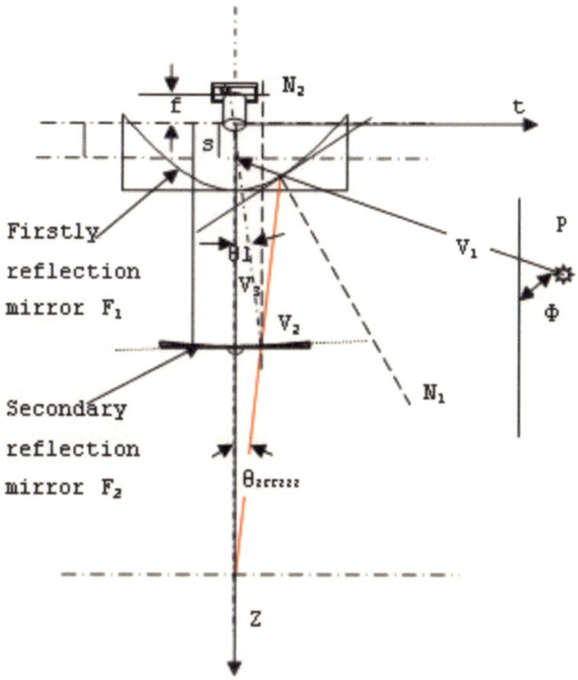

Fig. 3. Average angular resolution for two catadioptric imaging principle

The design of average angle resolution can be ascribed to the design of reflection mirror curve. As shown in Fig. 3, the incidence V_1 of a light source P reflects on the firstly reflection mirror $P_1(t_1,F_1)$, the reflected light V_2 reflects again on the secondary reflection mirror $P_2(t_2,F_2)$, the reflected light V_3 enters into the camera lens with the incidence angle of θ_1 then images on the camera unit (CCD or CMOS).
According to imaging principle, the angle between the first incidence V_1 and the spindle Z is ϕ, the angle between the first reflected light V_2 and the spindle Z is θ_2, the angle between the tangent through P_1 and the spindle t is σ, the angle between the normal and the spindle Z is ε the angle between the secondary reflected light V_3 and the main axis Z is θ_1, the angle between the tangent through P_2 and the spindle t is σ, the angle between the normal through P_2 and the spindle Z is ε_1. For these relations we can get the equation (1):

$$\begin{cases} \sigma = 180^0 - \varepsilon \\ 2\varepsilon = \phi - \theta_2 \\ \sigma_1 = 180^0 - \varepsilon_1 \\ 2\varepsilon_1 = \theta_1 - \theta_2 \end{cases} \tag{1}$$

Among them,

$$\tan\varphi = \frac{t_1}{F_1(t_1 - s)}, \tan\theta_2 = \frac{t_1 - t_2}{F_2 - F_1}, \tan\theta_1 = \frac{t_2}{F_2}$$

In the equation: F_1 is the firstly reflection mirror curve, F_2 is the secondary reflection mirror curve; s is the intersection of incidence V_1 and spindle Z.
Simplifying the equation by triangular relationship we can get:

$$F_1'^2 - 2\alpha F_1' - 1 = 0 \tag{2}$$

$$F_2'^2 - 2\beta F_2' - 1 = 0 \tag{3}$$

Among them,

$$\alpha = \frac{(F_1 - s)(F_2 - F_1) - t_1(t_1 - t_2)}{t_1(F_2 - F_1) - (t_1 - t_2)(F_1 - s)}, \beta = \frac{t_2(t_1 - t_2) + F_2(F_2 - F_1)}{t_2(F_2 - F_1) - F_2(t_1 - t_2)}$$

Solutions of (2), (3) can be:

$$F_1' = \alpha \pm \sqrt{\alpha^2 + 1} \tag{4}$$

$$F_2' = \beta \pm \sqrt{\beta^2 + 1} \tag{5}$$

Among them, F_1' is the differential of curve F_1, F_2' is the differential of curve F_2.
In order to make some certain linear relationship between the point on the imaging plane and the incidence angle, we need to build a linear relationship between the distance from pixel P to the spindle Z and the incidence angle ϕ, namely:

$$\phi = a_0 \cdot P + b_0 \tag{6}$$

In the equation: a_0, b_0 are arbitrary parameters.
If f is the focus of the camera unit, P is the distance from pixel to spindle Z, $P_2(t_2,F_2)$ is the reflex point on the secondary reflection mirror. According to imaging principle, we have:

$$P = f \cdot \frac{t_2}{F_2} \tag{7}$$

By substituting equation (7) into the equation (6), we can get:

$$\phi = a_0 \cdot (f \cdot \frac{t_2}{F_2}) + b_0 \tag{8}$$

The mirror curve satisfing equation (8) can meet the requirements of average angular resolution. According to the catadioptric principle by equation (8) we can get:

$$\tan^{-1}(\frac{t_1}{F_1 - s}) = a_0 \cdot (f \cdot \frac{t_2}{F_2}) + b_0 \tag{9}$$

We can get the numerical solutions F_1 and F_2 of the equation (2), (3),(9) by the forth-order Runge-Kutta algorithm (as shown in Fig. 4), so the firstly reflection mirror and secondary reflection mirror are of the average angular resolution.

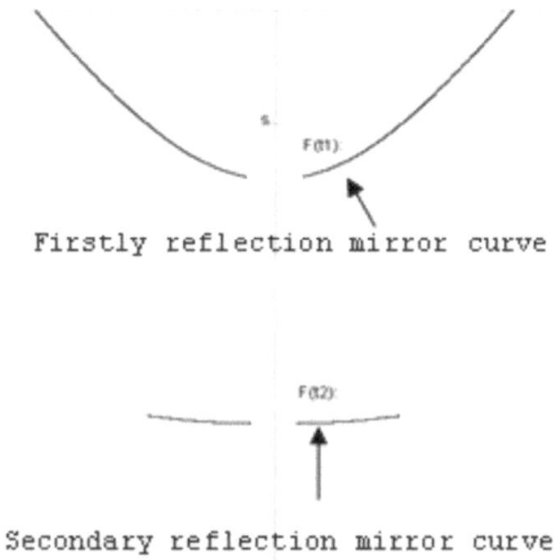

Fig. 4. Reflector curvilinear figure solution

3.3 Design of lens combination

From the ODVS viewpoint which is designed above, its view sheltered by the secondary reflection mirror that is video information before the secondary reflection mirror is invisible; in order to obtain this video information before the secondary reflection mirror. This chapter presents that a wide-angle lens is embedded in the center of the secondary reflection mirror. The wide-angle lens and the camera lens compose a combination lens device, as shown in Fig. 2. Fig. 5 shows the ubiety of the camera lens and the wide-angle lens. The wide-angle lens is configured in front of the firstly reflection mirror and in the secondary refection mirror. The central axises of camera lens, wide-angle lens, firstly reflection mirror and secondary reflection mirror are configurated on the same axis line. The objects through the hole in the firstly reflection mirror image between the wide-angle lens and the camera lens (known as the first imaging point). This imaging point through the camera lens images at the camera component.

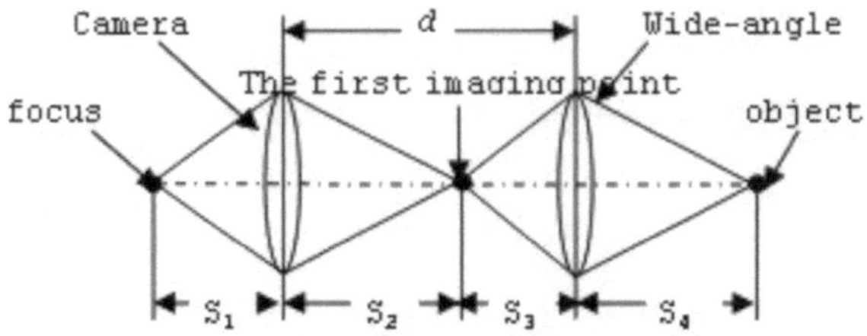

Fig. 5. Ubiety between camera lens and wide-angle lens

The focus of camera lens is f_1, the focus of wide-angle lens is f_2, the distance between camera lens and the camera lens focus is S_1, the distance between camera lens and the first imaging point is S_2, the distance from wide-angle lens to the first imaging point is S_3, and the distance from wide-angle lens to the object point is S_4, according to the lens imaging equation we can get the following relationships:

$$\frac{1}{f_1} = \frac{1}{S_1} + \frac{1}{S_2} \tag{10}$$

$$\frac{1}{f_2} = \frac{1}{S_3} + \frac{1}{S_4} \tag{11}$$

$$d = S_2 + S_3 \tag{12}$$

According to equation (12), as shown in Fig. 5 it should configure wide-angle lens with the distance d away from the firstly reflection mirror, and then we get the wide-angle imaging figure as the middle part of Fig. 5. But the present invention is configurating the wide-angle lens in the secondary reflection mirror, so the distance d between camera lens and the wide-angle lens is a constraint, and only by designing focus f_2 of wide-angle lens can we satisfy the requirements of equation (12). As shown in Fig. 4 taking the camera lens and the wide-angle lens into consideration, as a combination lens its focus can be got by

$$\frac{1}{f_3} = \frac{(f_1 + f_2 - d)}{f_1 f_2} \tag{13}$$

In addition, if the synthetic lens diameter is D, the magnification can be expressed by the following equation:

$$n = \frac{D}{f_3} \tag{14}$$

In order to make the view field of synthesized lens matching for the dead angle of ODVS, in this design it requires the following equation:

$$n = \frac{D}{f_3} = 2\theta_{1\max} \tag{15}$$

The θ_{1max} is the maximum angle between the secondary reflected light V_2 and Z axis.

4. 360 °×360 ° field of view for the world's surface ODVS

4.1 ODVS with back to back configuration

According to the design above, each ODVS view scope can reach 240°×360° and have the same average angular resolution. So as long as fixing two ODVS back-to-back and making sure the two ODVS' axis lines overlap, the view scope of the two combined ODVSs of no dead angle full sphere device can reach 360°×360°. There are about 60° overlap field where the two can obtain images of the same spatial object at the same time, as shown in Fig. 6.

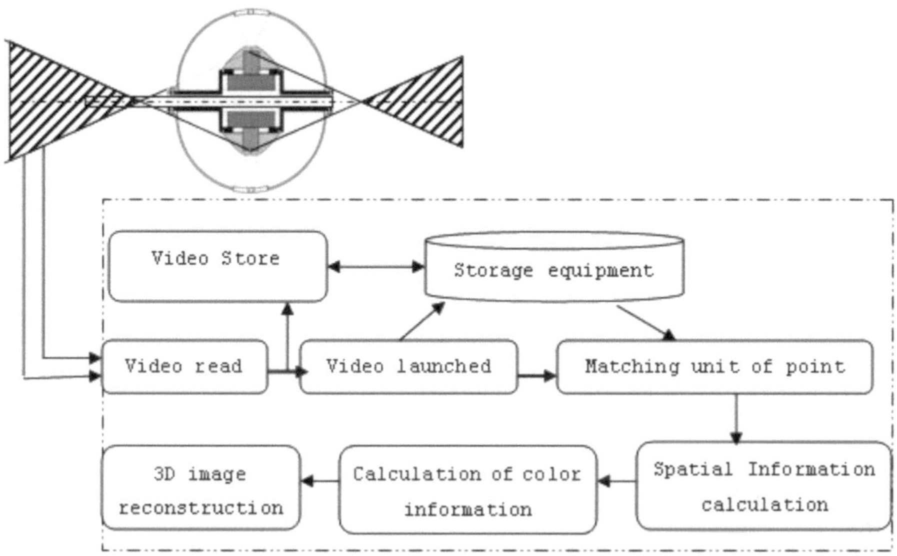

Fig. 6. Spherical ODVS with back to back and its image disposal flow

By combination of the camera lens and the wide-angle lens each ODVS captures image which locates in the centre of the entire image, as shown in Fig. 7(a), Fig. 7(b). Before unwrapping the omni-directional image we need to separate its central part alone; the calculation step at horizontal direction in the unwrapping algorithm is $\Delta\beta = 2\pi/l$; the calculation step at vertical direction is $\Delta m = \phi_{max} - \phi_{min}/m$; in the equation, ϕ_{max} is the scene lighting incidence angle corresponding to the biggest effective radius (Rmax), ϕ_{min} is the scene lighting incidence angle corresponding to the smallest effective radius (Rmin). The more details of the implement of the unwrapping are referred to Intelligent Omni-Directional Vision Sensors and Their Application.

As to the concrete realization, a connector is used to connect the two ODVSs together which are of the same average angular resolution and no dead angle, the camera's video cable and power cable are fetched out through the hole in the connector. as shown in Fig. 8. Each camera video cable of ODVS connects to video image access unit, because each camera of ODVS can get image information with view of 360°×240° and has the same average

(a) Panoramic image of upside ODVS (b) Panoramic image of downside ODVS

Fig. 7. Panoramic images captured by spherical ODVS

Fig. 8. Full sphere ODVS with back to back configuration

Fig. 9. Video image from combination lens of downside & upside ODVS

angular resolution in the vertical (incidence angle) direction, it can realize image information fusion between the two ODVSs easily. Video access unit reads video information of each camera separately and stores in storage space (ODVStmp1, ODVStmp2), the two ODVS images are shown in Fig. 7(a), 7(b). Video image unwrapping unit reads the original video information in storage space (ODVStmp1, ODVStmp2) constantly, and splits the circular video images captured by the combination lens, as shown in Fig. 9. Then the obtained image of each ODVS is unwrapped by the unwrapping algorithm. ODVS image after unwrapping is shown in Fig. 10. In the unfolding figure the horizontal axis is azimuth, vertical axis is incidence angle. The splicing principle is azimuth alignment of the upper and the lower ODVS image, so the image point of the same material point in the two stitching images are in a vertical line. In this chapter the spherical panorama after stitching does not include the overlapping part of the two ODVS, we only stitch when the incidence angle of ODVS is less than 90°. If you want to implement three-dimensional object point matching, spatial information calculation, three-dimensional image reconstruction, we need to calculate the overlapping part of the two ODVSs.

Fig. 10. Video unwrap mosaic image by two ODVS

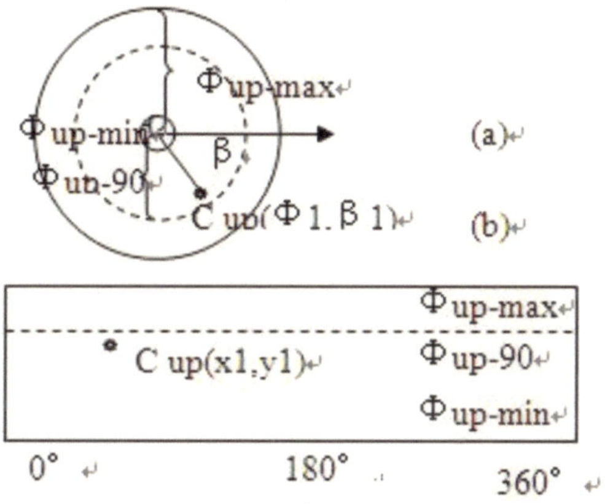

Fig. 11. Schematic diagram of panoramic vision photo graphed by upper ODVS

4.2 Match of the image point

Fig. 11 shows unwarped schematic diagram of upper ODVS. In unfolded image, x-axis expresses azimuth angle, y-axis expresses incidence angle. The principle of splicing is to match the azimuth angles of ODVS. It makes the same object from two unfolded images on the same vertical line in splicing image. If the longitudes of ODVS is justified during the design period, the ODVS can realiz the constraint of linear relationship in structure. After meeting the linear relationship, the problem search corresponding points in the entire unfolding iamge changes into searching in a vertical line. The reduction of search range provides foundation for the rapid match between point-to-point. From the viewpoint of latitude, if there is certain linear relation between the incidence angle and the pixels on image plane, the incidence angle of the ODVS can be calculated conveniently, and the problem can be simplified from searching corresponding points in a vertical line to a certain area of the vertical line. It should satisfy equation(16):

$$180^\circ \le \phi_1 + \phi_2 \le 2\phi_{max} \quad (16)$$

In this equation, ϕ_1 is the incidence angle of lower ODVS's imaging point, ϕ_2 is the incidence angle of upper ODVS's imaging point, ϕ_{max} is the maximum incidence angle of ODVS imaging point called elevation.

We mark the upper ODVS as ODVSup and the lower ODVS as ODVSdown. Assume that the object point C is in the range of the binocular vision, its relevant point of imaging point in the panorama in ODVSdown is Cup (Φ1,β1) (shown in Fig. 11(a)), its coresponding object point in the spherical launched plane is Cup(x1,y1) (shown in Fig. 11(b)). Φup-max is the elevation when then incidence angle of ODVSup is the biggest, Φup-90 is the value 90° of the incidence angle of ODVSup, Φup-min is the depression angle when the incidence angle of ODVSup is the smallest.

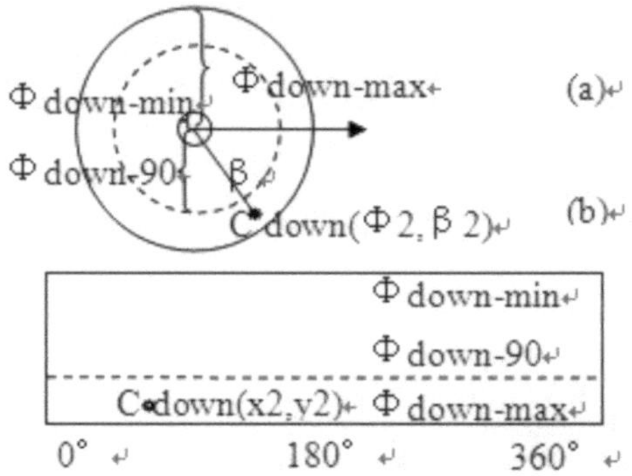

Fig. 12. Schematic diagram of panoramic vision photo graphed by lower ODVS

We can also know that object point C's relevant point of imaging point in the panorama in ODVSdown is Cdown(Φ2,β2)(shown in Fig. 12(a)), its object point in the spherical launched plane is Cdown(x2, y2) (shown in Fig. 12(b)).

The incidence angle bigger than 90° is called elevation while smaller is depression angle. In this chapter, we set the incidence angle of the ODVS as elevation, so it must have some area that both two ODVSs can reach which is named binocular vision scope. For the same object point in space, if it can be seen in the binocular vision scope, it must have two image relevant points (Cup(Φ1,β1) and Cdown(Φ2,β2)of the two panoramas of ODVS)which have the same azimuth angle β, that is, β1= β2.

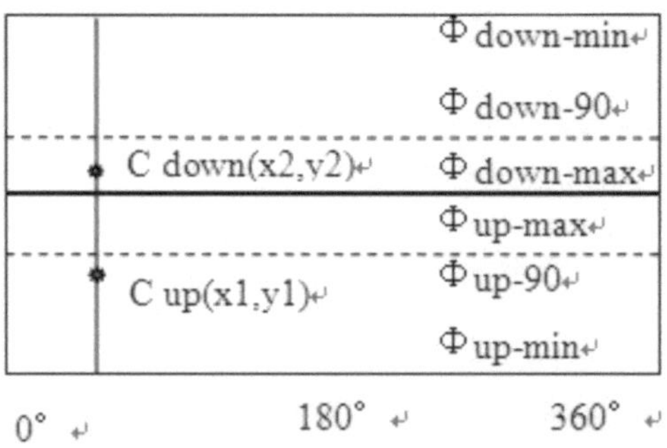

Fig. 13. Image point matching for two ODVSs

As a result, the X coordinate is the same corresponding to the spherical launched plane, that is x1=x2. So according to this principle, the azimuth angle of the two ODVS can be justified in the spherical launched plane, as shown in Fig. 13. Actually, the Fig. 13 is combination of the Fig. 11(b) and the Fig. 12(b), which can realize the justifying of the azimuth angles in the two spherical launched planes conveniently.

4.3 The coordinate of Gaussian sphere and central eye

Human-centered stereo omnidirectional vision is three dimension and high fidelity. We call the center of binocular vision's baseline as "central eye" which is used to describe the information of object point $c = C(r, \phi, \beta, R, G, B, t)$ in space. The meaning of each physical parameter is shown in Fig. 14.

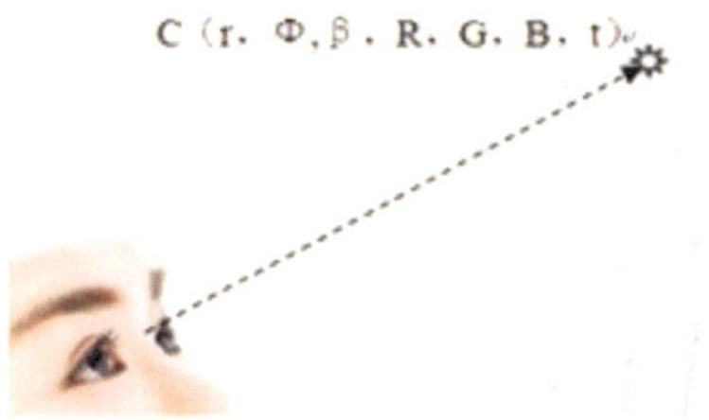

Fig. 14. Imaging point expression in Gaussian reference

The coordinate of central eye is used to be the origin *o* of Gaussian sphere coordinates in this design. We use seven parameters to describe the information of object point in space. *r* expresses the distance between origin *o* and object point; ϕ expresses the angle between Z axes and the line connecting origin *o* with object point; β expresses azimuth angle; *R* is the average value of central eye's red component; *G* is the average value of central eye's green component; *B* is the average value of central eye's blue component; *t* is time information. The equation(17) can express any object point in space,

$$c = C(r, \phi, \beta, R, G, B, t) \tag{17}$$

We adopt a scientific and uniform Gaussian sphere coordinate in binocular stereo vision system to express all object points by using seven physical parameters. It can provide a good technology foundation for model simplification and fast calculation in future. It also provides convenience for the follow-up geometric calculation.

4.4 Object point's spatial information and color information acquisition and calculation

The spatial information of object point is expressed by three parameters *r*, ϕ, β in Gaussian sphere coordinate. Because we use central eye as origin of Gaussian sphere coordinate, calculation of spatial information can be concluded to calculate the ubiety of object point and central eye. Among them *r* expresses the distance between origin *o* and object point. Compared with central eye, object point's longitude value is ϕ. Compared with central eye, object point's dimensionality value is β. According to the principle of binocular vision we can estimate the object point's depth information, as shown in Figure 15.

According to the imaging principle of binocular vision, we can get the distance from object point to the central eye that is depth information by only obtaining the incidence angle of object point of ODVS Φ1 and Φ2. Because two ODVSs are combined together by back-to-back manner, Φ1 and Φ2 can be counted by equation (18), (19):

$$\phi_1 = \phi_{\min} + (\phi_{\max} - \phi_{\min}) / m \cdot (m - y_1) \tag{18}$$

$$\phi_2 = \phi_{\min} + (\phi_{\max} - \phi_{\min}) / m \cdot y_2 \tag{19}$$

In the equation, m is the height of unfolded image; y_1, y_2 is the match point on y-axis in two unfolded images; ϕ_{min} is the minimum incidence angle; ϕ_{max} is the maximum incidence angle.
According to the triangular relationship, we can get the distance r between origin o and point C,

$$\begin{aligned} r = \overline{OC} &= \sqrt{\overline{AC}^2 + (dc/2)^2 - 2\overline{AC}(dc/2)\cos A} \\ &= \sqrt{[\frac{dc}{\sin(A+B)} \bullet \sin B]^2 + (dc/2)^2 - \frac{dc^2}{\sin(A+B)} \bullet \sin B \cos A} \\ &= \sqrt{[\frac{dc}{\sin(\phi 1+\phi 2)} \bullet \sin \phi 1]^2 + (dc/2)^2 + \frac{dc^2}{\sin(\phi 1+\phi 2)} \bullet \sin \phi 1 \cos \phi 2} \end{aligned} \tag{20}$$

In the equation A=180°-Φ2, B=180°- Φ1, dc is the distance between ODVSup's viewpoint and ODVSdown's viewpoint.The incidence angle Φ can be counted by the equation (21):

$$\phi = \arcsin(\frac{dc}{2r}\sin\phi_2) + \phi_2 - 180^{\circ} \tag{21}$$

Φ is the incidence angle of object point; dc is the distance between point A and point B in binocular system; r is the distance between object point and central eye; Φ2 is the incidence angle of ODVSup. Another parameter β can choose from one of the two ODVS's azimuth angle. t is the time from computer system.
The average value of each color components R, G, B of matching points of two unfolded image are adopted as central eye's color coding. First we obtain color components R_{ODVS1}, R_{ODVS2}, G_{ODVS1}, G_{ODVS2}, B_{ODVS1} and B_{ODVS2} of matching points of unfolded image, then the average value of each color component is counted as central eye's color coding. The equation is shown as follows:

$$\begin{aligned} R &= \frac{R_{ODVS1} + R_{ODVS2}}{2} \\ G &= \frac{G_{ODVS1} + G_{ODVS2}}{2} \\ B &= \frac{B_{ODVS1} + B_{ODVS2}}{2} \end{aligned} \tag{22}$$

In the equation, R is the average value of red component; R_{ODVS1} is red component of ODVS one; R_{ODVS2} is red component of ODVS two; G is the average value of green component; G_{ODVS1} is green component of ODVS one; G_{ODVS2} is green component of ODVS two; B is the average value of blue component; B_{ODVS1} is green component of ODVS one; B_{ODVS2} is blue component of ODVS two; the value range is 0~255.

4.5 Depth accuracy

The vertically-aligned binocular omnistereo systems have two viewpoints and a fixed baseline. For the stereo matching between the two converted panoramic views, any conventional algorithms is applicable. Once correspondence between image points has been established, depth calculation in both spherical and cylindrical panorama is easily counted by simple triangulation in equation (20). And the depth resolution mainly depends on camera resolution, the length of baseline.

$$\partial r = f(\frac{r^2}{dc})\partial \phi \tag{23}$$

Where, r is the distance between viewing object and Binocular Omnistereo Vision Sensor, dc is the length of baseline, $\partial \phi$ is similar to the camera resolution. It seems that larger baseline and higher camera resolution will get better depth accuracy. And depth estimation error is proportional to the 2 power of the distance between viewing object and Binocular Omnistereo Vision Sensor. The depth accuracy of the V-binocular omnistereo is isotropic in all directions, and the epipolar lines is simply vertical lines in omnidirectional image.

5. Experimental results

5.1 Full sphere view and without dead angle

Full sphere ODVS is shown in Fig. 8, the two ODVSs are fixed together back to back by a connector. Its view scope is same as the full sphere camera device as shown in Fig. 1(b). The original panoramic images of the upper and the lower ODVS are shown in Fig. 7(a) and Fig. 7(b). The center part of the image is the imaging of wide-angle lens, that is, the dead angle parts of the upper and lower ODVS of the secondary reflection mirror shown in Fig. 9(a) and 9(b). In Fig. 7(b) the ship brand is partly sheltered by the secondary reflection mirror of the lower ODVS, but the combination lens can also obtain the ship brand video information, shown in Fig. 9(b); Similarly, the lattice umbrella is partly sheltered by secondary reflection mirror of the upper ODVS, however, the lens combination can also obtain the lattice umbrella video information shown in Fig. 9(a).

By splicing the unwrapping images of the panoramic image Fig. 8(a) and 8(b) the fusion of the video images is shown in Fig. 10. From the experimental results of image processing we can see the full sphere ODVS in this article can be real-time and capture the entire 360°×360° spherical images within the surveillance video. Further improvements in the future are to solve the problem of fusion between wide-angle lens and ODVS image, using 360°×360° full sphere ODVS to implement three-dimensional reconstruction and ranging.

5.2 Measuring depth of viewing object

In order to get better depth accuracy range for special application requirements, we carry out experiments to measure depth of viewing object using V-binocular stereo ODVS of back-to-back configuration.

The panoramic images obtained by binocular stereo ODVS are transmited to computer through two USBs. After it computer will process these images, match the object points, and measure the depth of object point. Fig. 16 is shown the experimental device and environment a panoramic image of both the frames of upper ODVS and lowwer ODVS graphed by V-binocular stereo ODVS with back-to-back configuration, its sphere panoramic image resolution is 640×480, unwrapped panoramic image resolution is 1280×200. Experiments measuring depth between viewing object (in red cross mark) and central eye(origin O) are carried out using the binocular stereo ODVS experiment device, from short distance to long distance respectively. Fig. 17 shows parts of experiments for matching the object point and measuring the depth of object point. The software is developed by Java and operating system is Windows XP.

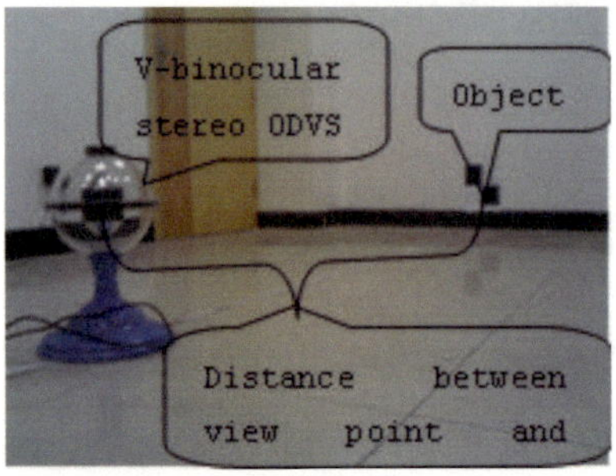

Fig. 16. Experiments for measuring depth of object

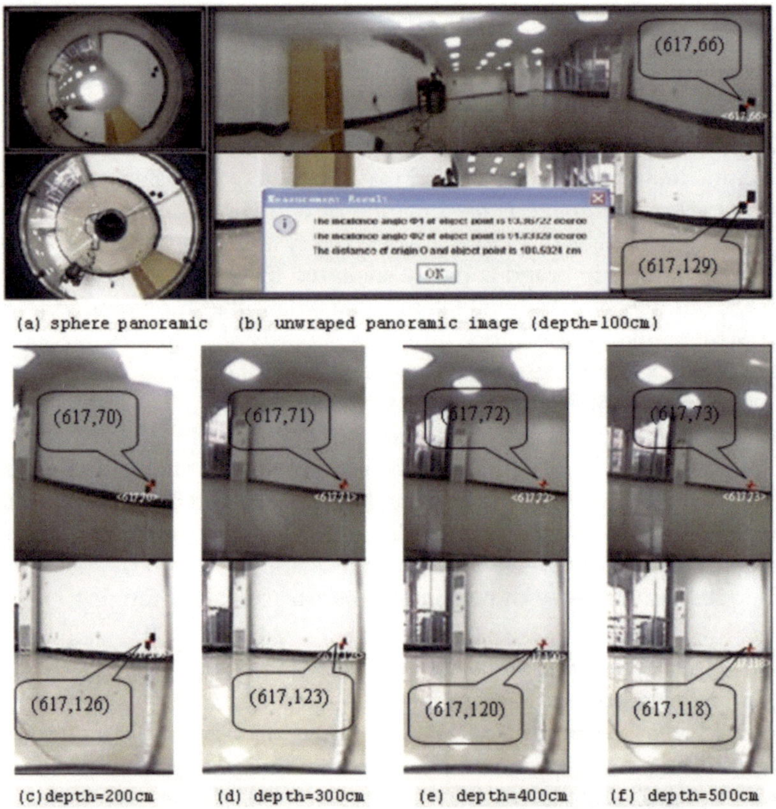

Fig. 17. Experiments for matching the object point and measuring the depth of object point

Actual depth (cm)	Up image plane coordinates $C_{up}(x_1, y_1)$	Angle of incidenceΦ1 (degree)	Down image plane coordinates $C_{down}(x_2, y_2)$	Angle of incidenceΦ2 (degree)	Depth estimation (cm)	Error ratio (%)
30.00	618,47	98.81	618,151	98.26	33.08	10.28
40.00	618,52	97.43	618,143	96.02	42.25	5.63
50.00	616,57	96.02	616,138	94.56	54.05	8.11
60.00	618,60	95.15	618,136	93.97	62.99	4.98
70.00	617,62	94.56	617,134	93.37	72.73	3.91
80.00	616,62	94.56	616,131	92.45	82.54	3.18
90.00	616,64	93.97	616,130	92.14	95.21	5.79
100.00	617,66	93.37	617,129	91.83	100.50	0.50
110.00	617,66	93.37	617,129	91.83	112.64	2.40
120.00	616,66	93.37	616,128	91.52	120.16	0.14
130.00	617,67	93.06	617,128	91.52	128.50	-1.15
140.00	616,67	93.06	616,127	91.21	138.44	-1.12
150.00	618,67	93.06	618,127	91.21	138.44	-7.71
160.00	619,68	92.76	619,127	91.21	149.68	-6.45
170.00	616,69	92.45	616,127	91.21	162.99	-4.12
180.00	619,69	92.45	619,126	90.89	179.38	-0.35
190.00	616,69	92.45	616,126	90.89	179.38	-5.59
200.00	617,70	92.14	617,126	90.89	198.92	-0.54
210.00	619,70	92.14	619,126	90.89	198.92	-5.28
220.00	618,71	91.83	618,124	90.25	298.44	35.65
230.00	617,71	91.83	617,124	90.25	298.44	29.76
240.00	616,71	91.83	616,124	90.25	298.44	24.35
250.00	617,71	91.83	617,124	90.25	298.44	19.38

Table 1. Experimental results of measuring depth between view point and object from 30cm to 250cm using V-binocular ODVS with Back-to-Back configuration in Fig. 16

Actual depth (cm)	Up image plane coordinates $C_{up}(x_1, y_1)$	Angle of incidenceΦ1 (degree)	Down image plane coordinates $C_{down}(x_2, y_2)$	Angle of incidenceΦ2 (degree)	Depth estimation (cm)	Error ratio (%)
100.00	617,67	93.37	617,129	91.83	100.50	0.01
200.00	617,70	92.14	617,126	90.89	198.92	-0.54
300.00	617,71	91.87	617,123	89.93	359.08	19.69
400.00	617,72	91.40	617,120	88.96	462.75	15.69
500.00	617,73	91.12	617,118	88.30	645.85	29.17
600.00	617,70	92.14	617,124	90.25	969.43	61.57
700.00	617,71	91.83	617,124	90.25	1113.63	59.09
800.00	618,71	91.83	618,123	89.93	1316.21	64.53
900.00	617,71	91.83	617,129	91.83	1610.93	78.99
1000.00	618,72	91.52	618,122	89.61	2055.70	105.57
1100.00	617,72	91.52	617,125	90.72	2884.77	162.25

Table 2. Experimental results of measuring depth between view point and object from 100cm to 1100cm using V-binocular ODVS with Back-to-Back configuration in Fig. 16

Table 1 are experimental resluts of measuring depth between view point and object with distance from 30cm to 250cm, and Table 2 are experimental resluts of measuring depth between view point and object from 100cm to 1100cm, both using V-binocular ODVS with Back-to-Back configuration, the baseline length of which is 9.80cm, in Fig. 16.

6. Discussion

In order to obtain real-time 360°×360° entire full sphere view scope video, this chapter presents a secondary catadioptric principle and structure of ODVS, and designs a catadioptric mirror, use fourth-order Runge-Kutta algorithm to obtain numerical solution of the reflection mirror by the design method of combination lens integrating ODVS with wide-angle lens to eliminate the inherent dead angle of the original ODVS, and then fixes the two ODVS devices without dead angle back to back, finally stitches the 360°×360° video image seamlessly by unwrapping algorithm. The experimental results show that the design of ODVS device can obtain real-time 360°×360° view scope video image. The software which we develop for the full sphere ODVS to do experimental studies runs in the operation system of Windows XP with CPU of 1.7Celeron and 512M RAM. When the resolution of camera is 640×480, the system can handle 15 frames per second, and basically satisfy the requirements of real-time video data acquisition.

Because each ODVS of the composition of full sphere ODVS adopts average angular resolution to design, the parameters of the two ODVS fixed back to back are fully consistent and the point of imaging plane and the incidence angle has a linear relationship, thus it can make sure the imaging of transition zone of the integrated ODVS is continuous.

For the reflection mirror design, this chapter uses Runge-Kutta algorithm to obtain the numerical solution of the reflection mirror of ODVS and validates the catadioptric mirror by the simulation experiment. This method can guide design of ODVS mirror, and provide a theoretical support to ODVS reflection mirror design.

Fig. 10 shows the unwrapping stitching image exists stitching error. The reason is that the central axis of the upper and the lower ODVS has error in manufacturing and assembly processing. It is difficult to ensure the two ODVS fixed back to back on the same axis line,

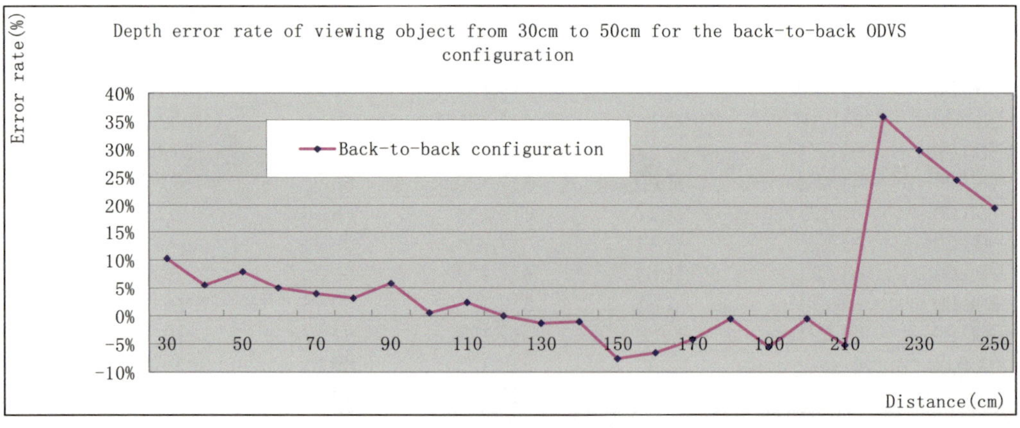

Fig. 18. Depth estimate error rate of viewing object from 30cm to 250cm for the V-binocular ODVS with back to back configuration

but this problem can be solved by ensuring the same axis angle when assembling in the technic schedule.
Depth error analysis of distance calculation is shown as Fig. 18. According to the principle of binocular stereo vision the position of object can be measured exactly. But the image is not continuous when it is obtained by imaging unit. The image is discrete data which takes pixel as a unit. There is minimum resolution ratio error in measurement due to camera's resolution. This problem can be improved by using high resolution camera.
According to the measurement results, depth estimation error will increase with the increase of distance from target object. Because in the same direction when the measuring distance increases, the variable quantity of incidence angle in two ODVS Φ1 and Φ2 is becoming smaller, and the incidence angle of upper and lower ODVS both tend to 90°. It makes the distance from target object of the equation (20) very sensitive to the change of incidence angle.

7. Conclusion

A novel dynamic omnistereo approach is presented by which viewpoints of two omnidirectional camera can form optimal stereo configuration for localizing moving objects. Further extension is made to the concept of omnidirectional imaging from viewer-centered to object-centered representation, thus it allows establishing omnidirectional models of large objects or even our planet. Numerical analysis is given on omnidirectional representation, epipolar geometry and depth error characteristics, which could be very useful for the research and applications of omnidirectional stereo vision.
The beneficial effects of 360°×360° full sphere ODVS designed in this chapter are mainly reflected in: 1)It can obtain real-time 360°×360° omni-directional 3D video images, then by geometry calculation get the whole panoramic image of the monitoring sphere. The monitor tracking objects will never be lost; 2)It uses the average angular resolution for the ODVS design. The whole image of monitor sphere is not heteromorphic solving the problem of catadioptric ODVS image distortion. It provides a complete theoretical system and model for the fast-moving target real-time tracking in large space. 3)Because each ODVS of the composition of full sphere ODVS uses the average angle resolution to design, the parameters of the two ODVS cameras are fully consistent with good symmetry. In the spherical coordinates the real-time video image obtained can rapidly match point and point providing more convenience for the subsequent three-dimensional image process. 4)The ODVS design uses catadioptric technology, so it exists the problem of fixed focus, the clarity is same in any area of the image; 5)It Uses a secondary catadioptric imaging technology and easily implement miniaturization. It can be widely used in military reconnaissance, aviation and navigation, virtual reality and so on .

8. Reference

Peleg, S.; Ben-Ezra, M. & Pritch, Y. (2001). *Omnistereo: Panoramic Stereo Imaging* [J].IEEE Transaction on Pattern Analysis any Machine Intelligence, 2001, 23(23): 279-290
Matthew Brown & David G. Lowe. *Automatic panoramic image stitching using invariant features*[J].International Journal of Computer Vision, 2007,74 (1):59-73.

Shum H Y & Szeliski R.(2000) *Systems and experiment paper: construction of panoramic image mosaics with global and local alignment*[J].International Journal of Computer Vision, 2000,36(2):101–130.

Nalwa Vishvjit Singh (Holmdel, NJ). *Panoramic Viewing System with a Composite Field of View* [P].United States Patent.6700711.Mar 2, 2004.

Peleg S & Herman J. *Panoramic mosaics by manifold projection*[J]. Proc.of IEEE conference on CVPR [C].San Juan.Puerto Rico,1997,pp.338-343.

David McCutchen. *Immersive imaging method and apparatus*[P].US Patent.6141034. October 31, 2000.

TANG Yi-ping. *Omni Directional Vision Sensors without dead angle.* Chinese Patent No.200710066757.0, .pages 446-451,2007-07-25.

TANG Yi-ping et al. *Research on Intelligent Omni-Directional Vision Sensors and Their Application*, CHINESE JOURNAL OF SENSORS AND ACTUATORS, Vol. 20, No. 6, pages 1316~1320,2007.

Koyasu H & Miura J,Shirai Y.(2002). *Recognizing moving obstacles for robot navigation using real-time omnidirectional stereo vision.* Journal of Robotics and Mechatronics,2002,14(2):147-156.

SU Lian-Cheng & ZHU Feng. *Design of a Novel Omnidirectional Stereo Vision System* [J]. ACTA AUTOMATICA SINICA ,2006,32(1):69-74.

Tomas Pajdla & Tomas Svoboda. *Epipolar Geometry for Central Catadioptric Cameras*[J]. International Journal of Computer Vision,2002,49(1):23–37.

Zhu Z et al. *Panoramic virtual stereo vision of cooperative mobile robots for localizing 3D moving objects.* Proceedings of IEEE Workshop on Omnidirectional Vision – OMNIVIS'00, Hilton Head Island,pages 29-36,2000.

3

A Wireless Camera Node with Passive Self-righting Mechanism for Capturing Surrounding View

Kuniaki Kawabata[1], Hideo Sato[2], Tsuyoshi Suzuki[2] and Yoshito Tobe[2]
[1]*RIKEN(The Institute of Physical and Chemical Research)*
[2]*Tokyo Denki University*
Japan

1. Introduction

Japan is a land of frequent earthquakes, and developing effective means for preventing and mitigating disasters in their aftermath is a matter of deep and widespread concern. The time and location of their occurrence is essentially unpredictable, and interest therefore centers on preventing and mitigating damage. A key prerequisite for effective mitigation is rapid, accurate appraisal of conditions in the stricken region. For this purpose, the development of systems for concurrent, parallel information gathering, capable of covering a broad range of affected areas and conditions, is critical. In the *DDT Project, 'Development of Advanced Robots and Information Systems for Disaster Response.'* of the Japanese Ministry of Education, Culture, Sports, Science and Technology (MEXT), the development effort for rescue robots and other next-generation basic technologies for disaster prevention and mitigation has included the development of interlinked rescue robots, airborne vehicles, sensors, and other elements of disaster area information gathering technologies (Tadokoro, 2009).
A related recent development has been the trend toward ubiquitous computing (Weiser, 1991), data carriers (Takeda, 1991), and related technologies, with research and development in progress for the creation of intelligent information environments to support and aid in daily life and living. In parallel with these advances, the authors have developed an intelligent data carrier (IDC) for rescue, designed to support the search for victims immediately after an earthquake (Kurabayashi et al., 2003); (Asama et al., 2005); (Kawabata et al. 2006); (Hada et al., 2006). The rescue IDC is a small device with wireless radio communication capability, for installation in living environments. In the wake of an earthquake, this device can send out voice calls to any who might be trapped in the rubble and record their responses. With multiple deployments, the IDCs enable parallel searches for victims throughout the stricken area. In a separate study, Takizawa et al. (2007) has applied RFID (Radio Frequency Identification) technology to the development of an information transmission system in which wireless tags are permanently installed along streets and other routes to collect information on the stricken area, so that victims trying to leave the area and rescue personnel can perform non-contact automated gathering of the information. In the wake of a disaster, however, the rescue IDCs may not be available where

they are needed. In the information transmission system of Takizawa as well, it is necessary to install the electronic tags in the environment in advance. In many cases, the sites in need of information gathering cannot be determined until after the disaster. It is therefore desirable to develop information terminals which can be readily deployed after a disaster, for efficient information gathering at appropriate locations.

Some sensor systems and devices have already been developed for deployment following hazards. Inoue et al.(2005) have developed a ball-shaped probe that can be thrown into rubble following a disaster, and evaluated the configuration for mobility in rubble. The search ball contains a camera with motor-controlled sensing direction, for information acquisition, but it is not effective for use in disaster areas requiring information acquisition and collection in parallel with multiple sites. Remington Arms Co. of the United States provides a product named the Eye Ball for on-site information gathering at crime scenes such as hostage standoffs and for on-site security. It is a ball-shaped camera that can be thrown into a target area and then autonomously adjust its attitude, like a self-righting Japanese *Dharma* doll, on a floor or other level surface. Under control signals from the outside, the Eye Ball rotates its internal camera to scan the area, thus enabling acquisition of information on the surrounding interior. The information is relayed using a video transmitter, however, this would make simultaneous operation of multiple sensors difficult because of the number of channels required for such a purpose.

Interest has grown rapidly in sensor network technology (Ando et al., 2005) for environmental information gathering and sharing by organically linked sensor nodes in a wireless network within a given area, and various efforts are in progress for developing related technologies. Fukatsu and Hirafuji (2005) have developed an environment monitoring system which incorporates fixed wireless nodes in a broad agricultural area, linked to a web browser. Fixed network systems such as these are effective in cases where the measurement sites are determined in advance, but in the case of disasters or other events, in which the appropriate sites and circumstances are largely unpredictable, a capability for ad hoc network construction is essential.

Wireless sensor network technology holds great promise for rapid information gathering and sharing over a broad disaster area, which requires rapid construction of an information infrastructure appropriate to the conditions in the area together with simultaneous parallel collection of information acquired at additional sites. In such circumstances, it is essential to include identification of the time and place of acquisition together with the information acquired by the sensors, to enable presentation of the information in a coherent, organized form for browsing and observation.

In this report, we propose the basic concept of a camera-based sensor node that can be readily deployed amidst rubble and irregular land surfaces, with the capability for wireless network construction to enable information gathering from a disaster area, and report on experimental trials held to verify the function and performance of prototype camera nodes based on this concept.

2. Design concept

Many studies have focused on sensor nodes for advance mounting on ceilings, streetlights, and other structures (Nakata & Kushiro, 2007). In a disaster, however, the position and orientation of pre-installed nodes may change, the nodes themselves may even be damaged or inoperable, and, in any event, the sites requiring information gathering and monitoring will be largely unknown until after the disaster strikes. A sensor node is therefore needed which can be readily deployed in an area following a disaster, in highly irregular topography. In such circumstances, moreover, the existing information infrastructure may be severely damaged and disrupted. An effective system should therefore be able to operate independently of ordinary infrastructure, with a capability for construction of a self-organizing information network following deployment, to enable reliable transmission of information from the sensors on their surroundings and the time and location of the acquired information.

In performing the specification design for a sensor node to meet these needs, we have identified the following as essential functions.

- Power supply self-contained for autonomous drive.
- Bilateral wireless communication and self-organizing network construction.
- Acquisition of information on surroundings, position, and time.
- Maintenance of specified sensor attitude, regardless of topography at placement site.

The sensor node must also contain its own power source, such as a battery, to enable continuous operation of its autonomous drive and other functions for a sufficient period in the absence of lifeline utilities and infrastructure, which may be the case in disaster areas.

For gathering and consolidation of information on the disaster area, an information infrastructure must be constructed in the actual area, with connection among the information terminals. The sensor must be capable of wireless two-way communication and participation in self-organized, on-site construction of the communication network. It must therefore also enable temporal and spatial coordination, as the information it acquires will otherwise be meaningless when consolidated with information acquired at other sites. For this reason, it must be capable of determining "when and where" it acquires the information, and attach it to the acquired data. For coherent information gathering in the disaster area, in short, the sensor nodes must be able to form a network and provide a means for reliable consolidation of the acquired information without information loss.

Sensor attitude and sensing direction are also essential considerations. Whether the information acquisition is directional or omnidirectional, the orientation of the sensor node at each site during data acquisition is important. If the sensor is directional and points toward the surface on which it has been placed, it may entirely preclude acquisition of meaningful information. One solution would be to deploy multiple sensors at a single site in accordance with the data acquisition characteristics of the sensor and thereby eliminate blind spots, but this tends to increase the difficulty of achieving compact hardware design and obtaining low energy consumption. Sensor attitude is, in any case, a key consideration, as the site surfaces may be uneven, and it is necessary to ensure attainment of appropriate sensor attitude regardless of the surface angle. In summary, for any extended period of use, it is desirable to minimize the size, weight, and complexity of the sensor node, its drive and control units, and thus its energy consumption, and to provide a means of effective sensor attitude control with the smallest possible number of sensor components while providing a broad field of information acquisition and sufficient level of information acquisition.

For effective information acquisition in a disaster area, a sensor node that satisfies all of these requirements is necessary.

3. Design and fabrication of camera node

We designed and fabricated of a sensor node prototype to meet the above requirements. A camera is used as the sensor, to enable intuitive visual observation and ascertainment of the acquired information by rescue personnel and others, and a fisheye lens was selected to provide surroundings information acquisition. To distinguish this sensor node from other types and versions, we refer to it below as the "camera node" or simply the "node". Its key design parameters included the ability to visually recognize objects and structures (assumed to be approximately 1.7 m in size) located 5 m from the camera node as well as movement at close-range distances of 1–2 m.

3.1 Passive self-righting mechanism

The external appearance and the internal structure of the fabricated prototype is shown in Fig. 1. The acrylic shell is 2.8 mm thick and 250 mm in diameter. The gross weight is 3.5 kg. The camera node consists of a core module composed of mounted computer and peripheral devices, sensors, battery, and other components, enclosed in the acrylic shell. Six ball rollers are mounted on the core module and maintain contact with the shell body. The core module is thus supported inside the shell by the ball rollers, yet free to rotate inside the shell under the force of gravity. This passive self-righting structure keeps the camera vertical and facing upward without the use of actuators or other devices, enabling acquisition of omnidirectional images with the same geometrical attitude regardless of the node orientation and the environment.

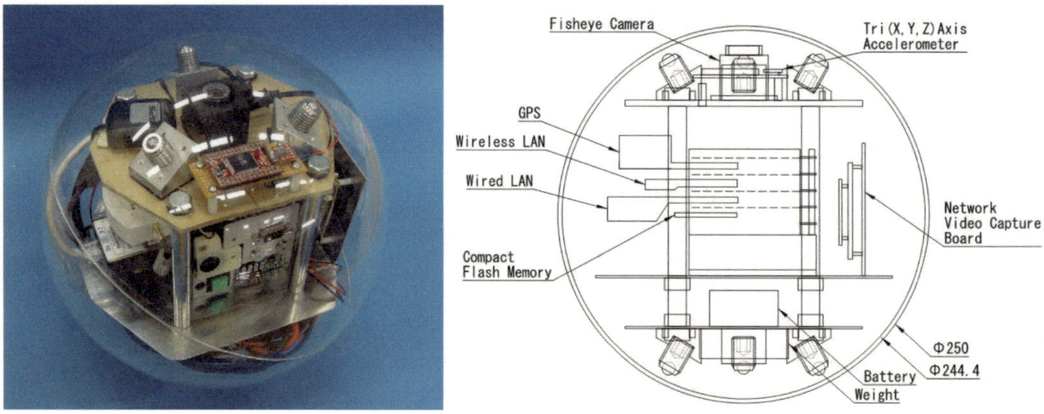

Fig. 1. A Prototype of Wireless Camera Node with Passive Self-righting Mechanism

The Cyclops (Chemel et al., 1999) and Omniclops (Schempf et al., 1999) are also spherical devices containing a camera and designed for uses similar to those envisioned in the present study, but the geometrical attitude of the camera is controlled by an electric motor and is thus essentially different from the passive control employed in our camera node, which enables higher energy efficiency.

3.2 Internal system components

The internal system components of the camera node are shown in Fig. 2 and Table 1. The computer module at the heart of the camera node, which performs the data processing and also serves as the mount for the sensor, contains an embedded Linux OS-based core from the Rescue Communicator (R-Comm, Mitsubishi Electric Information Technology) (Hada et al., 2006). Other functional components include a CF memory card, a wireless LAN adaptor, a wired LAN adaptor utilized for connecting image capture card, a CMOS camera with fisheye lens (OPT, NM-30) as the sensing device, and a GPS locator, mounted in four compact flash memory card slots (CF slots).

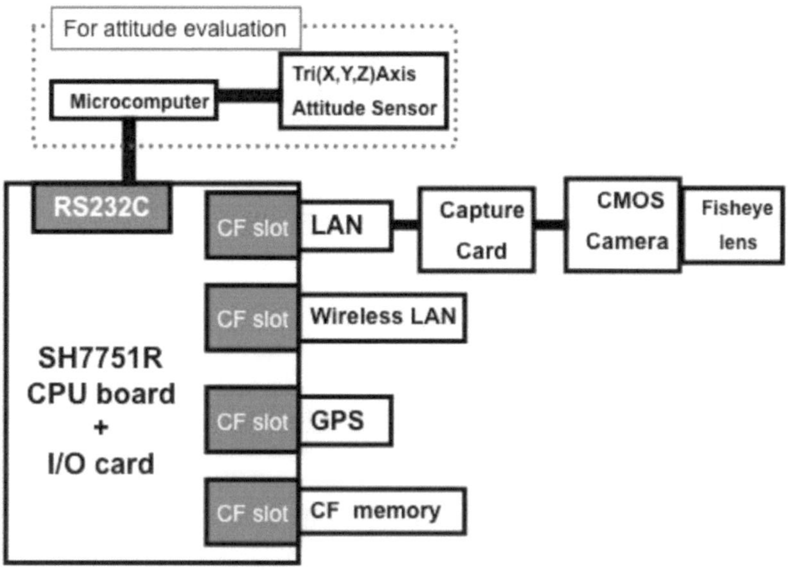

Fig. 2. System Configuration of Wireless Camera Node

CPU	SH7751R (internal bus 100 MHz, system bus 25 MHz)
OS	CELinux1.0 (Kernel2.4.20 base)
SDRAM	32[MB]
Flash ROM	8[MB]
Peripherals	Wireless LAN (IEEE802.11b), CMOS camera with fish-eye lens, GPS adaptor
Battery	+7.2[V], 3700[mA] (for sensors) +6[V], 2500[mA] (for computer)

Table 1. Specification of Wireless Camera Node

An internally mounted battery supplies the electric power necessary for the autonomous drive. Time management on the Linux OS and locating by GPS enables attachment of temporal and spatial identifiers to the acquired information (i.e., the video information). Files are saved with time, position, and other information embedded, for easy, intuitive understanding in subsequent browsing.

For network formation, the AODV-uu ad hoc on-demand distance vector (AODV) protocol is also incorporated to enable self-organizing network construction. It was confirmed that camera node operation was possible for about 5 h with the AODV in continuous operation.

The attitude sensor shown in Fig. 2 was installed to measure the attitude of the core module of the camera node in the following experiments.

(a) The manuscript must be written in English, (b) use common technical terms, (c) avoid abbreviations, don't try to create new English words, (d) spelling: Follow Merriam Webster´s Collegiate Dictionary, Longman or Oxford Dictionaries.

4. Experiments

The camera node was subjected to the following experiments, to verify its capability for achieving the basic functions described above.

4.1 Camera node placement experiment

We investigated the capability of the passive self-righting mechanism in the camera node to self-right of the camera, as illustrated in Fig. 3.

The camera node was released on a 15 degree incline in the environment shown in Fig. 3 and allowed to roll down the incline and across the floor until it stopped, as shown in Fig. 4. In this experiment, an attitude sensor was installed as illustrated in Fig. 2, to measure the roll (rotation about the X-axis), pitch (rotation about the Y-axis), and an absolute value of yaw (rotation about the vertical Z-axis) of the core module as shown in Figs. 5.

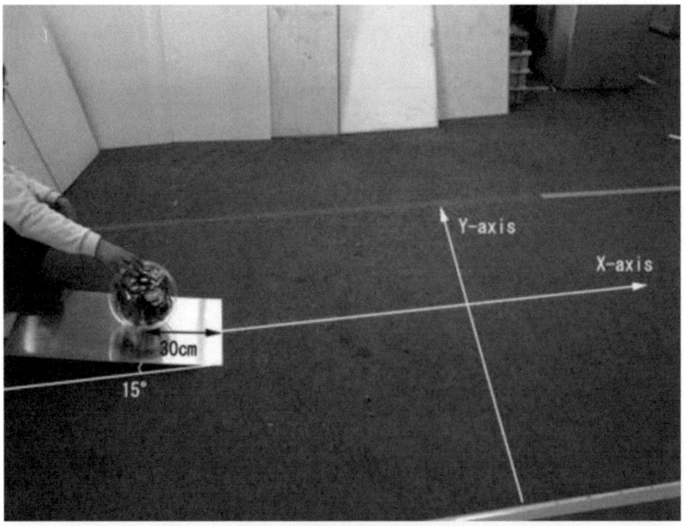

Fig. 3. Setup for Camera Node Setting-up Experiment

Fig. 4. Outlook of Setting-Up Experiment

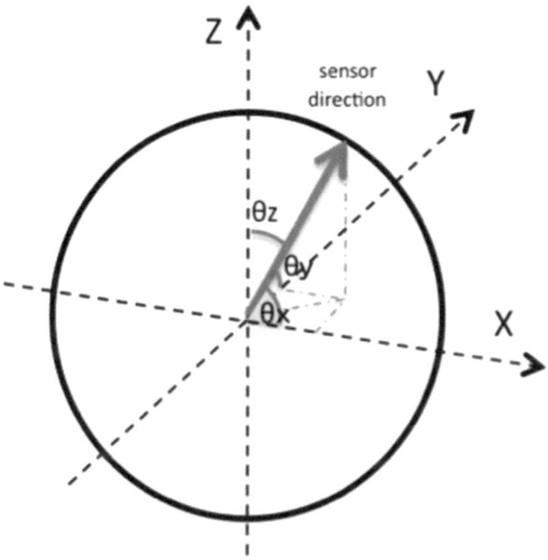

Fig. 5. Coordination for Camera Direction

The final attitude of the core, found from multiple trials, is shown in Fig. 6. The final attitude was generally within five degrees of the three axes. Although this depends on imaging conditions, given that the divergence is within five degrees, theoretical calculation shows that about one-half (2–3 pixels) of a 1.7-m object located 5 m from the lens (thus about 5 pixels for the whole-object length) will be captured with the orthogonal fisheye lens in the camera node, even if the divergence is in a direction involving partial loss of the target image. In the experiments, it was found that for an object extending over approximately 9–10 pixels in the full image, with an attitude divergence of five degrees in the direction of image loss, the object image still extended over approximately 6–7 pixels, thus confirming a sufficient capability for visual on-screen detection of object movement. These results show that the range of attitude error found in the experiment permits attainment of the initial performance objective of visual object recognition, and thus verify the effectiveness of the passive self-righting mechanism.

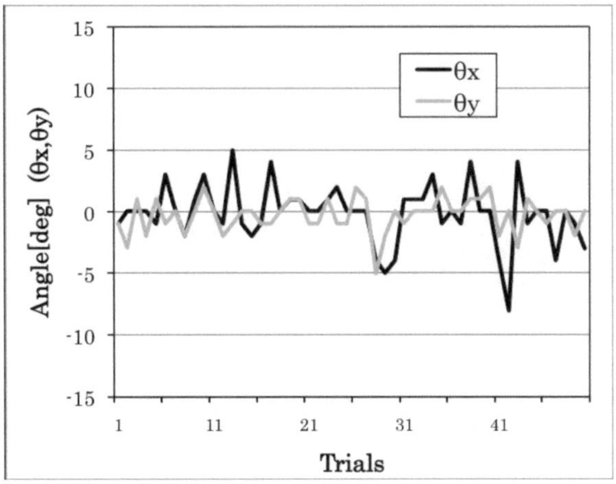

(a) Measured Sensor Attitude in X-axis and Y-axis

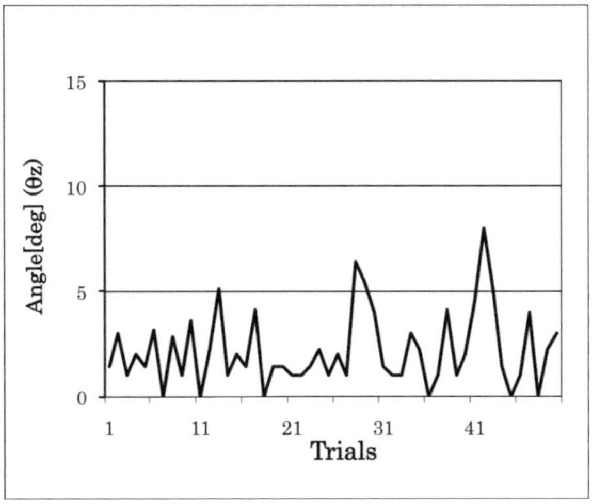

(b) Calculated Sensor attitude in Z-axis

Fig. 6. Experimental Result of Setting-Up a Camera Node

Similar results were obtained in an outdoor experiment as well when the camera node was rolled by hand, again confirming the vertical orientation of the camera by the passive self-righting mechanism.

The basic design concept assumes visual inspection of the acquired images to investigate the area around the camera node. As the vertical orientation of the camera with the fisheye lens enables information acquisition, the results of this experiment confirm the basic validity of this concept.

A further task remains concerning the shell body, made of acrylic plastic in the prototype. In the final version of the sensor node, the use of polycarbonate or some other material of high impact resistance is envisioned, to withstand possible impacts by falling objects due to aftershocks and falls by the node itself. A related task is the development of a systematic program for redundant deployment of the sensor nodes and reserve units for replacement of disabled units (Suzuki et al., 2008), to ensure preservation of the network connection and information gathering functions.

4.2 Basic experiment on video transmission and communication

We next performed a basic experiment on transmission of the video images via the ad hoc connections of the camera node. Two views of the outdoor experimental site are shown in Fig. 7. To facilitate investigation of the basic performance, we chose a location providing good visibility. In each trial, the camera node was placed at an arbitrary position, established an ad hoc network with the host PC, and, on a "shoot" signal from the host PC, performed video information acquisition for 5 s.

Fig. 7. Setup for Video Capturing and File Transferring Experiment
(In case of distance=15 [m])

Video captures of images sampled at 1-s intervals from a 5-s video file display on the PC, after shooting video and data transmission (transmission distance, 15 m) by the camera node, are shown in Fig. 8.

For each image, as indicated in the figure, information related to the acquired video is included in the video filename, in the form "date+time+GPS position information+imaging/image capture length (sec)+name of acquiring device.ASF (file format-specifying extension)". As shown in Fig. 9, the filename consolidates the data on the time that the video recording began the position, and the file format.

The images shown in Fig. 8(a) are video captures of the image obtained by the camera node using video streaming. They demonstrate the capability to visualize trees (about 2 m tall) and building windows at about a 10-m distance from the device. The images shown in Fig. 8(b) are from the same position, but include the image of a person walking past the camera node. The person passed the camera node at a distance of about 1 m, and this image clearly provides sufficient detail for confirming movement.

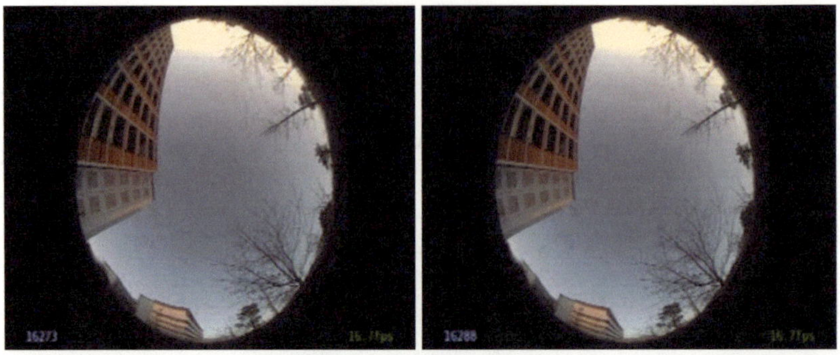

(a) Captured video filename: 2008.02.28.17.20.17.3546.5874,N,13936.6583,E.5.rcomm1.ASF

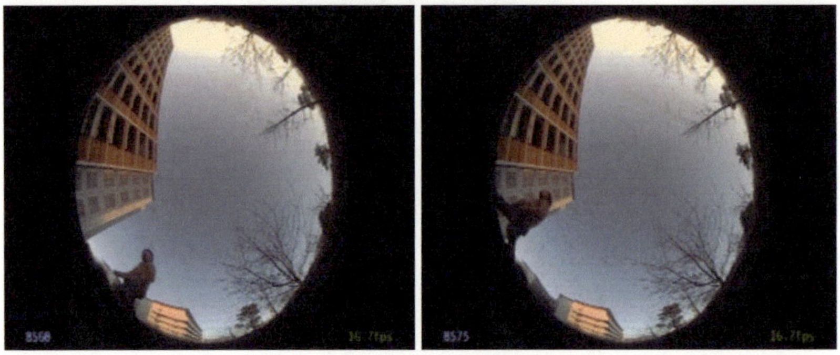

(b) Captured video filename: 2008.02.28.17.12.22.3546.6918,N,13936.5564,E.5.rcomm1.ASF

Fig. 8. Examples of Captured View by Developed Wireless Camera Node

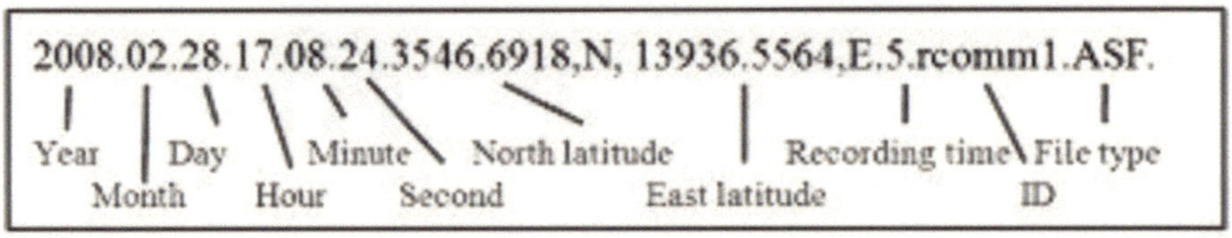

Fig. 9. A Format of filename for including the conditions

The experimental results verify that it is possible to transmit on-site information acquired by the embedded CMOS camera, together with the acquisition time and position and other related information, to a separate terminal via a network formed by ad hoc connection. The acquired image is distorted by the fisheye lens, but can be converted to a panorama view by lens reverse-modeling computation after acquisition.

We next investigated the video transmission capability of this system, in the aforementioned outdoor environment. The imaging data was acquired as 360-kB-sized video (resolution CIF standard 352×288 pixels) file in advanced streaming format (ASF), at distances of 15 and 30 m from the camera node to the PC, outdoors, using file transfer protocol (FTP).

At the transmission distance of 15 m, the duration of the experiment was 10 min and 35 sec, in which 49 video files were transmitted. The mean time per file was thus 12.96 s (transmission rate: 0.23 Mbit/s). Similarly, at the transmission distance of 30 m, the experiment duration was 10 min and 52 s with transmission of 43 files, and thus an mean time per file of 15.16 s (0.19

Mbit/s). These mean times include the entire transmission process based on AODV and FTP, as indicated in Fig. 10. As shown, some variation occurred in file transmission time, but the results clearly confirm the capability for stable transmission.

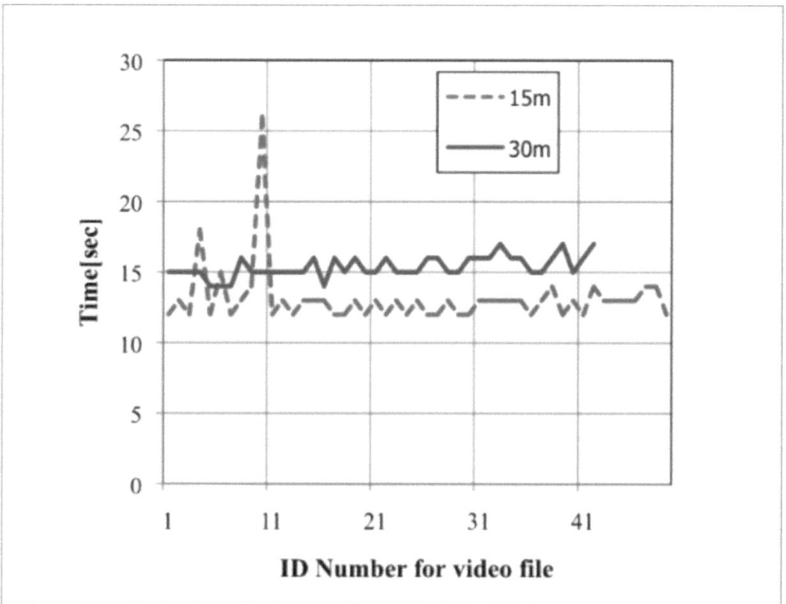

Fig. 10. Video File Transferring Performance

The experimental results thus verify the capability of the camera node for effective acquisition and transmission of information on the surroundings at the camera node site.

4.3 Experiment on information gathering in ad hoc network

The next experiment was performed to verify the basic capability for multihop transmission of site information (i.e., video images) acquired by individual camera nodes via the ad hoc wireless camera network constructed by two or more camera nodes. As shown in Fig. 11, the experiment was performed in the minimal two-hop configuration at outdoor environment, using a notebook PC with a wireless LAN adaptor and two camera nodes (Node 1 and Node 2; Fig. 12). Direct communication between the PC and Node 2 was blocked by the building, necessitating two-hop transmission. The PC served as the host for consolidation of the acquired image data, Node 1 as the relay station, and Node 2 as the information acquisition node and FTP uploader to the host PC via Node 1.

A file size of 360 kB was used for the video data (ASF format, 352×288 resolution, video playback time 5 sec), uploaded in a hop configuration with data acquisition by Node 2, transmittted to Node 1 and then from Node 1 to the PC, followed by a 15-s interval and then initiation of the next transmission, in a repeating sequence over a 40-min time period.

Table 2 is a typical routing table for the output by Node 2 (IP address 192.168.1.249) using AODV-UU in the video transmission. As this table shows, the destination was 192.168.1.200, which is the IP address of the PC, and the next hop designation was 192.168.1.103, the IP address of Node 1, thus confirming that the data transmitted by Node 2 was routed to the PC via Node 1. In the experiment, Node 2 transmitted captured videos, all of which were received by the PC. Thus, the remote site information was transmitted over two hops with no difference in file size, indicating that the information acquired on-site was transmitted effectively via the ad hoc wireless network constructed by the camera nodes. Fig. 14 shows network performance for transmitting the video files. Average time of transferring video files is 23.1[sec] and average throughput value is 16.2[KByte/sec].

Fig. 15 shows the behavior related to actual packet transmission. Retransmitting data and route error were happened frequently. Camera node retransferred the video data and deliver video data via wireless ad-hoc network.

Finally, Fig. 16 shows the examples for browsing collected video files that are registered to Geographic Information System (GIS), actually 'Google Earth', based on GPS information. As mentioned above, GPS information is included in each file name and it is utilized to register the data to GIS. When the operator click the thumbnail on the interface, it is to play specified video file.

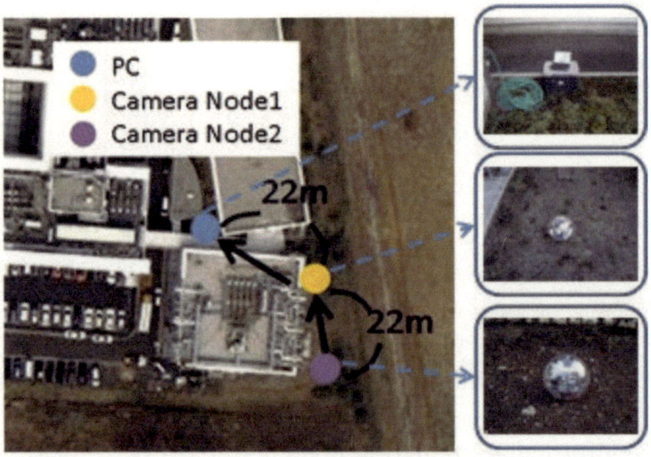

Fig. 11. Set up for Two-hop Communication Experiment

Fig. 12. Experimental Devices (Laptop PC, Camera Node1 and Camera Node2)

# Time: 17:41:42.244 IP: 192.168.1.105, sequence no: 136 entries/active: 2/2					
Destination	Next hop	HC	St.Sequence No.	Expire Flags	Interface Precursors
192.168.1.200	192.168.1.110	2	VAL 183	2940	Eth0
192.168.1.110	192.168.1.110	1	VAL 34	2934	Eth0

Table 2. Organized Routing Table

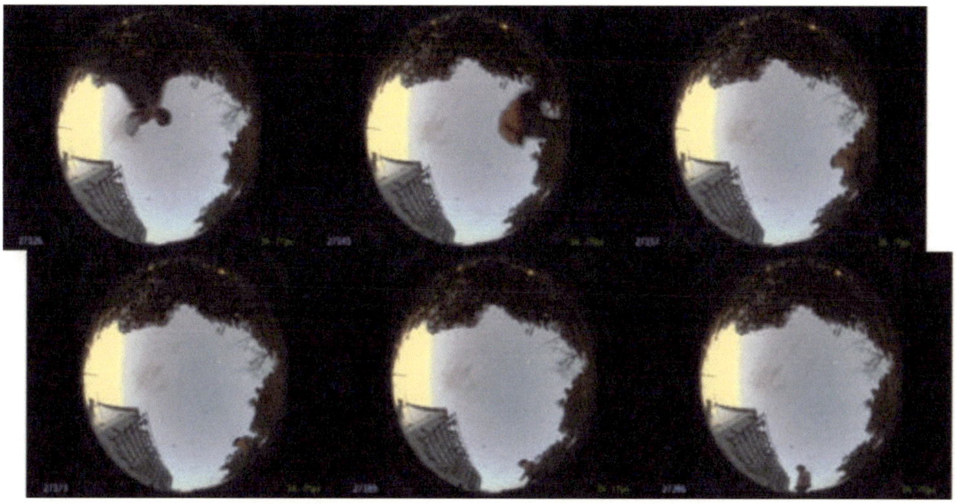

Captured video file name: 2008.02.28.17.12.22.3546.6918,N,13936.5564,E.5.rcomm1.ASF

Fig. 13. Examples of Captured and Transferred View by Camera node 2

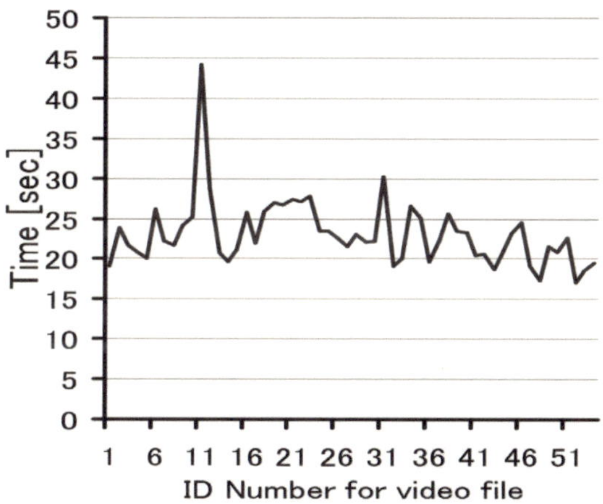

Fig. 14. Network performance

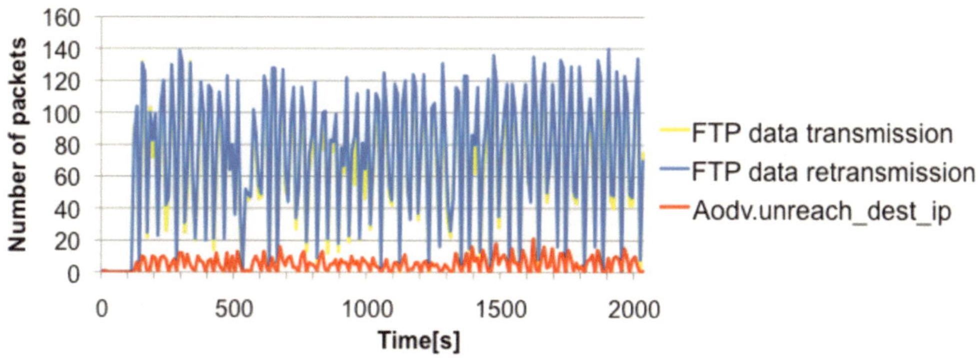

Fig. 15. Behavior of network packet

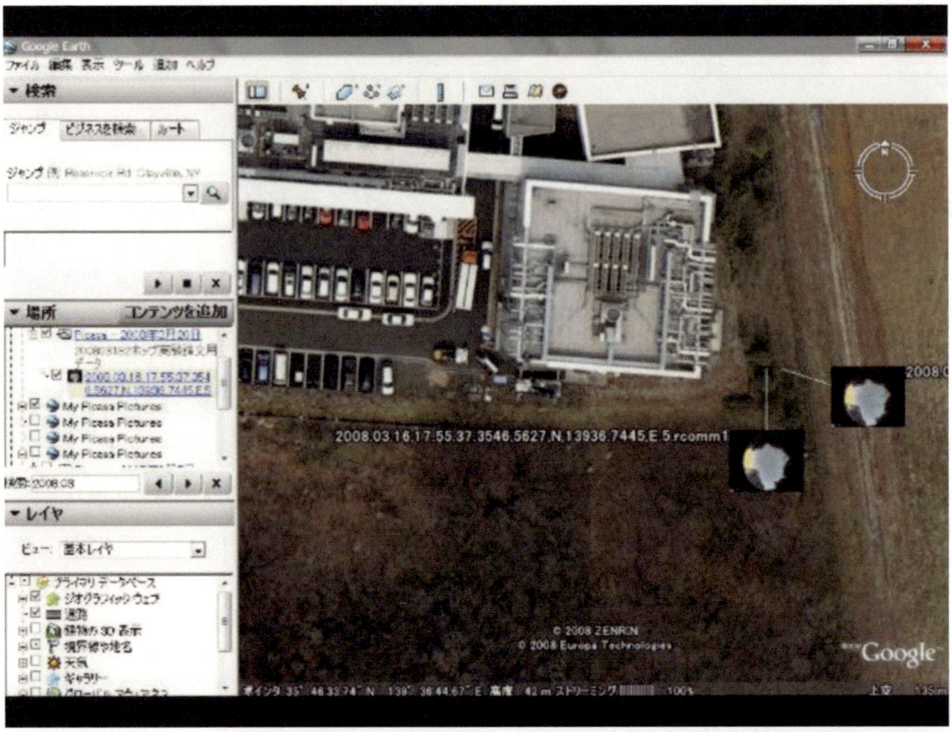
Google Earth
ファイル 編集 表示 ツール 追加 ヘルプ
検索
ジャンプ
ビジネスを検索
ルート
場所
コンテンツを追加
My Picasa Pictures
レイヤ
2008.03.16.17.55.37.3546.5627.N.13936.7445.E.5.rcomm1
© 2008 ZENRIN
© 2008 Europa Technologies
Google

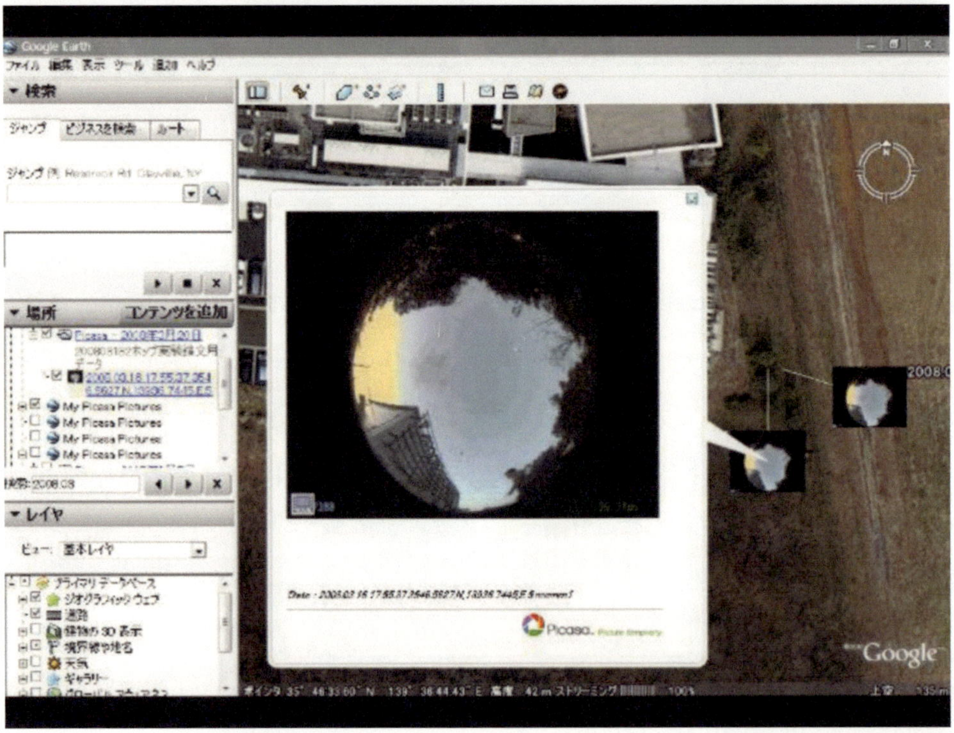
Google Earth
ファイル 編集 表示 ツール 追加 ヘルプ
検索
ジャンプ
ビジネスを検索
ルート
場所
コンテンツを追加
My Picasa Pictures
レイヤ
Picasa
Google

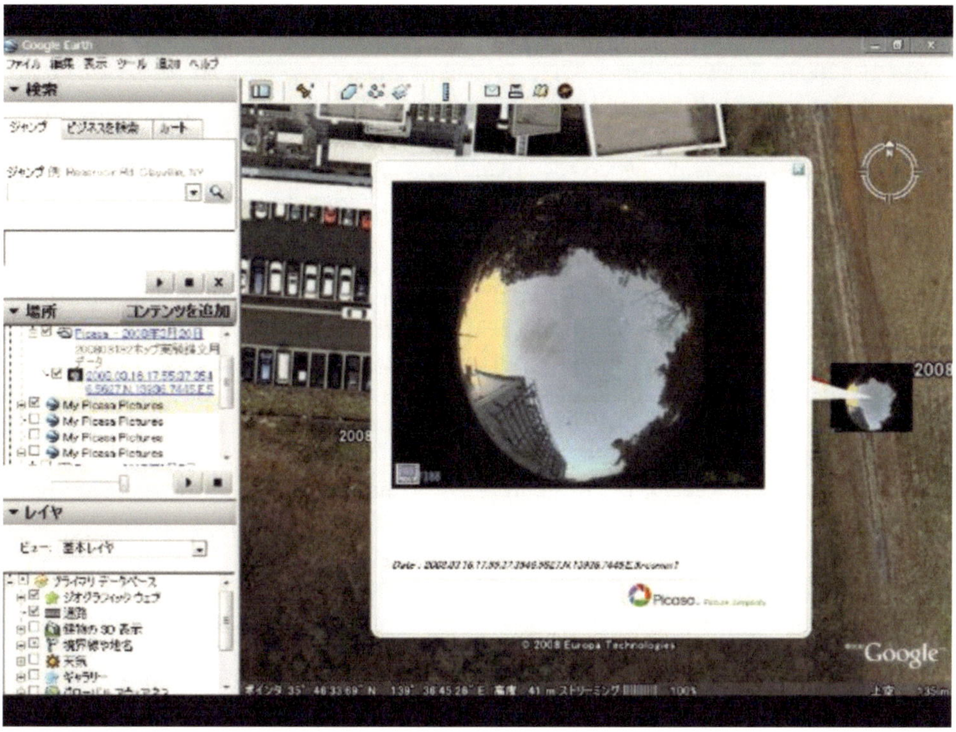

Fig. 16. Registered video files to GIS

5. Conclusion

In this report, we have proposed a sensor node and related wireless network for information gathering in disaster areas. We have described a "camera node" prototype developed on this basis, containing a camera with a fisheye lens, a passive self-righting mechanism to maintain the camera orientation, and the systems capability for construction of an ad hoc wireless network, together with a GPS adaptor and an embedded computer timer to identify its position and imaging time. The camera node is relatively easy to deploy and enables acquisition and consolidation of temporally and spatially coherent information on disaster areas. These functions were verified in experiments with this camera sensor prototype. Utilizing prototypes data transmission experiment was done and ad-hoc network construction and stable video data transmission were also verified.

We are planning to incorporate modifications to enable more accurate adjustment of the embedded camera attitude. In addition, although a transparent acrylic shell was used in the prototype for the experiments described in this report, we are considering the use of polycarbonate or other impact-resistant material for the shell to increase its durability under dropping or impact from falling debris and rubble. We intend to investigate the development of systems for deployment, retrieval, and redeployment of the camera-bearing nodes and networks by robots or other automated equipment, utilizing the relative ease and simplicity of deployment characteristic of these sensor nodes and the consequent freedom from a need for complex deployment control equipment or procedures. Investigation is also in progress for further reduction of their size and weight, and discussions will be necessary to determine their optimum size for use in disaster areas.

6. Reference

Tadokoro, S. (2009). *Rescue Robotics: DDT Project on Robots and Systems for Urban Search and Rescue*, Springer, ISBN-10: 1848824734, London

Weiser, M., (1991). The Computer for the Twenty-First Century, *Scientific American*, 94-10

Takeda H. (1991).Data Carrier, *Nihon kogyo shinbun sha, (in Japanese)*

Kurabayashi, D., Noda, K., Asama, H., Kawabata, K., Kaetsu, H., and Hashimoto, H. (2003): Information Assistance for Search-and-Rescue by Intelligent Data Carriers and a Data Retrieval Blimp, *Journal of Robotics and Mechatronics*, 15, 5 , 521-527

Asama, H., Hada, Y., Kawabata, K. (2005). "Overview of Information Infrastructure and Ubiquitous Devices for Victim Search" *Proceedings of the 2nd International Conference on Ubiquitous Robots and Ambient Intelligence (URAmI'05)*, KRW056

Kawabata, K., Hada, Y., Kaetsu, H., Asama, H. (2006)."Ubiquitous Victim Search Device : Intelligent Data Carrier for Rescue", *Proceedings of IEEE Conference on Robotics and Automation*, 4306-4308

Hada, Y., Kawabata, K., Kaetsu, H., Koguchi, H., Asama, H., (2006). "Rescue Communicators for Grobal Victim Search and Local Rescue Planning", *Proceedings of IEEE/RSJ International Conference on Intelligent Robots and Systems*, 3510-3513

Takizawa, O., Shibayama, A., Hosokawa, M., Takanashi, K., Murakami, M., Hisada, Y., Hada, Y., Kawabata, K., Noda, I., Asama, H., (2007). Hybrid Radio Frequency Identification System for Use in Disaster Relief as Positioning Source and Emergency Message Boards, *Mobile Response*, LNCS 4458, 85-94, ISNN: 0302-9743

Inoue, K., Yamamoto, M., Mae, Y., Takubo, T., Arai, T. (2005). Search Balls: Sensor Units for Searching Inside of Rubble, *Advanced Robotics*, 19, 8 , 861 - 878

Ando, S., Tamura, Y., Tobe, Y., Minami, M., (2005), *Sensor Network Technology*, Tokyo Denki Press *(in Japanese)*

Fukatsu, T. & Hirafuji, M. (2005). Field Monitoring Using Sensor-Nodes with a Web Server, *Journal of Robotics and Mechatronics*, 17, 2, 164-172

Nakata, M., & Kushiro, N., (2007). Practical Solution for Constructing Sensor Network in Building and Home Control System, *Journal of the Robotics Society of Japan*, 25, 4, 530-533

Chemel, B., Mutshler, E., Schempf, H. (1991). Cyclops : Miniature Robotic Reconnaissance System, *Proc. of the 1999 IEEE International Conference on Robotics and Automation*, 2298-2302

Schempf, H., Mutshler, E., Chemel, B., Nayar, S., Piepgras, C., Crowley, W., Boehmke, S. (1999). Evolution of Urban Robotic System Development, *Proceedings of the 1999 IEEE/ASME International Conference on Advanced Intelligent Mechatronics*, 689-694

Hada, Y., Kawabata, K., Kaetsu, H., Koguchi, H., Asama, H. (2006). Rescue Communicators for Grobal Victim Search and Local Rescue Planning, *Proceedings of IEEE/RSJ International Conference on Intelligent Robots and Systems*, 3510-3513

Suzuki, T., Sugizaki, R., Kawabata, K., Hada, Y., Tobe, Y. (2008). Development and Management of Wireless Sensor Network using Mobile Robots for Gathering Environment Information", *Distributed Autonomous Robotic Systems 8*, Asama, H.; Kurokawa, H.; Ota, J.; Sekiyama, K. (Eds.), 63-72, ISBN: 978-3-642-00643-2

4

A Machine Vision System for Automated Headlamp Lens Inspection

S. Satorres Martínez, J. Gómez Ortega,
J. Gámez García and A. Sánchez García
Electronic Engineering and Automation Department. University of Jaén
Jaén, Spain

1. Introduction

Headlamps on vehicles are primarily responsable for illuminating the traffic space during periods of low visibility, such as night or precipitation. In addition, headlamps are also considered as a cosmetic part, playing an important role in the car styling. Because of this, carmakers request a great precision for surface defect detection in all the headlamp components.

One of these components is the cover lens (Fig. 1). This part used to be made of glass but polycarbonate lenses have become today's standard. In comparison to glass, plastic lenses have the advantages of higher resistance to impact, lower weight, small manufacture tolerances and much greater freedom of design thanks to the possibility of undercuts [Wördenweber et al. (2007)]. But for scratch resistance, policarbonate lenses must be coated. Failures during the manufacturing and coating process lead to different kind of defects known as *aesthetic defects*. Although this kind of defects do not entail any functional disadvantage, may be considered as aesthetically displeasing.

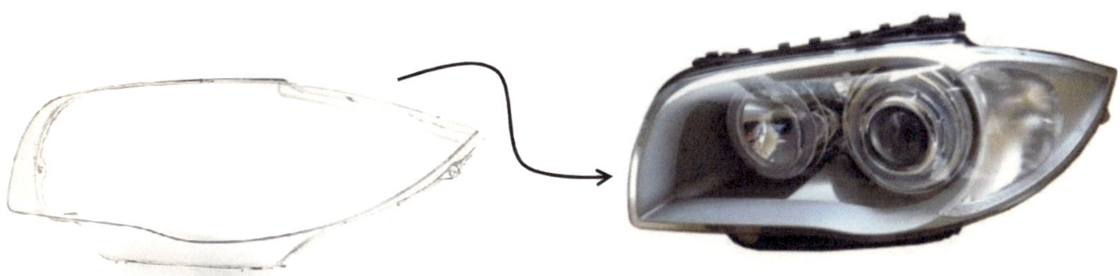

Fig. 1. The Serie 1 BMW headlamp and its cover lens.

Nowadays, the quality control of the lenses is made by manual means. The results of this process depend on *human factors* as subjectivity and visual tiring, that may lead to a dissatisfactory quality control. For this reason, a fully automated inspection system is highly desirable.

This chapter presents a machine vision system capable of revealing, detecting and characterizing *aesthetic defects* on headlamp lenses. Due to its geometry and dimensions, this part requires multiple vision sensor poses to completely observe it and, our proposal, performs an automatic selection of these poses. For this task, a sensor planning system that computes the number and sensor locations has been developed. This system includes useful information provided by the human inspector, as the maximum defect size that should be located in every lens area, to fix better the sensor poses. In order to code the expert information for including it in the sensor planning system, a fuzzy rule based system is also developed. To compute the number and distribution of vision sensors, the planning system applies a genetic algorithm.

Furthermore, as some kind of defects and the lens have the same optical properties, special lighting conditions are required to enhance defects and to simplify the subsequent processing algorithms. To solve this problem, we also introduce in this chapter the special lighting conditions required, presenting the lighting techniques capable of revealing defects, with different optical properties, on transparent parts. Once the acquisition stage is finished, the images should be processed to extract suitable information. So, the computer vision algorithms involved in delivering this kind of information should be defined.

The chapter is organized as follows. In the next section, the task that the machine vision system has to accomplish is described; also a former work that offers a global solution to the automated inspection of lenses. Section 3 presents the proposed machine vision system describing, in detail, all its components. Finally, the machine vision is experimentally tested using a commercial lens model and the results are offered in Section 4, whereas Section 5 outlines the conclusions of this work.

2. Problem description: the headlamp lens inspection

To date, the quality control of headlamp lenses is visually made by an expert operator, or simply, by an inspector, that checks the absence of aesthetic defects on the lens surface. He also decides if it has to be rejected or packaged for further processing. The aesthetic defect sizes may vary from tenths of millimeter to centimeters and, according to their shape, can be divided into the following groups (Fig. 2):

- punctual defects (bubbles, blisters and black points);
- lineal defects (threads, scratches);
- surface defects (excesses of varnish, orange skin).

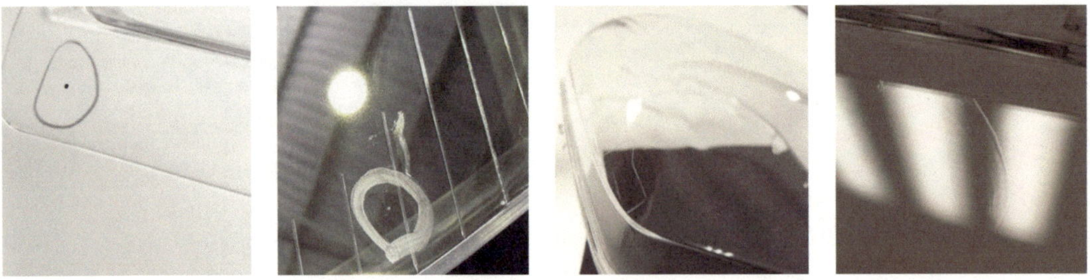

Fig. 2. Aesthetic defects. From left to right: punctual and opaque defect (a black point), punctual and transparent defect (a blister), lineal defect (a scratch) and surface defect (excesses of varnish).

Moreover, to meet the customer requirements, and also to establish a standard in this manual process, the inspector must follow the *inspection guideline*. This guideline is a document which presents the acceptance and rejection criterions for the lens. The time invested to inspect the lens and the visual path that the inspector must follow during the inspection are also described in this document. Normally, a sketch of the lens divided into colored areas is presented to define the rejection criterions. Every color indicates different inspection requirements, so the defect dimension that has to be located in each lens area differs from one to another (Fig. 3).

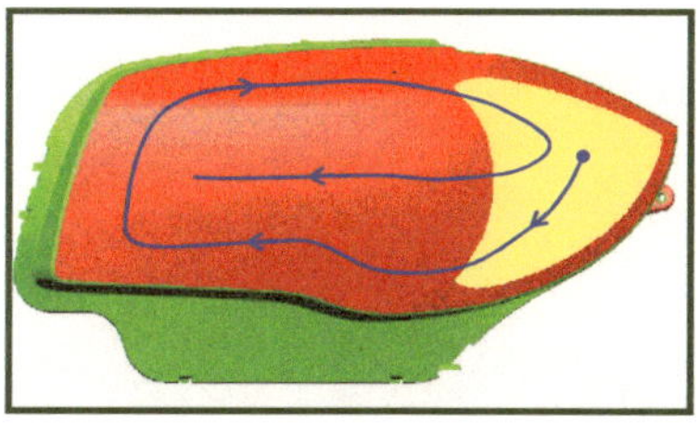

Defect geometry	Red	Yellow	Green
Punctual mm	0.7 •	1 •	1.5 •
Surface mm	Not visible P/V	6 ● ■	10 ● ■
Linear mm	1 -	2 –	5 –

Fig. 3. Information presented in the inspection guideline.

Due to the complexity of the defects to be detected: small size, different optical properties—transparent, opaque—and geometries, it is desirable to offer a robust solution capable of automating the lens inspection process. In this respect, machine vision provides innovative solutions for automatic surface inspection systems [Malamas et al. (2003)] and this technology had been used in the first attempt to automate the lens inspection. The development was a machine vision prototype known as VIGILE (Visual Intelligent Glass Imperfections Looking Equipment)[Automation & Robotics (2001)]. It was supposed that by successive scanning of the surface of the lens, that was laid down on a specific automatically adaptable carrier, VIGILE detected different types of defects using three stations of inspection. This machine vision system could be adapted to inspect four model of lenses. Finally, this prototype was not commercialized because it did not fit to the lens manufacturers expectations.

Our proposal presents substancial differences respect to the VIGILE system. Firstly, for the image acquisition the lens surface is not scanned; instead of this, a set of suitable sensor poses is computed through a sensor planning system. Secondly, defects with different optical properties are not identified in several stations of inspection. In our machine vision system, only one lighting device with flexibility for selecting different lighting techniques is utilized. As regards the image processing, the information about the computer vision algorithms included in the VIGILE was not available. In our case, and thanks to the lighting system, the images are processed utilizing algorithms with a very low computational burden, allowing the real time inspection.

3. The machine vision system

To accomplish the automated inspection of lenses, a machine vision system has been developed and it is presented in figure 4. This system consists of the following components:

- an anthropomorphic 6-DOF Stäubli RX60 industrial manipulator and a CS8 controller;
- a firewire monochrome vision sensor GUPPY F-080B;
- a TFT monitor as lighting system;
- a host PC to mainly compute the sensor poses, to control the lighting system and to process the images.

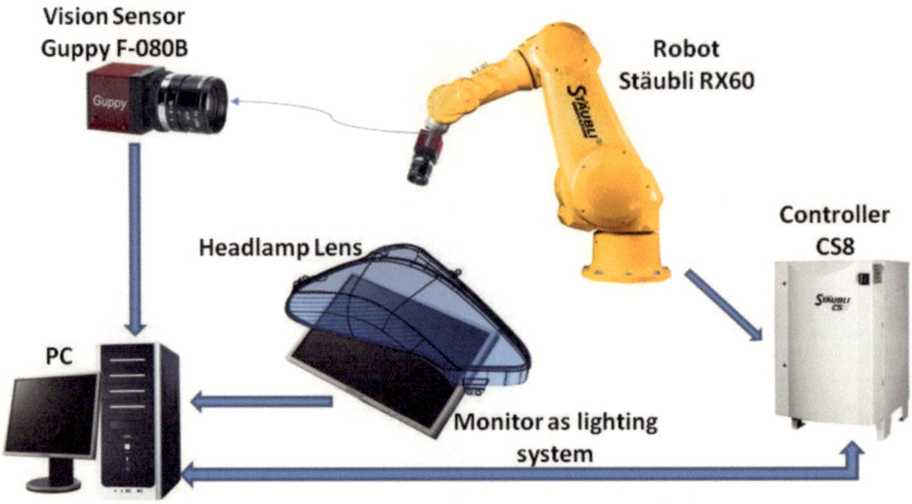

Fig. 4. The machine vision system.

The attention is first focused in the image acquisition. The monochrome vision sensor is mounted, as end-effector, on the industrial manipulator. This enables flexibility and accuracy in the vision sensor poses being easily adaptable to different lens models. The vision sensor poses are computed off-line using a host PC. Also, the computer vision algorithms are executed in it.

As regards the lighting system, the machine vision includes a TFT monitor. This device enables flexibility for selecting different lighting solutions, specially adapted to enhance all the types of aesthetic defects [Satorres Martínez et al. (2009c)]. The next subsections are dedicated to introduce the steps that had been carried out to finally automate the lens inspection process. They are:

- planning the sensor poses;
- selecting the lighting system;
- the image processing.

3.1 Planning the sensor poses

In occasions, one single viewpoint is not enough to sample the whole surface of a part. This is the case of a headlamp lens, that due to its geometry, size and the dimension of defects that have to be located in its surface requires multiple sensor poses to observe it.

The problem of automating the sensor vision poses in order to select suitable viewpoints for the object inspection is know as sensor planning or sensor placement [Sheng, Xi, Tan, Song&Chen (2003)]. Several researchers have proposed sensor planning approaches that fall into two main categories [Tarabanis, Allen & Tsai (1995)]: *generate-and-test* and *synthesis*. The *generate-and-test* approach [Kakikura (1990)], [Yi et al. (1990)] simplifies the sensor planning into a search problem in a restricted solution space. Although it is straightforward and easy to implement, the computational cost is very high due to the large number of candidate viewpoints.

Contrary to the *generate-and-test*, the *synthesis* approach [Cowan & Kovesi (1988)], [Tarabanis, Tsai & Allen (1995)] requires a deeper understanding of the relationships

between the parameters to be planned—sensor poses and optical parameters—and the goals to be achieved. Task constraints are characterized analytically and the sensor parameter values, that satisfy these constraints, are directly determined from the analytical relationships. However, this approach has two main drawbacks. Firstly, constraint equations in high dimensional space that are not easy to solve; and secondly, it is very difficult to mathematically express the exact solution regions to these equations. Other ongoing work combines the previous methodologies for solving the problem [Sheng, Xi, Song & Chen (2003)], or study it under a multi-objective framework [Dunn (2005)].
In the proposed machine vision system a sensor planning system, that automatically generates a set of vision sensor poses for inspecting the lens, has been developed. This system is deeply described in [Satorres Martínez et al. (2009d)] but its main components are stated below.

3.1.1 The sensor planning system

The Sensor Planning System (SPS) (Fig. 5) requires several inputs to achieve its goal. First, a detailed specification about the environment (e.g., the object under observation, the available sensors, other useful information for the inspection task) should be provided. Then, the SPS automatically determines the vision sensor parameter values (e.g., number of sensors and their poses) to take images from the whole headlamp lens. In order to determine an optimal set of vision sensor poses the SPS uses a genetic algorithm. Therefore, the system inputs and the corresponding output are the following:

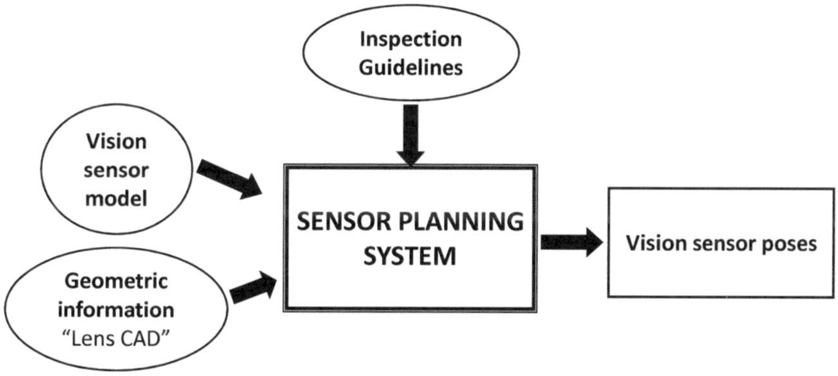

Fig. 5. The sensor planning system.

1. System inputs.
   The a priori known information is taken into account in the viewpoint computation:
   a. geometric and physical information of the headlamp lens that is extracted from its CAD model;
   b. a vision sensor model that approximates its geometrical properties. The model adopted is the pin-hole lens model. This model assumes that light rays travel in straight lines and all the rays entering the vision sensor system pass through a single point [Forsyth & Ponce (2003)];
   c. the *inspection guideline* that provides the acceptance and rejection criterions for lenses. As this document is defined by experts in lens inspection to model this knowledge, for including it in the SPS, a Fuzzy Rule-Based System (FRBS) has been developed. This FRBS was initially presented in [Satorres Martínez et al. (2009a)].

2. System output.
   For each viewpoint the SPS computes four positional parameters (Fig. 6):
   a. three degrees of freedom of viewpoint's position. These are the vision sensor Cartesian coordinates in the world coordinate system;
   b. one degree of freedom of viewpoint's orientation (θ_{Z_c}). This angle corresponds to the vision sensor rotation around its optical axis. The other degrees of freedom in the viewpoint's orientation, θ_{X_c} and θ_{Y_c} angles, are not considered, since the optical axis of every point of view is set to look inward to the nearer lens area.

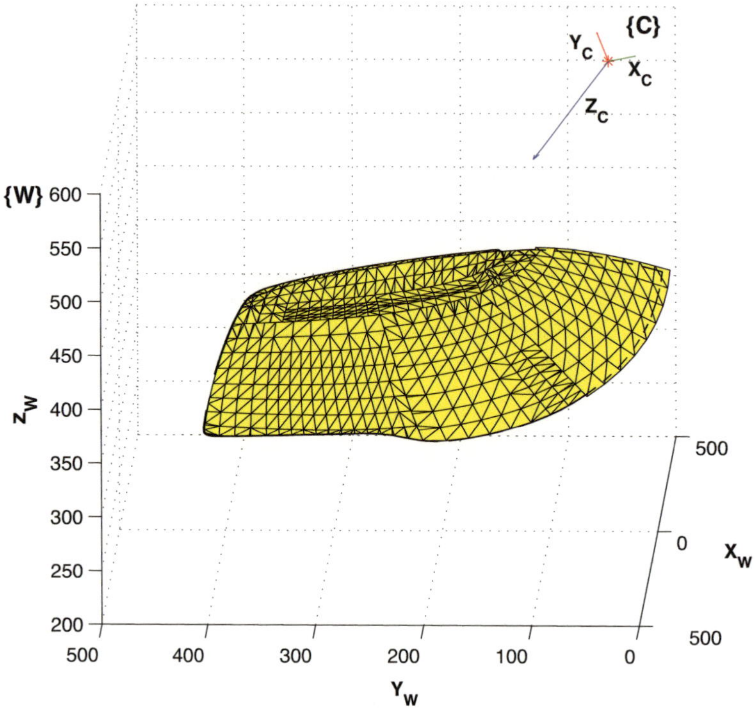

Fig. 6. A vision sensor pose and the lens CAD model.

Moreover, an admisible viewpoint should satisfy the following constraints that are checked in the following order:

a. *visibility*: this constraint ensures that there is no occlusion between the viewpoint and the lens surface to be inspected;
b. *field of view*: vision sensors have limited field of view by the size of the sensor area and the focal length of the lens. The homogeneous transformation matrix is used to compute the surface points that will be projected inside the sensor area. This mathematical modeling gives a direct relation between the camera and world coordinate systems. So, the image coordinates x and y of a point in the world coordinate system ${}^{w}P$ are obtained from:

$$x = \frac{{}^{c}P_1}{{}^{c}P_4} = \frac{a_{11} \cdot X + a_{12} \cdot Y + a_{13} \cdot Z + a_{14}}{a_{41} \cdot X + a_{42} \cdot Y + a_{43} \cdot Z + a_{44}} \quad (1)$$

$$y = \frac{^{c}P_2}{^{c}P_4} = \frac{a_{21} \cdot X + a_{22} \cdot Y + a_{23} \cdot Z + a_{24}}{a_{41} \cdot X + a_{42} \cdot Y + a_{43} \cdot Z + a_{44}} \tag{2}$$

where a_{ij} are the elements of the homogeneous transform matrix ${}^{c}_{w}T$ that relates the vision sensor and the world coordinate systems through a rotation, translation and perspective transform [Satorres Martínez et al. (2009d)]. A point in the world coordinate system ${}^{w}P$ can be referenced in the vision sensor coordinate system ${}^{c}P$ as:

$$\begin{bmatrix} {}^{c}P \\ \cdots \\ 1 \end{bmatrix} = {}^{c}_{w}T \cdot \begin{bmatrix} {}^{w}P \\ \cdots \\ 1 \end{bmatrix} \tag{3}$$

c. *viewing angle*: implies that the curvature of the field of view can be chosen by selecting a limit between the viewing direction and the normal of the surface points;
d. *resolution*: ensures that the smaller size of defect accepted in every lens area with length l is imaged to at least p pixels on the image plane. Considering the lens model (Fig. 7), the following can be formulated:

$$x_s = \frac{h}{f} \cdot p \cdot x_c \leq l \tag{4}$$

where x_s is the scene feature size, h is the distance from the camera lens to the surface to be inspected, f is the focal length and x_c is the pixel size.

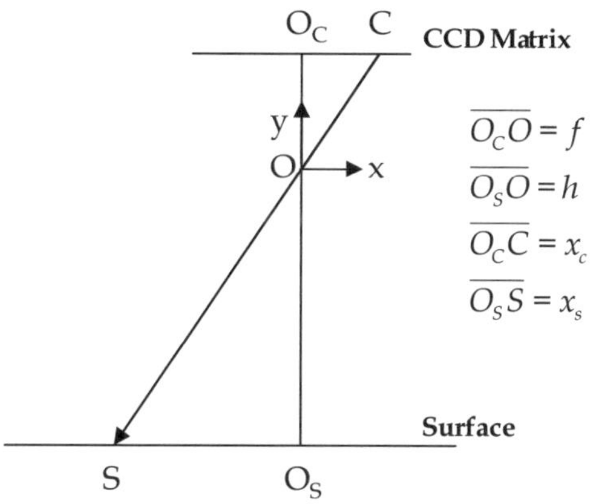

Fig. 7. Resolution constraint.

3.1.2 Optimal sensor placement

With respect to the genetic algorithm, developed for the optimal vision sensor placement, two main aspects are worthy of mention:

- representation of candidate solutions to the problem in a "genetic" form (*chromosome representation*);
- establishment of a *fitness function* that rates each solution in the population.

The genetic operators to produce new individuals from the exiting ones are widely used in evolutionary computing [Eiben (2003)] and also are deeply described in [Satorres Mart´ınez (2010)].

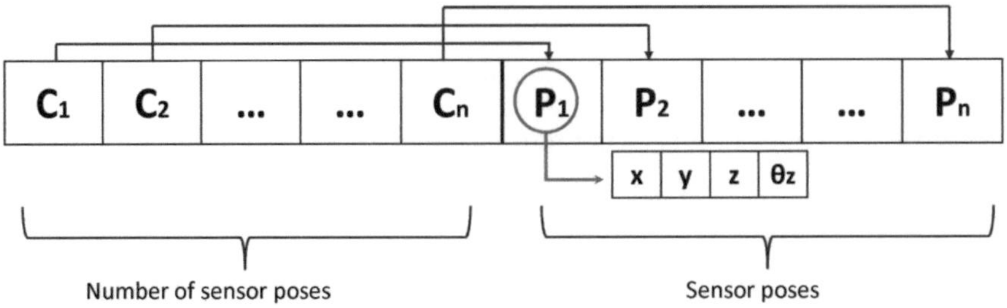

Fig. 8. Chromosome structure.

1. Chromosome representation.
   The chromosome contains two different type of genes (Fig. 8): control genes and parametric genes [Chen & Li (2002)]. Parametric genes ($P_i = (x,y, z, \theta_z)$) mean the sensor poses with $x,y, z \in \mathbb{R}$, $\theta_z \in [-\pi,\pi]$, and control genes (C_i) are a binary variable meaning the number of viewpoints. The activation of the parametric genes is governed by the value of the control genes.
   When "1" is assigned to a control gene, the associated parametric gene to that particular active control gene is activated. The parametric genes are inactive when the corresponding control genes are "0".
   To determine the chromosome length, the maximum number of viewpoints must be estimated through [Chen & Li (2004)]:

$$N = \frac{2 \cdot S_{lens}}{S_{view}} \tag{5}$$

   where S_{lens} is the lens surface area size and S_{view} is a single view size. So, the length of a chromosome is expressed as: $N + k \cdot N$, where N is the maximum number of viewpoints and k is the number of parameters planned for each point of view. With this chromosome representation, all individuals in the population have the same size, but the number of active viewpoints may be variable.
2. Fitness function.
   Each individual of the population is evaluated by a fitness function (Eq. (6)), that is given as a weighted sum of two contradictories objectives, each of which characterizes the quality of the solution with respect to an associated requirement. Thus, the fitness function is written as

$$F = w_1 \cdot OBJ_1 + w_2 \cdot (1 - OBJ_2) \tag{6}$$

   where w_i are the weighting coefficients and OBJ_i are the objectives that have to be satisfied being summarized as follows:
   a. **OBJECTIVE 1** (OBJ_1):
      Minimizing the number of viewpoints (C_i):

$$OBJ_1 = \min \frac{\sum_{i=1}^{n} C_i}{n_C} \tag{7}$$

      where the number of occurrences of "1" in the control genes is equivalent to the number of viewpoints for each chromosome, and n_C is the number of control genes.

b. **OBJECTIVE 2** (OBJ_2):
Maximizing the accuracy of the vision inspection, that is, how the resolution of every camera pose fits to the resolution required to inspect its scanned lens area.
To evaluate this objective a two-dimensional binary array, known as the *quality matrix* (q_m), is created by:

$$q_m(i,j) = \begin{cases} 1 & \text{if } s_j \text{ fulfill the constraints for } v_i \\ 0 & \text{otherwise} \end{cases} \tag{8}$$

q_m will be an array of $r \times c$ dimensions, where r is the number of viewpoints and c is the number of CAD finite elements. If $q_m(i, j) = 1$ the surface point s_j is viewable from the viewpoint v_i and also fulfills the aforementioned constraints.
Nevertheless, a column of 0's in the quality matrix means that there is some surface point that cannot be seen by the available sensor poses and therefore it is not possible to create a plan that can view the entirely of the lens. Conversely, if there are not nonzero-columns, a plan to view the whole lens exists.

3.2 The lighting system

In computer vision applications, the provision of a correct and high-quality illumination is absolutely decisive [Telljohann (2008)]. Hence, the light needs to be provided in a control manner to accentuate the desired features of the surface avoiding disturbances which could alter the quality of the acquired image. So, an inadequate lighting system selection involves the development of complex computer vision algorithms to extract information from the images, or even imply an unfeasible vision task [Jahr (2008)]. Finding the best setup is usually a result of experiments with commercial lighting systems. Next subsection shows the main experiences obtained evaluating several lighting techniques to enhance aesthetic defects on the lens surface.

3.2.1 Lighting techniques

There is a rich variety of lighting techniques that may be used in machine vision. From the available commercial lighting systems, the most recommended for this application are the back-light and the diffuse dark field systems and both of them have been studied.
The diffuse back-light achieves non-directional uniform illumination resulting in a bright image, whereby surface features appear in gray levels. This technique is normally used for viewing the silhouette of opaque objects and for inspecting transparent ones. But this light is suitable when the contrast between different surface qualities is high so, in the lens, only not-transparent surface defects are revealed (Fig. 9).
Concerning the dark field illumination, the angle of the incident light rays to the surface normal vector is very large. This results in a dark appearance of the surface, but salient features, such as scratches, appear bright in the image. Hence, this type of illumination is used to detect small particles in flat parts. In addition, applied this lighting system to the less curvature areas in the lens only revealed surface dirt as dust (Fig. 10).
Another lighting technique, that it is utilized for inspecting reflective surfaces is the structured lighting [Seulin et al. (2001)] and [Aluze et al. (2002)]. Adapting this technique for inspecting the lens surface, the transparent aesthetic defects can be enhanced. So, the lighting principle in which it is based this kind of structured back-light system is the following (Fig. 11): the orientation of a surface imperfection is different from the flawless

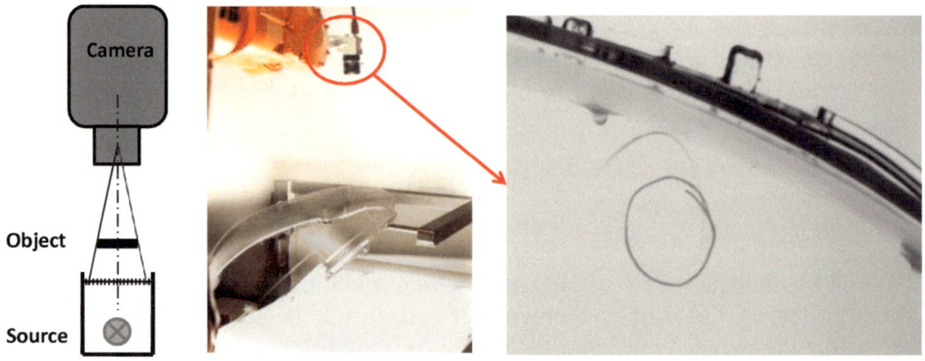

Fig. 9. Diffuse back-light. From left to right: principle of lighting; robotic platform with back-light illumination; the image acquisition.

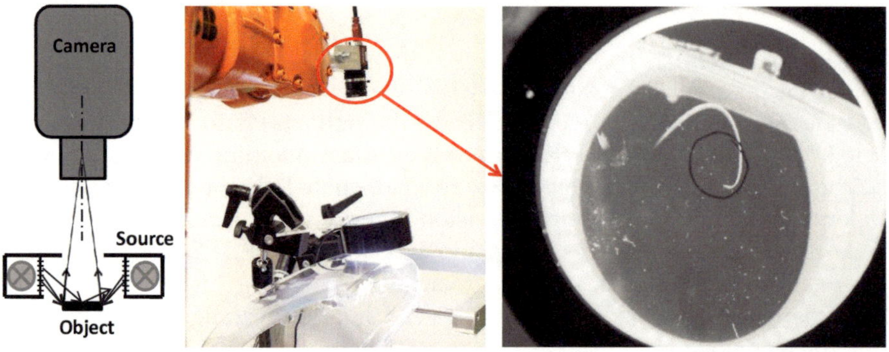

Fig. 10. Diffuse darkfield. From left to right: principle of lighting; robotic platform with darkfield illumination; the image acquisition.

Fig. 11. Structured lighting. From left to right: principle of lighting; robotic platform with structured lighting; the image acquisition.

ones, so incident ray lights are not scattered in the same direction [Coulot et al. (1997)]. Therefore, a defect, because of its orientation, appears in the capture image as a set of luminous pixels among a dark zone. It is interesting to point out that the imperfections are properly revealed when they are next to the light transitions. So, to ensure the defect detection in the whole lens surface, the light stripes have to scan all over the sensor field of view.

As it can be seen, two lighting techniques should be applied for enhancing aesthetic defects: the backlight (for opaque defects) and the structured back-light (for transparent ones). This flexibility is achieved with our lighting system: a TFT monitor.

3.2.2 The TFT monitor as lighting system

In the proposed machine vision system a TFT monitor has been adopted as lighting. Previous work have also used this kind of illuminator but for different purposes as surface measurement [Guo (2007)], surface reconstruction [Kutulakos (2008)] or subsurface crack detection [Chan (2008)]. In our case, the TFT monitor has been included in the vision system mainly for:

- flexibility: one device provides two lighting techniques;
- easy to generate and to modify: the light pattern—the white and black stripes—can be adapted to reveal defects with different sizes;
- accurate pattern movement: from every sensor pose several images with different stripe displacement should be acquired. With this lighting system the stripe movement is done by software so, the movement is not subjected to mechanical imprecisions.

In addition, the set of images acquired from every sensor pose should be processed using computer vision algorithms with a very low computational burden. This issue is also achieved processing an image composed from this sequence. In previous work, this image has been denoted as *aspect image* [Satorres Martínez et al. (2009b)] and a determined procedure has to be applied for obtaining it.

3.3 The image processing

The whole inspection process, starting in the image acquisition and finishing in the defect characterization, is exposed in the flowchart presented in figure 12. As shown, the acquisitions are synchronized with the stripe movements and when the white stripe covers the dark stripe width completely, the image sequence is finished. From this set of images, the *aspect image* is obtained and all the subsequent processing algorithms are applied on predefined regions of this composition. Once the set of pixels, labeled as possible defects, are extracted from the background, the decision of rejecting the lens is based on the measurement parameters—such as the defect size—considered in the manual inspection process and presented in the *inspection guidelines*.

3.3.1 The aspect image

Let consider a one-dimensional representation of the lighting system being a square waveform ($P(x)$) and the white stripe T_B has to scan the whole period of the wave (T)(Fig.13), where:

- Δ: displacement between stripes in two consecutive images.
- α: duty cycle.

To obtain an image where the background appears with medium gray level and defects as high gray level, the mean image of the N waveform sequence has to be computed as:

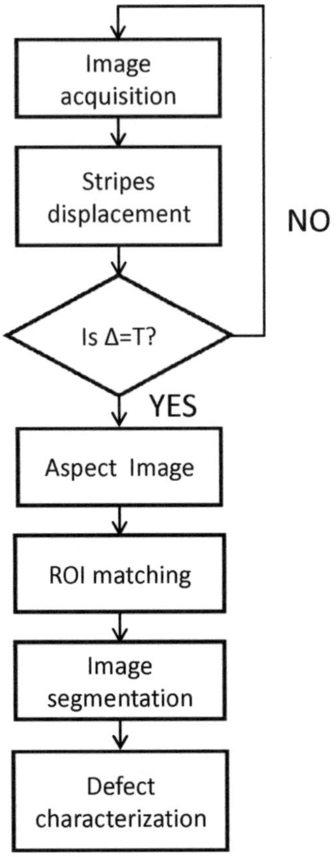

Fig. 12. The image processing flowchart.

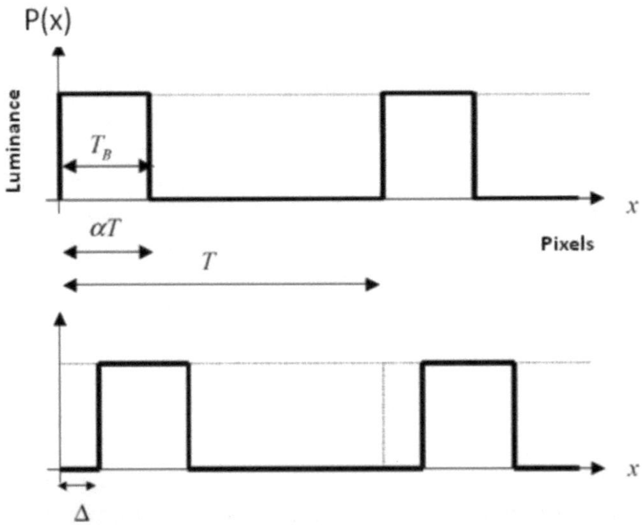

Fig. 13. Lighting system geometric information

$$M(x) = \frac{1}{N} \cdot \sum_{n=0}^{N-1} P(x - n \cdot \Delta) \quad n \in \mathbb{N} \tag{9}$$

$$\Delta = \frac{\alpha \cdot T}{s} \quad s \in \mathbb{N} \quad 1 \leq s \leq \alpha \cdot T \tag{10}$$

where $M(x)$ is called *aspect image* and the homogeneity of the background is critical in the defect segmentation. So, the imaging conditions have to be chosen in order to provide *aspect images* with a background the more homogeneous as possible.

3.3.2 Defect segmentation

Image segmentation can generally be described as separating images into various regions or objects in which the pixels have similar characteristics [Russ (2007)]. This is an important task, in that the image interpretation relies strongly on its results. In our case of study, and previous to the segmentation step, the image regions, where the processing algorithms have to be applied, should be defined.

In computer vision applications, these regions are known as Regions Of Interest (ROI) and if they are not defined, false detection could perturb the defect characterization. This definition is particularly important on the lens edges or on the lens surfaces that are not completely smooth. As we perform the inspection in a robotic platform, repetitive vision sensor positioning is achieved. So, for every sensor pose, a binary mask is defined where pixels labeled with "1" are later processed.

Because of the well contrasted *aspect image* and the homogeneity of its background, no preprocessing algorithms are required. Dealing with this sort of image, the automatic thresholding methods are widely used for segmentation [Ng (2006)]. The basic idea of these methods is, based on the gray-level distribution derived from the image histogram, to select a threshold value for separating objects of interest from the background.

The aspect image histogram presents an unimodal distribution because most of the pixels are included in the background and have a similar medium gray-level. Only aesthetic defects present a high gray-level but constitute a disproportionately small number of pixels of the whole image. There is a thresholding algorithm suitable for segmenting images that present an unimodal histogram distribution. This is the Rosin algorithm [Rosin (2001)] that estimates an automatic threshold by computing the following expression:

$$U_{opt} = arg\ max \left[\frac{\left| (x_f - x_s) \cdot (y_s - h(g)) - (x_s - g) \cdot (y_f - y_s) \right|}{\sqrt{(x_f - x_s)^2 + (y_f - y_s)^2}} \right] \tag{11}$$

where (x_s, y_s) correspond to the dominant peak of the histogram and (x_f, y_f) are relative to the secondary population that may not produce a discernible peak but it is well separated from the large peak. The values g and $h(g)$ are the gray-level and the number of pixels with gray-level g, respectively.

3.3.3 Defect characterization

Once the defects are extracted from the flawless area, they have to be measured to determine if the lens could be accepted or, however, has to be rejected. The measurement parameters and the acceptance thresholds are extracted from the *inspection guidelines* and they correspond to the ones used in the manual inspection process. These parameters are normally the following:

- The size in mm^2 of the defect. This measure is to characterize punctual defects.
- The longitude in *mm* of the major axis of the defect. Useful for characterizing lineal defects.
- The number of defects.

Because the vision sensor is posed normal to the lens surface, the number of active pixels "1*s*" corresponding to a defect, is a linear function of the defect occupancy surface. Hence, no perspective correction is required to measure the defect that have been extracted in the previous step.

4. Results

On this section different types of results, that have been obtained during the validation of the machine vision system, are presented. Firstly, a set of sensor poses computed with the sensor configurations defined in the table 1 is obtained with our planning system. The planning results were subsequently utilized to acquire the images from the whole lens surface. Later, the effectiveness of the lighting system for enhancing aesthetic defects is demonstrated using defective lenses that have been rejected in the manual inspection process. The lighting system configuration is also presented in table 1. Finally, related to the computer vision algorithms, their performances are assessed by processing a serie of aspect images acquired using a commercial model of lens. For this lens model, the minimum defect size that has to be detected is a punctual defect of 1*mm* of diameter.

Vision Sensor	
Parameters	**Values**
Resolution	1034×778
Pixel size	0.00465*mm*
Focal length	25*mm*
Spatial resolution	0.1*mm*/*pixel*
Lighting System	
Parameters	**Values**
T_B	6 *pixels*
T	18 *pixels*
Δ	1 *pixel*

Table 1. Sensor and lighting system configuration

4.1 The sensor planning system

The set of sensor poses is presented in the figure 14. This set has been obtained adjusting higher the weighting coefficient (w_2) in the fitness function. In this case, the second objective has been prioritized so, from all the sensor poses, the spatial resolution should be enough to guarantee the aspect defect detection. As can be seen, with 22 sensor poses the whole lens surface is inspected and in all the sensor poses the spatial resolution is enough to ensure the defect detection. The table 2 shows the two extreme sensor poses with their distances to the

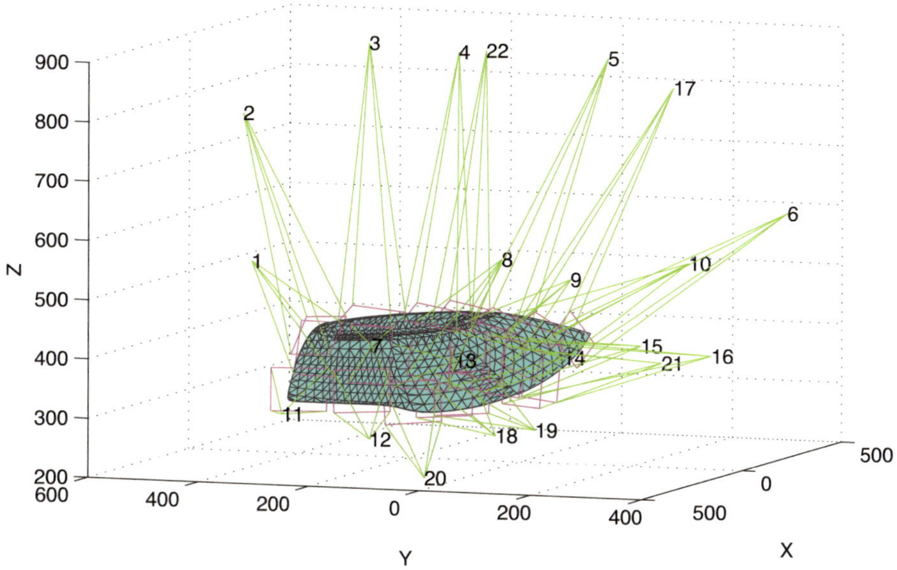

Fig. 14. The planning results.

lens surface and the defect size that could be detected from them. In fact, in the sensor pose with a greater distance to the lens surface the defect size that could be detected is 0.96 *mm* which is lower than the defect size that has to be located for this lens model.

Sensor pose	Distance from the vision sensor to the lens surface (*mm*)	Defect size (*mm*)
6	483	0.8
20	520	0.96

Table 2. Sensor poses and their distances to the lens surface.

4.2 Enhancing aesthetic defects

A TFT monitor as lighting system has been utilized in the machine vision system for enhancing the aspect defects. This device offers two lighting techniques that could be adapted to reveal opaque and transparent defects. Figure 15 shows two types of punctual defects and how they are enhanced with the our lighting system. For the opaque punctual defect (Fig. 15a) the TFT monitor projects an homogeneous background performing as a conventional back-lighting system. However, the transparent defects are only enhanced projecting a stripe pattern (Fig. 15b). Later, and thanks to the image composition this type of defects are clearly contrasted from the lens surface (Fig. 15c).

4.3 Characterizing aesthetic defects

Once the aspect image is achieved it has to be processed for deciding if the lens has to be rejected or accepted. The figures 16 and 17 show the aspect image segmentation and how the regions of pixels extracted in each figure have been labeled. In both cases, if the number of pixels in a region is higher than 50, the corresponding region, is considered as an aesthetic defect. According to the sensor configuration and the distances from the vision sensor to the lens surface, this region size coincides with a defect length or diameter of 1*mm*. In this respect, all the segmented regions in figure 16b have a dimension lower than 50 pixels and because of this are labeled as *OK*. On contrary, one of the segmented regions in the figure 17b has a dimension higher than 50 pixels. For this reason, an aesthetic defect has been located in this aspect image labeling the region as *KO*.

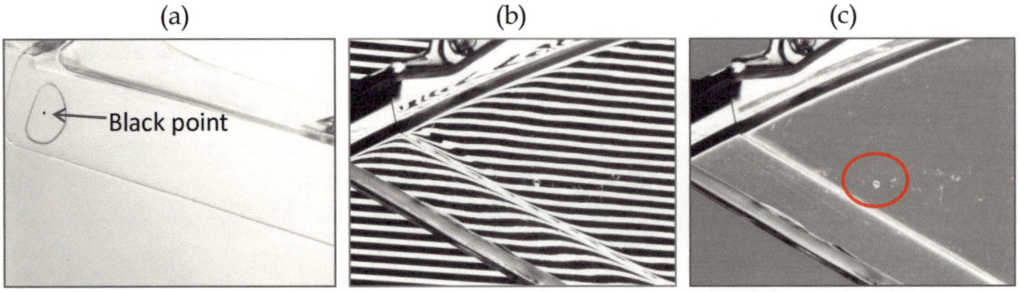

Fig. 15. Enhancing aesthetic defects: (a) Opaque punctual defect; (b) Transparent punctual defect with the stripe pattern; (c) Transparent punctual defect in the aspect image.

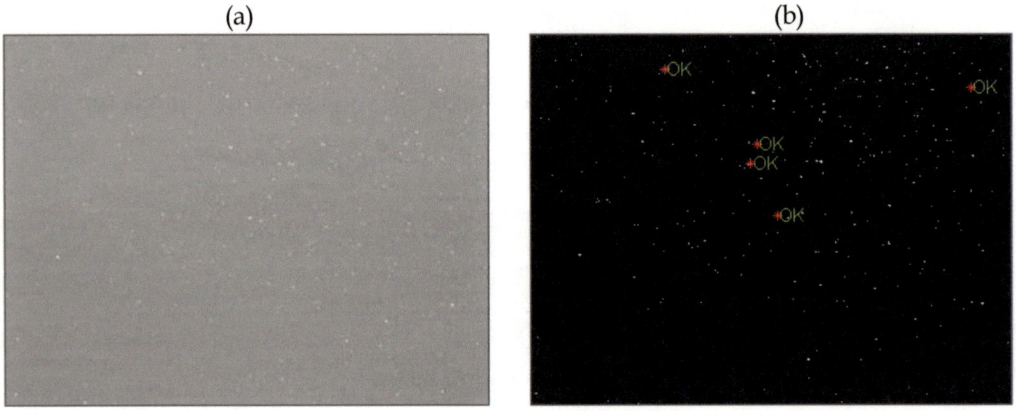

Fig. 16. Processing results: (a) Aspect image without aesthetic defects; (b) Aspect image segmentation and characterization.

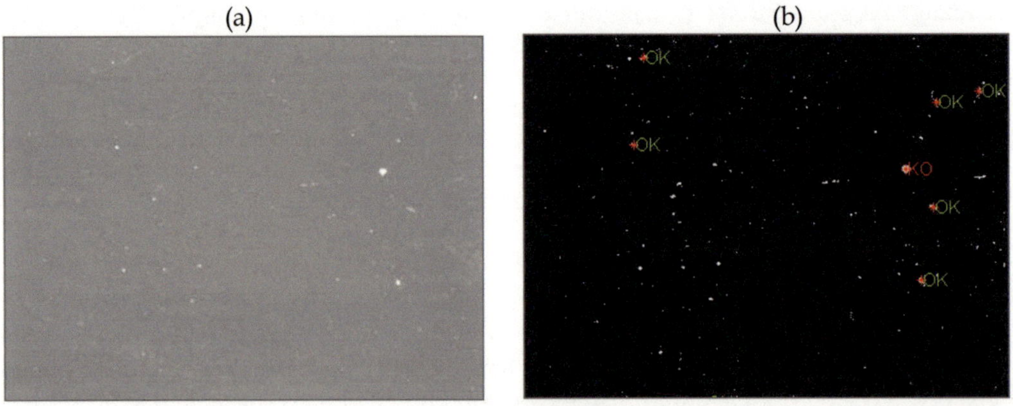

Fig. 17. Processing results: (a) Aspect image with a transparent punctual defect; (b) Aspect image segmentation and characterization.

5. Conclusions

This chapter is dedicated to develop a machine vision system for the automated inspection of headlamp lenses. The quality control of this part is a complex task that nowadays is made by manual means. Its complexity is due to the fact that, the proportion between the aesthetic defect size and the lens dimension is high. Moreover, some defects may be transparent, as the lens surface, and revealing them require a particular lighting conditions.

Both issues are taken into account in the proposed machine vision system. Firstly, to observe the whole lens surface several vision sensor poses should be defined. In this work, the sensor poses are computed automatically through a sensor planning system. In some lens models, the aesthetic defect size is variable depending on the lens zone where it was located. This information is utilized in the planning system allowing to fit better the number of sensor poses. It is worth noticing that the machine vision system could be easily adapted to inspect different lens models.

Secondly, the lighting system enables the detection of transparent and opaque defects using different lighting techniques. It is possible using a TFT monitor and projecting two light patterns: an homogeneous white background or white and black stripes. The first pattern enhances the opaque defects and the second reveals the transparent ones. On the other hand, the image processing has been carefully studied. The computer vision algorithms are applied to an image composition named as *aspect image*. In this image, the aesthetic defects appear well contrasted and the image background is totally homogeneous. So, the defect segmentation is fast to compute using a global thresholding algorithm. Finally, with our system, a set of a commercial model of headlamp lenses have been analyzed demonstrating that the automated inspection of this part is a feasible task.

6. References

Aluze, D., Merienne, F., Dumont, C. & Gorria, P. (2002). Vision system for defect imaging, detection, and characterization on a specular surface of a 3d object, *Image and Vision Computing* 20: 569–580.

Automation & Robotics (2001). http://www.ar.be/index.htm.

Chan, F. (2008). Reflective fringe pattern technique for subsurface crack detection, *NDTE International* 41: 602–610.

Chen, S. & Li, Y. (2002). A method of automatic sensor placement for robot vision in inspection tasks, *Proc. IEEE Int. Conf. on Robotics and Automation* 3: 2545–2550.

Chen, S. & Li, Y. (2004). Automatic sensor placement for model-based robot vision, *IEEE Transaction on Systems, Man and Cybernetics - Part B: Cybernetics* 34(1): 393–408.

Coulot, C., Kohler-hemmerlin, S., Dumont, C., Aluze, D. & Lamalle, B. (1997). Simulations of lighting for an optimal defect detection by artificial vision, *IEEE/ASME International Conference on Advanced Intelligent Mechatronics* pp. 117-122.

Cowan, C. & Kovesi, P. (1988). Automatic sensor placement from vision task requirements, *IEEE Transaction on Pattern Analysis and Machine Intelligence* 10(3): 407–416.

Dunn, E.;Olague, G. (2005). Pareto optimal camera placement for automated visual inspection, *IEEE/RSJ International Conference on Intelligent Robots and Systems* pp. 3821-3826.

Eiben, A.E.;Smith, J. (2003). *Introduction to evolutionary computing*, Springer.

Forsyth, D. & Ponce, J. (2003). *Computer Vision: A Modern Approach*, Prentice Hall.

Guo, H.; Tao, T. (2007). Specular surface measurement by using a moving diffuse structured light source, *Proceedings of SPIE- The International Society for Optical Engineering* 6834(68343E).

Jahr, I. (2008). *Lighting in Machine Vision. Handbook of Machine Vision*, A. Hornberg, Wiley-VCH Verlag GmbH.

Kakikura, S. S. T. M. (1990). Automatic planning of light source placement for an active photometric stereo system, *IEEE International Workshop on Intelligent Robots and Systems* pp. 559–566.

Kutulakos, K. (2008). A theory of refractive and specular 3d shape by light-path triangulation, *International Journal of Computer Vision* 76: 13–29.

Malamas, E., Petrakis, E., Zervakis, M., Petit, L. & Legat, J.-D. (2003). A survey on industrial vision systems, applications and tools, *Image and Vision Computing* 21: 171–188.

Ng, H.-F. (2006). Automatic thresholding for defect detection, *Pattern Recognition Letters* 27: 1644- 1649.

Rosin, P. (2001). Unimodal thresholding, *Patter Recognition* 34(11): 2083–2096.

Russ, J. (2007). *The Image Processing Handbook*, fifth edition edn, Taylor and Francis.

Satorres Martínez, S. (2010). *Inspección automática de defectos en cristales de faros para automóviles mediante vision por computador*, PhD thesis, University of Jaén.

Satorres Martínez, S., Gómez Ortega, J., Gámez García, J. & Sánchez García, A. (2009a). An automatic procedure to code the inspection guideline for vehicle headlamp lenses, *IEEE International Conference on Mechatronic* .

Satorres Martínez, S., Gómez Ortega, J., Gámez García, J. & Sánchez García, A. (2009b). A dynamic lighting system for automated visual inspection of headlamp lenses, *14th IEEE International Conference on Emerging Techonologies and Factory Automation* .

Satorres Martínez, S., Gómez Ortega, J., Gámez García, J. & Sánchez García, A. (2009c). A machine vision system for defect characterization on transparent parts with non-plane surfaces, *Machine Vision with Applications (in review process)*.

Satorres Martínez, S., Gómez Ortega, J., Gámez García, J. & Sánchez García, A. (2009d). A sensor planning system for automated headlamp lens inspection, *Expert Systems with Applications* 36(5): 8768–8777.

Seulin, R., Merienne, F. & Gorria, P. (2001). Dynamic lighting system for specular surface inspection, *Machine Vision Applications in Industrial Inspection IX* 4301: 199–206.

Sheng,W., Xi, N., Song, M. & Chen, Y. (2003). Cad-guided sensor planning for dimensional inspection in automotive manufacturing, *IEEE/ASME Transaction on Mechatronics* 8(3): 372–380.

Sheng, W., Xi, N., Tan, J., Song, M. & Chen, Y. (2003). Minimum viewpoint planning for dimensional inspection of sheet metal parts, *Proceedings IEEE/ASME International Conference on Advanced Intelligent Mechatronics* pp. 1049–1054.

Tarabanis, K., Allen, P. & Tsai, R. (1995). A survey of sensor planning in computer vision, *IEEE Transaction on Robotics and Automation* 11(1): 86–104.

Tarabanis, K., Tsai, R. & Allen, P. (1995). The mvp sensor planning system for robotic vision tasks, *IEEE Transaction on Robotics and Automation* 11(1): 72–85.

Telljohann, A. (2008). *Introduction to Building a Machine Vision Inspection. Handbook of Machine Vision*, A. Hornberg, Wiley-VCH Verlag GmbH.

Wördenweber, B., Wallascheck, J., Boyce, P. & Hoffman, D. (2007). *Automotive Lighting and Human Vision*, Springer-Verlag Berlin Heidelberg.

Yi, S., Haralick, R. M. & Shapiro, L. G. (1990). Automatic sensor and light source positioning for machine vision, *Proc. 10th Int. Conf. Pattern Recognition* pp. 55–59.

5

Bayesian Uncertainty Evaluation in Vision-Based Metrology

Markus Brandner
Graz University of Technology
Austria

1. Introduction

Metrology as the science of measurement is omnipresent in today's society. Many applications in a variety of fields ranging from economy to science have a strong demand for reliable methods to quantify and compare measurement results. Depending on the specific application, this comparison can cover measurements acquired within the same minute by the same operator using the same measurement instrument under the same environmental conditions, or measurements acquired within a month by different operators and measurement instruments on two different continents. In either case, metrology has to provide means to ensure the validity of the comparison of those measurement results. Two aspects of metrology are of importance to us in the context of this paper: The *traceability* of the measurement result and the evaluation of the quality of the measurement result by means of its associated *measurement uncertainty*.

Traceability: The measurement process is defined as a quantitative comparison of an unknown physical quantity - the *measurand* - with a known standard (cf. DIN1319 (1995)). Measurement results can thus only be compared on an international level provided compatible standards are available and used. Consequently, our society requires a world-wide system of physical standards which is accepted by and accessible to every nation. The first attempts to internationally standardise physical quantities date back to 1875, when the *Bureau International des Poids et Mesures* (BIPM) was founded on the basis of the Metre Convention (BIPM (2008)). At that time, international prototypes of the metre and the kilogram where physically built. The evolution of these references triggered the installation of seven base quantities. Since the 11th General Conference on Weights and Measurements in 1960, this system of base units is referred to as the *International System of Units* (SI) (BIPM (2006)). Today, standards are maintained and made available to the public of participating member states and associated economies by means of a hierarchical structure of international and national metrological institutes as outlined in Figure 1. The highest quality standards are available at BIPM and are used to derive secondary standards operated by national metrological institutions. These institutions, in turn, are responsible to pass standards on to subordinate laboratories and eventually to instrument manufacturers. This concept of *traceability* ensures that every measurement can be referred back to a physical standard by an unbroken chain of comparisons (International vocabulary of basic and general terms in metrology, VIM (1993)). An example of such a comparison chain is provided in Figure 2. An optical instrument is used to measure the position x of a

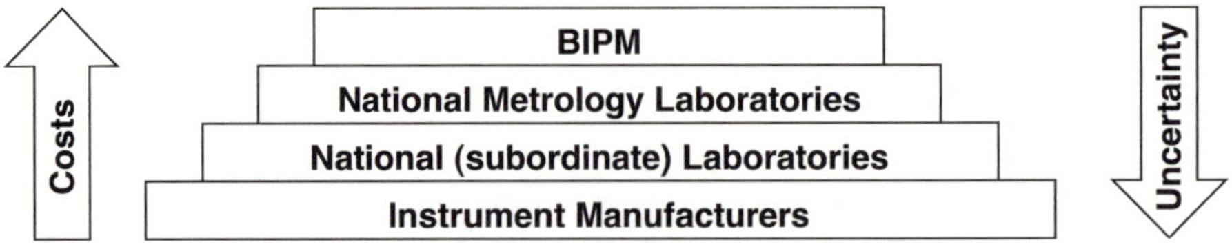

Fig. 1. Hierarchy of metrological institutions responsible to maintain the SI system. The costs and the quality of the standards kept at the different layers increase from bottom to top. Similarly, the uncertainty of the different standards increase from top to bottom. Any measurement taken by an instrument which is properly calibrated can now be traced back to the base standard kept at BIPM.

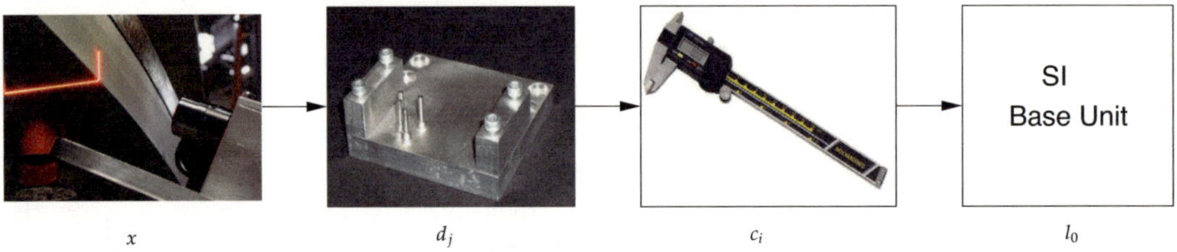

Fig. 2. The concept of traceability shown at the example of an optical measurement system. The length standard applied within the measurement system can be traced back to the meter standard.

mechanical part in 2D. A chain of comparisons links the measurement results of this instrument back to the length standard: The geometry of the instrument is calibrated using a calibration target. During this calibration procedure, the positions $\boldsymbol{d}_j$ of different geometric features such as bores and bolts serve as geometric references. These reference positions are determined during the manufacturing process of the target using a measurement device such as the shown calliper. By means of these measurements, the components of the vectors $\boldsymbol{d}_j$ are referred to the metric reference $\boldsymbol{c}_i$ of the calliper. Finally, the calliper is calibrated by the instrument manufacturer using standards that can likewise be referred to the length standard l_0 - symbolised in this example by the image of the metal bar representing the metre standard. Consequently, the measurement results obtained using the optical instrument can be traced back to the metre standard. Only through this specific setting, the measurement results are of practical use within a manufacturing process based on the current SI. The lack of traceability in such an environment would inevitably lead to false tolerances and hence defective parts.

Measurement Uncertainty (MU): The BIPM defines metrology as '*the science of measurement, embracing both experimental and theoretical determinations at any level of uncertainty in any field of science and technology*'[1], which highlights a second important aspect of metrology: the treatment of measurement uncertainty. The term *uncertainty of a measurement* refers to a parameter that is assigned to each measurement and represents the spreading of the measurement values '*. . . that could reasonably be attributed to the measurand*' (VIM (1993)). While the measurement of a scalar quantity results in a single *best estimate,* uncertainties are commonly expressed by means of an interval around this best estimate. Figure 3 depicts this

[1] see also www.bipm.org.

situation. The measurand Y is determined resulting in the best estimate y. Assuming that deviations around this best estimate are symmetrically distributed to either side of y, we obtain an interval parameterised by the *expanded uncertainty* U_y. The interval is assigned a coverage probability p, such that

$$\mathrm{Prob}(\{y - U_y < Y \leq y + U_y\}) = p, \quad (1)$$

where common probabilities are chosen to lie in the range of $p = 95...99\%$.

A frequent misconception outside the metrology community is the ambiguous use of the term *measurement error*. While the measurement uncertainty does not require the true value y_{True} of the measurand Y to be known, the *measurement error*, in contrast, is determined as

$$y_{\mathrm{Error}} = y - y_{\mathrm{True}}, \quad (2)$$

which can only be evaluated once y_{True} is available. As this is never the case for any physical measurement[2], the measurement error is only seen as a theoretical concept with little practical implications.

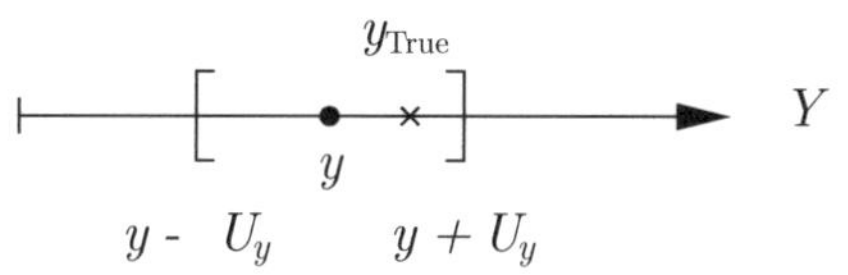

Fig. 3. The measurement uncertainty of a scalar measurand Y is expressed by an interval around the best estimate y which is parameterised by a coverage probability.

1.1 Vision-based measurement systems

Optical metrology utilises the interaction of light with an object in order to measure unknown quantities. Measurement principles based on the propagation of light are inherently non-contacting and mostly non-invasive. Thus, optical metrology is frequently used in applications where the measurand can either not be physically connected to a sensor (e.g. the measurement of mechanical stress and strain on a rotating blade of an aircraft turbine) or feedback of the measurement system to the measurand has to be kept to a minimum (e.g. measurements in the nano-scale). Further benefits of optical metrology include the potential to operate in large measurement volumes as well as the ability to set the focus of the measurement precisely at the point of interest through the line-of-sight principle that applies to light rays. While the large field of optical metrology covers the use of different light sources, sensors, and measurement principles, a sub-class of optical measurement systems uses 2D digital sensors to capture images and to perform signal processing on these images in order to deduce geometric properties of scenes or derived measurands. This sub-class is referred to as the class of *vision-based measurement systems*. Historically, these systems are also known as digital photogrammetric systems. In the context of this paper we refer to vision-based measurement systems with the following properties:

- Digital images are acquired using 2D image sensors (cameras).
- Greylevel features are used as primary source of information.

[2] The situation is different for simulation experiments, where y_{True} might be given.

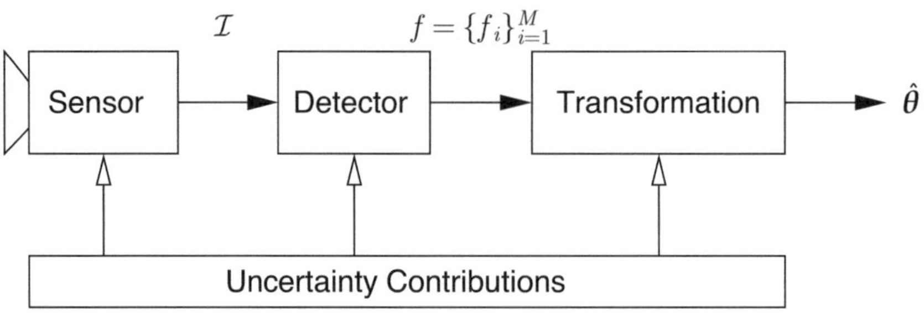

Fig. 4. Components of a typical vision-based measurement system. The best estimate of the unknown quantity $\hat{\theta}$ is obtained given an 2D intensity profile $\mathcal{I}$ acquired by the sensor.

- These features are used to derive measurands and their uncertainties.
- The measurement results are traceable to a standard and uncertainty estimates are provided.

The typical processing steps found in such systems are sketched in Figure 4: The camera maps the scene onto its image plane and acquires a 2D intensity profile $\mathcal{I}$. A feature detector is then used to identify features f (e.g. circular blobs) and to estimate their respective parameters (e.g. blob area and centre of gravity). These parameters are then being further processed by means of a transformation in order to obtain the best estimate of the unknown parameter $\hat{\theta}$.

Two examples of vision-based measurement systems are shown in Figure 5. A close-up of the inside of a two-camera system used to measure 2D displacements is shown in Figure 5a. Traceability and the proper characterisation of measurement uncertainties in this application are of importance as the measurement results are used in a research project aiming at the investigation of the long-term behaviour of different materials. A proper decision taken on the basis of these measurements has a significant economic impact on the customer.

The Augmented Reality (AR) system shown in Figure 5b augments a user's view of the real world by adding computer generated content that is spatially registered with the real content. In this application, a monocular vision-sensor provides position and orientation (i.e. pose) data that are fused with data obtained by an inertial measurement unit mounted on the same rigid platform. The temporal stream of poses is further used by the AR software to render artificial content within the user's field of view. The successful information fusion in this particular setup requires all sensor data to be referred to the same length and time standards. As far as vision-based pose estimation is concerned, this prerequisite is achieved by a vision-based measurement system.

1.2 Related work

Efforts have been undertaken in metrology in order to develop a general frame-work that can be used to identify the quantity of the measurand and to provide means to judge on the quality of this result. These developments led to the introduction of the *Guide to the Expression of Uncertainty in Measurement* (GUM, most recent document JCGM (2008a)). The foremost aim of the GUM developments was to provide a recommendation for the treatment of measurement uncertainty that is *universal, internally consistent,* and *transferable* (JCGM (2008a)).

The standard GUM extensively uses the concept of *degrees of freedom* to fuse information from different sources. This concept is a constant point of criticism in the literature (cf.

(a) (b)

Fig. 5. Vision-based measurement systems. (a) Measurement application used to measure displacement and creep of material samples. (b) Vision-based pose estimation applied to Augmented Reality.

Lira (2001)). In particular, the fusion of quantities derived using statistical methods (e.g. averaging over a number of measurements) with quantities denoting an expert opinion (e.g. prior knowledge about interval boundaries) are not satisfactorily covered by the GUM proposal. Weise & Wöger (1999) and later Kacker & Jones (2003) resort to the consistent use of Bayesian statistics in the context of uncertainty computations. Both approaches remove an inconsistency in the GUM interpretation of coverage probabilities. Kacker & Jones (2003) provide a modified set of rules based on the GUM recommendations that are built upon the Taylor approximation of the measurement equation. Their proposed modifications cover the propagation of first and second order moments neglecting modifications of the underlying distributions. Weise & Wöger (1999) instead propagate distributions providing a framework that is more generally applicable. The recent *GUM Supplement 1* document (GUMS1, JCGM (2008b)) makes explicit the Bayesian foundations of the GUM. Thus removing inconsistencies in the information fusion of the guide.

Different approaches to the treatment of uncertainty in the domain of computer vision have been reported in the literature (e.g. Havelock (1989); Kanungo et al. (1995); Triggs (2001); Ochoa & Belongie (2006)). Using the central limit theorem (CLT, Papoulis & Pillai (2002)) as a key argument, the use of the Gaussian assumption is suggested - and often validated - by many researchers. Heuel (2003) and Criminisi (2001) show that Gaussian densities can be applied to represent homogeneous geometric entities. In an earlier work (Brandner (2006)) we apply first order propagation of Gaussian quantities to a vision-based tracking application. Based on the exclusive use of Gaussian densities to describe both physical quantities and prior information, the Bayesian extensions of the GUM document are easily implemented in analytic form.

From a practical point of view, the proper evaluation of measurement uncertainties relies on the quality of the underlying process model. In many situations these models are complex and not straight-forward to derive. Sommer & Siebert (2006) propose a systematic solution to the model building problem in metrology. The authors use three building blocks to identify and visualise influencing factors and uncertainty contributions. Based on the cause-

and-effect approach, *Parameter Sources*, *Transmission Units*, and *Indicating Units* are employed to obtain the measurement equation. This equation is then reversed to obtain the GUM-compliant model equation. Finally, the measurement uncertainty of the unknown quantity can be derived.

1.3 Contribution

In this work we fuse the existing Gaussian characterisation of geometric entities within the field of uncertain perspective geometry with the uncertainty concepts of the GUM document. In order to highlight the quality of the obtained geometric quantities this concept is referred to as *metrological geometry*.

We present a modelling technique based on the cause-effect diagram which makes explicit the statistical dependencies between different geometric entities. Further, we show that for many problems in vision-based metrology an analytic frame-work for the propagation of Gaussian uncertainties can be applied. All processing steps can be carried out analytically, thus avoiding any simulation-based computations with the potential lack of real-time performance. The frame-work is consistent with the Bayesian extensions to the standard GUM. Using a number of simple building blocks we propose simple modelling steps to analytically derive the measurement uncertainty in vision-based applications explicitly covering inter-parameter dependencies.

The remainder of this chapter is structured as follows: based on a brief review of the GUM recommendations in the following Section 2 we introduce a common nomenclature and derive the requirements for a vision-based metrological application in Section 3. The subsequent Section 4 presents our approach to the modelling process and introduces the basic building blocks of a vision-based measurement system which are then applied to a simple example in Section 5. The paper concludes with a summary in Section 6.

2. The guide to the expression of uncertainty in measurement

Given a measurement process, the current GUM represents a general frame-work that can be used to evaluate the uncertainty of a physical quantity that results from that measurement. However, the GUM does not provide any means to determine appropriate models. In the following paragraphs we review the basic concepts of the GUM in order to provide the background required to develop the concept of the metrological geometry in Section 4.

2.1 Uncertain quantities

Assuming a measurand denoted by Y depends on a number of input quantities X_i, the GUM frame-work allows us to determine the uncertainty of a measurement result y taking into account the uncertainties of the contributing input quantities. Quantities in this context are treated as variables and their uncertainty is represented by a state-of-knowledge distribution. The best estimate of a quantity Y and its uncertainty are represented by the mean value and the standard deviation of the underlying PDF $f_Y(\cdot)$, respectively. Thus, the best estimate of the measurand Y is given by

$$E\{Y\} = \mu_Y = \int_{-\infty}^{+\infty} \eta f_Y(\eta) d\eta \tag{3}$$

and the associated standard deviation is given by

$$\sigma_Y = \sqrt{E\{[Y - \mu_Y]^2\}}. \tag{4}$$

Depending on the method used to determine the uncertainty of input quantities the GUM distinguishes between two families of uncertainty evaluations: *Type A* uncertainties are determined by statistical methods while uncertainties obtained *by other means* are classified as *Type B*.

The determination of a quantity Y by means of N repeated independent observations[3] y_i represents an example of a Type A uncertainty evaluation. The estimated arithmetic mean value of the observations is given by

$$\overline{y} = \frac{1}{N}\sum_{i=1}^{N} y_i \tag{5}$$

and the associated standard deviation of the arithmetic mean $\overline{y}$ is given by $s_y = s/\sqrt{N}$, where s denotes the empirical standard deviation of the observations and is given by

$$s = \sqrt{\frac{1}{N-1}\sum_{i=1}^{N}(y_i - \overline{y})^2}. \tag{6}$$

The GUM recommends to use the arithmetic mean $\overline{y}$ as best estimate for the quantity Y and to use the standard deviation s_y as *standard uncertainty*[4] u_y.

Type B uncertainties are used to treat input quantities whose uncertainty is determined by methods other than statistics. An example is the uncertainty associated with the calibration of an instrument. In this case best estimate, standard uncertainty, and degrees of freedom are given by the calibration laboratory. Other examples are the uncertainty of the transformation parameters and the detector used in the above example of a vision-based measurement system. In both cases the characterisation of the uncertainty is based on the experience of the experimenter and, thus, on *non-statistical* evaluations.

2.2 The measurement process

The evaluation of the uncertainty associated to the measurand is based on a mathematical model

$$Y = f(X_1, X_2, \ldots, X_N) \tag{7}$$

of the measurement process, where Y denotes the measurand and the X_i represent input quantities. This relation is referred to as the *model equation*. The best estimate of the measurand is given by replacing all input quantities in Equation 7 by their respective best estimates such that

---

[3] We will use the terms observation and measurement interchangeably.

[4] Following a suggestion by Sommer & Siebert (2006) we use u_y as symbol for the standard uncertainty associated to the measurement result y rather than the GUM nomenclature $u(y)$ which suggests that the standard uncertainty is a function of the best estimate.

$$y = f(x_1, x_2, \ldots, x_N). \tag{8}$$

Based on the estimates of the input values and their associated standard uncertainties, the *standard uncertainty* u_y is derived. Summarising the input quantities and their best estimates into a vector $X = (X_1, X_2, \ldots, X_N)^T$ and a vector $x = (x_1, x_2, \ldots, x_N)^T$, respectively, the measurement equation is developed into a Taylor series to obtain (cf. Weise & Wöger (1999))

$$Y = f(\mathbf{X}) \approx f(\mathbf{x}) + \sum_{i=1}^{N} \frac{\partial f(\mathbf{x})}{\partial X_i}(X_i - x_i) + \tag{9}$$

$$+ \sum_{i=1}^{N}\sum_{j=1}^{N} \frac{\partial^2 f(\mathbf{x})}{\partial X_i \partial X_j}(X_i - x_i)(X_j - x_j) + \ldots. \tag{10}$$

Assuming small deviations $(X_i - x_i)$, the higher order terms of the Taylor expansion are neglected leading to the simplified approximation

$$Y \approx f(\mathbf{x}) + \sum_{i=1}^{N} \frac{\partial f(\mathbf{x})}{\partial X_i}(X_i - x_i). \tag{11}$$

The partial derivatives of the measurement equation are referred to as *sensitivity coefficients* $c_i = \frac{\partial f(\mathbf{x})}{\partial X_i}$. Using Equation 11, the variance of the measurement result y is obtained by

$$u_y^2 = \left(E\left\{ \sum_{i=1}^{N} c_i (X_i - x_i) \right\} \right)^2 = \sum_{i=1}^{N} c_i^2 u_{x_i}^2 + 2\sum_{i=1}^{N-1} \sum_{j=i+1}^{N} c_i c_j \rho_{ij} u_{x_i} u_{x_j}, \tag{12}$$

with u_{x_i} denoting the standard uncertainties of the input values. The correlation coefficients $\rho_{ij} = Cov(x_i, x_j)/u_{x_i}u_{x_j}$ account for inner dependencies of the contributing input values. As u_y results from combining the input parameter uncertainties it is called the *combined standard uncertainty* of the measurement result y.

The GUM further suggests to report an interval within which a large fraction p of the distribution of values attributed to the measurand Y fall. Given a symmetric distribution of Y, this interval is obtained through the symmetrical extension of the best estimate y by the *expanded uncertainty* U_y to either side as shown for a scalar quantity in Figure 3. Assuming knowledge about the distribution of Y, the expanded uncertainty is obtained by $U_y = k \cdot u_y$ where k is a coverage factor. The fraction p is denoted the *level of confidence* associated to the *coverage interval* $(y \pm U_y)$.

The uncertainty estimates are based on realisations of random variables and, therefore, are subjected to uncertainty, too. Only for the evaluation of the expanded uncertainty, the standard GUM uses the concept of degrees of freedom of the input quantities and suggests to estimate an *effective number of degrees of freedom* of the resultant distribution based on the Welch-Satterthwaite (WS) equation (JCGM (2008a)).

2.3 Bayesian evaluation of measurement uncertainties

The standard GUM document has often been a target of criticism due to the lack of a clear distinction between the use of classical statistics and Bayesian statistics in the evaluation of measurement uncertainties. As opposed to the classical statistics approach which treats measurands as constants and the observations (e.g. made during Type A evaluations) as

realisations of random variables with known distributions, Bayesian statistics is build upon the philosophy that the measurand is itself a random variable and the observations are seen as constants (Kacker & Jones (2003); Gelman et al. (2003)). The important difference between the two approaches is that the state-of-knowledge distribution in the Bayesian theory does not represent an approximation but is assumed to be exact. Consequently, there is no uncertainty involved in evaluating the coverage intervals. Classical statistics, on the other hand, requires the handling of degrees of freedom and their controversial combination by means of the WS equation. In the Bayesian theory the state-of-knowledge of every quantity is given by distributions which must not be confused with frequency distributions in the sense of classical statistics (Weise & Wöger (1999), p.225). Prior knowledge about quantities and their associated lack of knowledge is represented by prior distributions (or simply: priors). In the case of complete lack of knowledge, these distributions are replaced by non-informative priors (Iversen (1984); Gelman et al. (2003); Jaynes (1968)).
Recently, the Supplement 1 document clearly shows that the GUM concept of measurement uncertainty evaluation is based on the Bayesian idea. We will subsequently refer to the fully Bayesian interpretation of measurement uncertainties as GUM/Bayes.

2.4 Multidimensional measurands

The concept of GUM/Bayes as presented above straight forwardly extends to multiple dimensions (cf. Lira (2001)). During this extension the best estimate of a vector-valued quantity is given by the mean vector comprising the expected values of the individual components. Thus, for a vector-valued quantity

$$\boldsymbol{Q} = (Q_1, Q_2, \ldots, Q_n)^T \tag{13}$$

the best estimate is given by the mean vector

$$\boldsymbol{\mu}_q = E\{\boldsymbol{Q}\} = (E\{Q_1\}, E\{Q_2\}, \ldots, E\{Q_n\})^T = (\mu_{q_1}, \mu_{q_2}, \ldots, \mu_{q_n})^2. \tag{14}$$

The standard uncertainty of the scalar quantity is extended towards the *uncertainty matrix*

$$\mathrm{U}_q = \Sigma_{QQ} + (E\{\boldsymbol{Q}\} - \boldsymbol{q})\,(E\{\boldsymbol{Q}\} - \boldsymbol{q})^T, \tag{15}$$

where Σ_{QQ} represents the covariance matrix of the measurand. Equation 15 covers the general case of arbitrary estimates $\boldsymbol{q}$. Using unbiased estimators, the uncertainty matrix simplifies to

$$\mathrm{U}_q = \Sigma_{QQ}\,. \tag{16}$$

These extensions suffice to determine the combined standard uncertainty of the measurement result. Analogous to the scalar case the expanded uncertainty represents a multidimensional interval. Based on an n-dimensional measurand $Q \in S^{(n)}$, where $S^{(n)}$ denotes the n-dimensional space, Iuculano et al. (2003) extend the concept of an coverage interval as defined in the GUM to a limited domain $C^{(n)} \in S^{(n)}$. Assuming the PDF of the measurand is denoted by $f_Q(\cdot)$ the coverage probability associated with $C^{(n)}$ is given by

$$p = P\{\boldsymbol{Q} \in C^{(n)}\} = \int_{C^{(n)}} f_Q(\boldsymbol{q})d\boldsymbol{q}. \tag{17}$$

It is not *a priori* defined what the shape of such a region in $S^{(n)}$ looks like. The GUM suggests to apply two criteria for the choice of the interval boundaries: the minimum width interval or the interval given by equal density values. While the recommendation for Monte Carlo (MC) simulation in the Supplement 1 document JCGM (2008b) suggests to revert to the minimum width interval for general densities, this can not be straight forwardly applied to $S^{(n)}$. Restricting our attention to multidimensional Gaussian distributions we find that ellipses (or hyper-ellipsoids in higher dimensions) meet the requirements of coverage regions. These regions are delimited by contours of constant density and are consistent with the GUM suggestions. This choice is supported by Iuculano et al. (2003) who show for square and circular regions $C^{(n)}$ that the analytically derived coverage probabilities for Gaussian and uniform distributions are in agreement with ground truth data obtained from Monte Carlo simulations.

3. Requirement analysis for a measurement uncertainty frame-work

In order to identify the requirements for an uncertainty propagation frame-work we use the following measurement example: A vision-based measurement system is used to measure the 2D displacement of a mechanical lever. In order to robustly capture the displacement, a circular blob marker is attached to the lever. This marker now translates within a known plane which is fixed with respect to a perspective sensor. The goal of the measurement process is to estimate the position of the marker and, consequently, the displacement of the lever in world coordinates based on measurements taken in the sensor image. We restrict this example to a measurement based on a single image acquisition. The uncertainty associated with this estimate must be identified. Figure 6 shows a sketch of the geometry of the measurement system.

The blob marker is represented by its centre vector $\mathbf{p} = (x,y)^T$. The allowed set of positions is restricted to lie within the plane Π_{World} by construction of the measurement system. The sensor now maps the blob onto the image plane Π_{Image}. In order to measure the position of the lever the following processing steps are performed: a single image is acquired, the blob centre $\mathbf{a} = (u,v)^T$ is estimated, and the corresponding centre $\mathbf{p}$ is determined. The points $\mathbf{p}$ and $\mathbf{a}$ are related to each other by means of a parameterised transformation function

$$\mathbf{p} = g(\mathbf{a};\, \theta), \tag{18}$$

where θ denotes the parameter vector characterising the measurement setup. For every practical realisation of the above example the measurement result is subjected to uncertainties. Important sources of uncertainty can be found in every processing step, e.g.

- *Sensor:* After the mapping of the marker onto the sensor plane using principles of geometric optics the sensor performs both a spatial and an intensity discretisation. The effects of this discretisation steps can be modelled by means of additive noise sources.
- *Detector:* Although blob detection may seem to be straight forward at a first glance, it already exhibits a fundamental problem in optical metrology: it is, in general, not possible to accurately model the image acquisition system which is a prerequisite for the estimation of parameters such as the blob centre. We assume in this example that the uncertainty introduced by the blob detector is characterised by the experimenters experience.

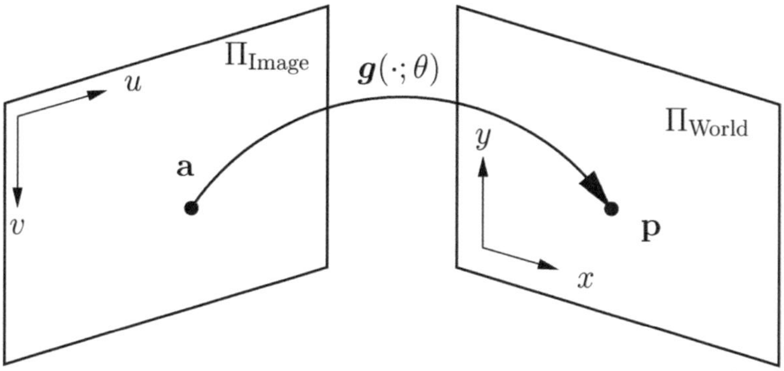

Fig. 6. Example application: The position of a point **p** in world coordinates is based on a detected point centre **a** in image coordinates. Both coordinate systems are related to each other by means of a transformation function $g(\cdot;\ \theta)$.

- *Transformation:* The measurement of **p** requires that the parameters of the transformation $g(\cdot;\ \theta)$ are known in advance. Given that these parameters necessarily are obtained by a calibration procedure they are subjected to uncertainties, too. Commonly, the parameter vector θ is assumed to be a realisation of a random process and the corresponding moment estimates are obtained during the calibration process.

Using this example we can already identify the requirements on a frame-work for the treatment of uncertainties which will later be applied to vision-based metrology applications. The following properties are required:

1. *Treatment of multivariate measurands:* Many of the measurands in the vision-based metrological application are multivariate variables such as point positions or parameters of a line.
2. In particular, many of the geometric entities are represented in a projective space. Consequently, the uncertainty frame-work needs to properly cover multivariate variables.
3. *General applicability to geometric entities:* In order to be of general use in the given context the uncertainty frame-work is required to be applicable to geometric entities of any type.
4. *Common handling of different types of input uncertainties:* As shown in the example there are two distinct types of uncertainties to be taken into account when computing the uncertainty of the measurement result: input parameter uncertainties such as noise effects that are described by means of statistics and uncertainties that are given based on experience. An example of the later class of uncertainties are general judgements on the quality of the calibration of a measurement setup.
5. *Propagation through different processing blocks:* Even this simple example consists of several processing blocks covering the sensor transfer function, feature detection, and the subsequent application of the transformation.
6. *Processing speed:* While in many metrological applications the determination of uncertainties can be solved off-line using simulation-based approaches, some applications require the real-time determination of parameter uncertainties. Examples include measurement systems with a varying number of input parameters. As opposed to simulation-based approaches, an analytical method can usually meet the processing speed requirements as it has a fixed processing time and is of lower complexity.

7. *Single measurements:* Repeated measurements are generally used to reduce the contribution of random effects. This requires that the measurements can be repeated under similar conditions. The relatively large sampling intervals and the amount of data being processed within a single image puts a limit on the minimum time interval between two consecutive acquisitions in vision-based applications. Thus, single measurement situations are frequently encountered in vision-based metrology which calls for a specific treatment of measurement uncertainty.
8. *Dealing with correlations:* Features extracted from a single image inherently show a certain degree of correlation due to the common conditions under which the image has been acquired. These correlations can have a significant impact on the uncertainty of the measurement result.

4. Metrological geometry

Homogeneous coordinates are frequently used in computer vision to represent geometric entities (Hartley & Zisserman (2004)). In contrast to the Euclidean representation, entities in projective spaces lead themselves to simple formulations and constructions. Given prior work by Criminisi (2001), Heuel (2003), and Förstner (2004) we observe that a multivariate Gaussian model is applicable to the problem of representing homogeneous entities in projective spaces. Using the bilinear transformation to construct new entities, this specific representation of parameter uncertainty provides a consistent tool. However, the validity of the approach only covers situations where the mean values of the parameters are large compared to their standard deviations. Heuel (2003) discusses conditions which suffice to obtain bounded parameter biases. By itself, the concept of uncertain projective geometry does not represent a frame-work for a proper expression of uncertainties. The missing elements cover the proper interpretation of a PDF as well as the metrologically sound derivation of standard, combined, and expanded uncertainties based on parameter densities. These elements are provided by GUM/Bayes as shown in Section 2 for the general case of multivariate quantities. In particular, GUM/Bayes covers the incorporation of prior knowledge and the appropriate treatment of correlated quantities.
Although most of the integrations suggested by GUM/Bayes can only be solved through time-consuming numerical algorithms such as Monte Carlo integrations, the restricted subset of quantities modelled by multivariate Gaussian densities leads itself to solutions which can be obtained analytically. If we further restrict any prior information to be represented by Gaussian quantities, we obtain a frame-work for the treatment of uncertain quantities based on the propagation of first- and second-order moments.
Consequently, we propose a fusion of the uncertain projective geometry with the GUM/Bayes approach in order to derive the concept of *metrological geometry* as outlined in Figure 7. Combining the ideas of uncertain projective geometry with the GUM/Bayes approach to the treatment of measurement uncertainty allows us to simplify and unify the modelling process for problems in geometric metrology. In summary our approach covers the following situations:

- Homogeneous entities represented by Gaussian random vectors. For example, a homogeneous point in 2D is given by

$$\underline{\mathbf{x}} \sim \mathcal{N}(\mathbf{x}, \Sigma_{\underline{\mathbf{xx}}}). \tag{19}$$

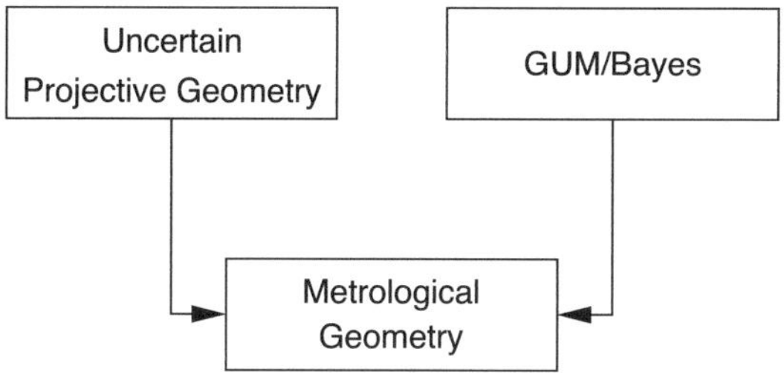

Fig. 7. Uncertain projective geometry and GUM/Bayes are combined to obtain a consistent frame-work for the treatment of uncertainties in vision-based metrological applications.

- Mapping of homogeneous entities including the propagation of parameter uncertainties. Mapping functions include: geometric transformations such as translations, rotations, and perspective mappings. Further, geometric construction (e.g. point results from intersecting two lines) and Euclidean and spherical normalisation are covered.
- Measurement updates of geometric entities with prior knowledge based on Gaussian random vectors.
- Correlations between geometric entities.

As opposed to the general recommendations provided by the original GUM document, the determination of the measurement uncertainty can be greatly simplified when considering only Gaussian uncertainties. Only a small number of building blocks is required to obtain a valid metrological model following a simple modelling procedure.

In the subsequent paragraphs we propose a unified nomenclature and present guidelines which cover the basic steps required to identify the model equation for vision-based metrological problems. In particular, we introduce components of a graphical model which greatly simplifies the setup of the model equation.

4.1 Nomenclature in metrological geometry

The nomenclature used in uncertain projective geometry differs from the nomenclature used in the GUM document. In particular, the GUM denotes physical quantities by upper case letters and their realisations (e.g. measurement results) by the corresponding lower case letters. While uncertain projective geometry uses covariance matrices for multivariate entities, the GUM document distinguishes between standard, combined, and expanded uncertainties in the univariate case and provides an uncertainty matrix in the multivariate case.

In the subsequent modelling process, we will use a unified nomenclature which assigns underlined symbols to quantities in a metrological sense. Their corresponding non-underlined version is used to denote realisations of the quantity. If it is clear from the context, we will also use the non-underlined symbols to denote the best estimates of the corresponding quantities. Thus, $\underline{c}$ is a scalar quantity and c is the corresponding realisation or best estimate. Following GUM we use u_c to denote the standard uncertainty of the best estimate and U_c as expanded uncertainty associated to a given coverage factor k. Similarly, a vector-valued quantity is referred to as $\underline{\mathbf{x}}$. The best estimate of $\underline{\mathbf{x}}$ is given by $\mathbf{x}$. The uncertainty matrix $\mathrm{U}_{\mathbf{x}}$ of $\mathbf{x}$ corresponds to the covariance matrix $\Sigma_{\underline{\mathbf{xx}}}$ of the quantity. It is now straight forward to make explicit the correlation between two different quantities $\underline{m}$ and $\underline{n}$ by means of their cross-covariance matrix $\Sigma_{\underline{mn}}$. The multivariate equivalent to the expanded uncertainty is obtained by finding constant density curves of the PDF which corresponds to a given coverage probability *p*. For 2D Gaussian quantities these curves are ellipses of general orientation as outlined for different coverage probabilities in Figure 8.

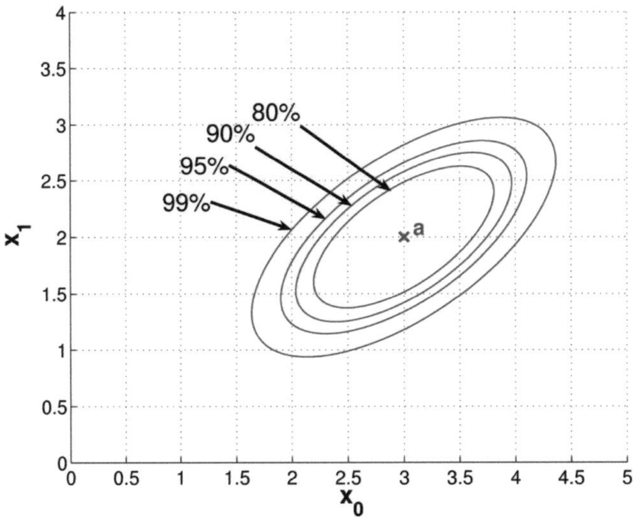

Fig. 8. Visualisation of the expanded uncertainty of a 2D Gaussian quantity $\underline{\mathbf{a}}$. Curves of constant probability density are ellipses in general configuration centred around the best estimate **a**. Different regions for varying coverage probabilities are shown.

4.2 The modelling process

The model equation as given by Equation 7 expresses the functional relationship between the measurand $\underline{Y}$ and the input quantities $\underline{X}_1, \ldots, \underline{X}_N$. However, the structure of the model equation usually does not directly reflect the processing steps involved in the measurement process. If we assume that the measurand $\underline{Y}$ is determined by reading the result of the quantity $\underline{X}_3$, Equation 7 can be reformulated such that X_3 is given by

$$\underline{X}_3 = f_M(\underline{Y}, \underline{X}_1, \underline{X}_2, \underline{X}_4, \ldots, \underline{X}_N), \tag{20}$$

which is referred to as the *measurement equation*. Sommer & Siebert (2006) suggest to base the model building process on this measurement equation as it physically relates the *cause*, i.e. the measurand $\underline{Y}$, to an *effect*, i.e. the reading $\underline{X}_3$. We propose to perform the following steps in order to evaluate the measurement uncertainty of a vision-based metrology system using this model equation:

- **Description of the Measurement Task:**
  A complete description of the measurement task is the most important step of the modeling process. This description includes the input quantities and – most importantly – the measurand.
- **Cause-Effect Relations:**
  All quantities included in the above description must be brought into a form following the idea of the cause-effect approach. It is helpful to visualise these relations using a simple graph as shown in Figure 9.

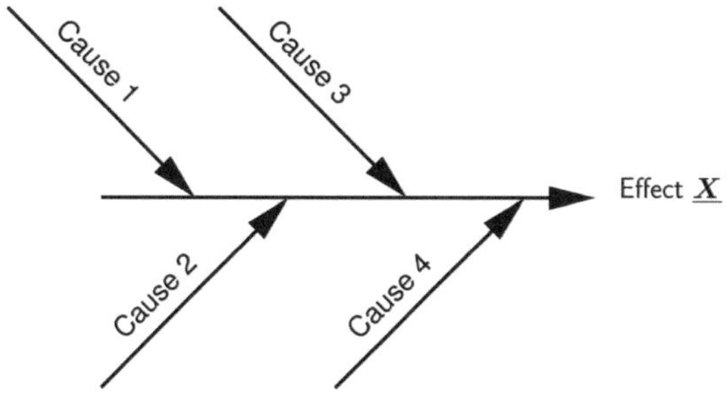

Fig. 9. Graphical representation of the cause-effect relationship.

- **Measurement Model:**
  In the next step, the measurement model is derived using cause-effect relations identified in the previous modelling step. The measurement model now relates *indications* or *observations* made by the sensor to the measurand. In most cases, it is not necessary to develop the measurement model in full detail. Rather, a coarse overview of the processing steps involved in the measurement process is sufficient as the next step in the modelling procedure aims at a fully qualified uncertainty model.
- **Model Equation:**
  The model equation relates all observations and other input quantities to the measurand. This core equation of the metrological system includes all quantities and their respective uncertainties. This step can be simplified by developing a graphical model. Due to the fact that all geometric quantities in our frame-work are represented by Gaussian random variables and linear transformations thereof are again Gaussian random variables, the graphical model[5] is composed of a small number of building blocks as outlined in Figure 10. We distinguish between the following blocks:
  - *Source:* Uncertain quantity characterised by its best estimate and the uncertainty matrix. The source block is frequently used to represent prior information.
  - *Transformation using constant parameters:* Simple transformations such as scaling functions are covered by this more general class of transformations. The uncertainty of the output quantity is only caused by the uncertainty of the input quantity.
  - *Transformation of uncorrelated quantities:* Transformations with stochastic parameters extend the previous building block by the ability to model uncertainty contributions caused by uncertainties of the parameters. Examples for this class of transformations are geometric constructions such as the intersection of two lines resulting in an uncertain point. The lack of correlation between the input quantities is depicted by input quantities that enter the block on different sides or equivalently by small rectangles attached to the input quantities denoting the range of correlated quantities.
  - *Transformation of correlated quantities:* As opposed to the previous class of transformations, this block explicitly covers correlations between quantities. Examples of this class of transformations are geometric constructions using entities which are based on a common source of uncertainty such as points commonly subjected to uncertain lens distortion. Graphically, correlation is indicated by grouping all correlated input quantities onto the same side of the block.

[5] We note that the terminology graphical model here refers to a simple and intuitive visualisation concept rather than to a model representation as used in the machine learning literature.

In summary, the components of the graphical model and their respective laws for the propagation of uncertainties are shown in Figure 10. Our set of components is chosen to allow for a straight forward derivation of the measurement equation. In contrast to Sommer & Siebert (2006), we explicitly differentiate between transformations using deterministic and stochastic parameters. We further consider parameter correlations in the graphical model and include the Bayesian information update into the modelling process.

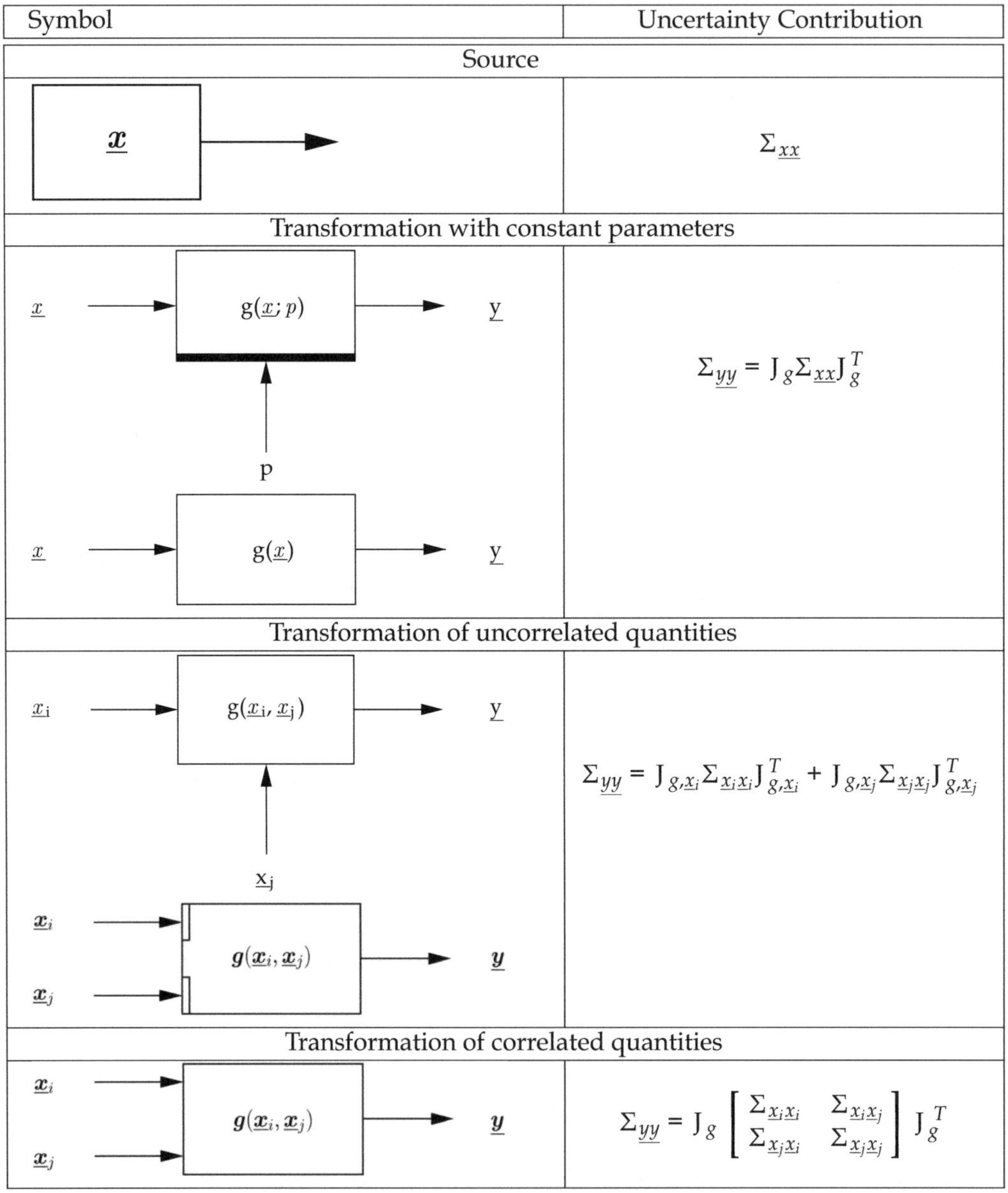

Fig. 10. Building blocks of the graphical model. Uncertainty contributions are expressed by means of their respective uncertainty matrices. The matrices J denote the Jacobians of the respective transformation functions.

4.3 Limitations of the approach

The transformation of Gaussian quantities results in another Gaussian quantity only for linear transformations. As soon as the transformation exhibits a non-linear contribution, the resultant quantity starts to deviate from the Gaussian assumption with the degree of deviation depending on the degree of non-linearity introduced by the transformation function. From the metrological point of view, these deviations from the Gaussian are of concern for the following reasons:

1. Non-linearities cause the PDF of the output quantity to deviate from the Gaussian shape. This might effect reasoning modules which operate based on the Gaussian assumption.
2. The analytic derivations of Bayes' law are only applicable to Gaussian quantities. Any deviation from this Gaussian assumption will lead to approximate solutions and, therefore, inaccurate uncertainty estimates.
3. Non-linearities introduce a bias of the best estimate of the output quantity. The bias generally is a function of the best estimates of the input quantities as well as of the input uncertainties.

These effects usually strongly depend on the degree of correlation between the input quantities. A detailed discussion of situations where our approach fails due to one of the above listed causes is given in Brandner (2009).

5. Application example

In the present section we apply the presented modelling procedure to the estimation of homography parameters. The resultant processing block is further applied to a vision-based creep test sensor. We briefly outline the measurement model of this sensor in order to highlight some properties of the proposed modelling approach.

5.1 2D Homography with uncertainties

Among the family of perspective transformations, *2D homographies* relate coplanar points to their respective images under a central projection. In other words, a set of coplanar homogeneous points $\mathbf{a}_i = (a_{x,i}, a_{y,i}, a_{h,i})^T$ in Π_1 is mapped onto another set of coplanar points $\mathbf{b}_i = (b_{x,i}, b_{y,i}, b_{h,i})^T$ in Π_2 for $i = 1...N$ as sketched in Figure 11a. Algebraically, corresponding tuples of points in Π_1 and Π_2 are related to each other by

$$\mathbf{b}_i = \mathrm{H}\mathbf{a}_i \tag{21}$$

where the 3 ×3 matrix H is a 2D homography and defined up to a scalar factor. Thus, H has 8 degrees of freedom (cf. Hartley & Zisserman (2004), p. 44). Consequently, the equality in Equation 21 is defined up to a non-zero scaling factor. In a metrological context, homographies can be used to model geometric constellations where features are bound to positions within a know plane (Ma et al. (2005); Stuflesser & Brandner (2008); Brandner et al. (2008)). Stacking the elements of the homography matrix H into a column vector **h** allows us to rewrite Equation 21 to obtain

$$\mathrm{G}\mathbf{h} = 0, \tag{22}$$

where the matrix G depends on the input points in both planes. In the case of $N = 4$ point pairs in non-degenerate configurations (cf. Hartley & Zisserman (2004)) the non-trivial

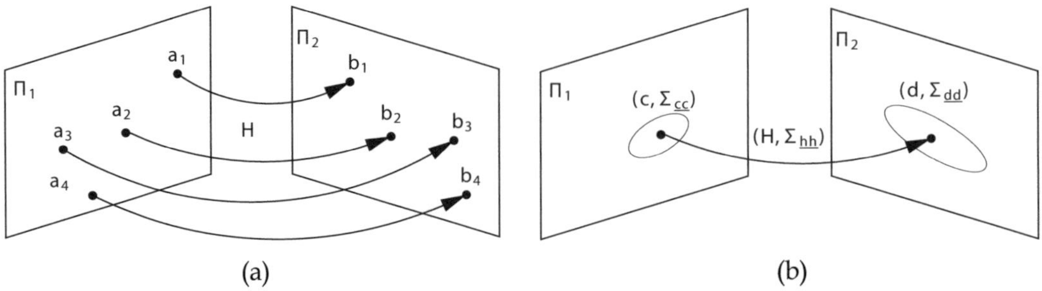

Fig. 11. Planar homography as a special case of a perspective transformation. (a) The homography H relates coplanar points $\mathbf{a}_i$ in Π_1 to their coplanar image points $\mathbf{b}_i$ in Π_2. (b) Given an uncertain point $(\mathbf{c},\Sigma_{\mathbf{cc}})$ and the parameters of the homography including their uncertainties $(\mathrm{H},\Sigma_{\mathbf{hh}})$, the resultant point and its associated uncertainty $(\mathbf{d},\Sigma_{\mathbf{dd}})$ can be obtained using first order uncertainty propagation (see text).

solution to the system in Equation 22 is exact. For the case of $N > 4$ the system is over-determined. Taking into account uncertainties of the input quantities, the solution in general is only approximate. Different optimisation strategies are known to numerically solve Equation 22. A representative of linear, direct least-squares estimators is the *Direct Linear Transform* (DLT) estimator. The cost functional minimised by the DLT is an *algebraic distance*. Due to its simplicity and numerical stability the DLT algorithm is widely used for homography estimation. The algorithm solves the system $\mathrm{G}\mathbf{h} = 0$ for non-trivial solutions, i.e. solutions $\mathbf{h} \neq 0$, by minimising $\|\mathrm{G}\mathbf{h}\|$. In order to avoid trivial solutions the minimization procedure is subjected to the constraint $\|\mathbf{h}\| = c$ for an arbitrary non-zero constant c. Although the exact value of c is irrelevant to the estimation process it is commonly set to $c = 1$ which can be realised by a norm constraint within the optimisation target, i.e.

$$\frac{\|\mathrm{G}\mathbf{h}\|}{\|\mathbf{h}\|} \to \min. \tag{23}$$

The solution of the minimisation problem in Equation 23 is given by the eigenvector that corresponds to the smallest eigenvalue of $\mathrm{M} = \mathrm{G}^T\mathrm{G}$ (cf. Hartley & Zisserman (2004)). A numerically robust solution is obtained via singular value decomposition (SVD) of M. We now cover uncertain input quantities as well as homography parameter uncertainties.

Consider the example shown in Figure 11b: An input data point $\mathbf{c}$ is transformed from plane Π_1 onto plane Π_2 using the homography H. The different sources of uncertainty contributing to final point estimate $\mathbf{d}$ are summarised in the cause-effect diagram shown in Figure 12. Using the processing blocks introduced in the previous section we can sketch the measurement model as shown in Figure 13a. This special configuration is characterised by the complete absence of any inter-parameter correlation. The resultant uncertainty of the output quantity $\mathbf{d}$ can be derived using

$$\Sigma_{\underline{dd}} = \mathrm{H}\Sigma_{\underline{cc}}\mathrm{H}^T + \mathrm{B}_c\Sigma_{\underline{hh}}\mathrm{B}_c^T, \tag{24}$$

where B_c represents an appropriate Jacobian function. Equation 24 greatly simplifies analytical derivations and, therefore, is frequently used by researchers in the field to

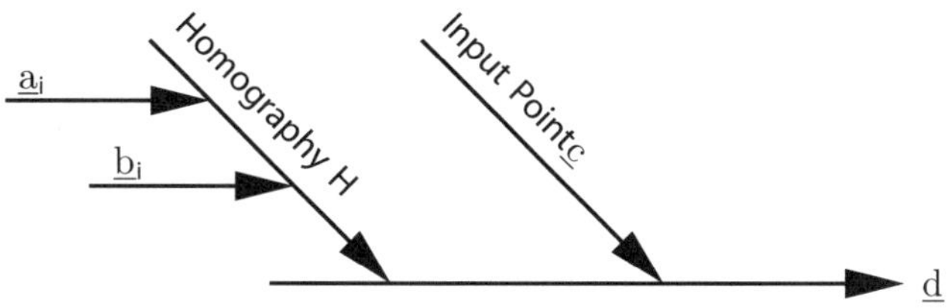

Fig. 12. Cause-effect diagram of the point measurement application shown in Figure 11b. Both uncertainties of the points used to estimate the homography parameters and uncertainties of the input point **c** contribute to the uncertainty of **d**.

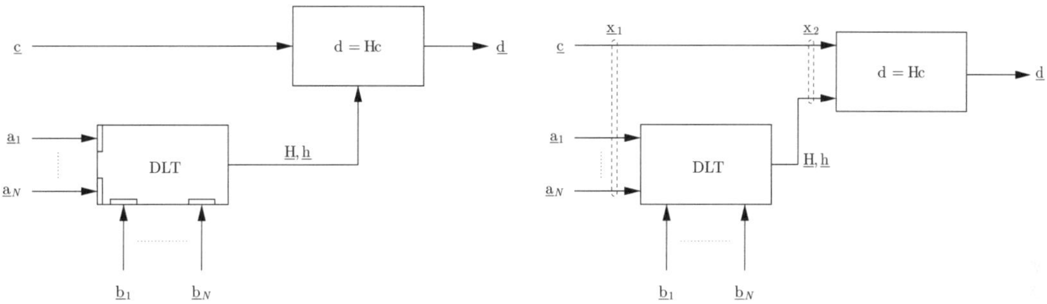

(a) (b)

Fig. 13. Graphical models of a measurement application based on a 2D/2D homography as shown in Figure 11b for different degrees of correlations between the involved parameters. Two point sets $\underline{\mathbf{a}} = \{\underline{\mathbf{a}}_i\}$ and $\underline{\mathbf{b}} = \{\underline{\mathbf{b}}_i\}$ are used to estimate H. This homography is in turn used to map a point $\underline{\mathbf{c}}$ onto its image $\underline{\mathbf{d}}$. (a) All contributing parameters are uncorrelated. (b) Common situation in planar metrology: The point set $\underline{\mathbf{a}}$ and $\underline{\mathbf{c}}$ are acquired simultaneously resulting in parameter correlation.

propagate uncertainties (cf. Criminisi (2001)). Apart from neglecting correlations between transformation parameters and geometric entities that are being mapped, Criminisi (2001) also assumes statistical independence within the point sets $\underline{\mathbf{a}}_i$ and $\underline{\mathbf{b}}_i$ that are used to estimate the homography parameters.

Correlations between parameters are often caused by uncertainties common to two or more quantities or by un-modelled systematic effects. A frequent source of systematic effects in computer vision are geometry-based biases in feature detectors. Thus, a more appropriate model for the homography example is given in Figure 13b. Apart from allowing for intra-parameter correlations within the set of model points $\mathbf{a}_i$, the model also covers correlations between the model points and the test point **c**. This situation occurs during *single acquisition* measurements, i.e. both the points used to estimate the homography parameters and the points used to apply the homography are detected within the same image. Under such circumstances, correlations need to be considered. It can be shown (cf. Brandner (2009)) that the measurement uncertainty of the resultant point **c** is obtained by

$$\Sigma_{\underline{dd}} = \mathrm{J}\begin{bmatrix} \Sigma_{\underline{cc}} & \Sigma_{\underline{ca}}\mathrm{K}_{\mathrm{a}}^{T} \\ \mathrm{K}_{\mathrm{a}}\Sigma_{\underline{ca}}^{T} & \Sigma_{\underline{hh}} \end{bmatrix}\mathrm{J}^{T}, \tag{25}$$

where J represents a Jacobian matrix and K_a a weigthening matrix, respectively. By inspection of Equation 25 we observe that the correlations between the point sets $\mathbf{a}_i$ and $\mathbf{c}$ enter the uncertainty calculi via their respective covariance matrix. The correlation introduced by the application of the homography is taken into account by means of the transformation J.

5.1.1 A numerical example

In order to validate the implementation of the previously described method to analytically estimate both the homography parameters and their associated uncertainties we compare the results with the estimates obtained using a Monte Carlo analysis. Figure 14 depicts a sample image where corner features are used to estimate the homography between the planar target and the image plane. The corners are detected and their respective positions $\mathbf{b}_i$ are estimated using a morphological detector. In this experiment an isotropic additive Gaussian noise source with variance σ^2 =1pixel^2 is superimposed to the true corner positions. Thus, assuming equal noise properties for each corner the covariance of $\mathbf{b}_i$ is given by

$$\Sigma_{\underline{b}_i\underline{b}_i} = \Sigma_{\underline{bb}} = \begin{bmatrix} 1 & 0 \\ 0 & 1 \end{bmatrix}. \tag{26}$$

Similarly we assume that the model uncertainty is characterised by an isotropic additive Gaussian noise source with variance $\sigma^2 = 0.01\text{cm}^2$. The four corners of the rectangle and the lower-left corner of the triangle are used to estimate the homography H and the associated covariance matrix Σ_{hh}. The red ellipses in Figure 14a represent the 95% probability regions around each detected corner. Clearly, the point correspondences used to estimate the homography show smaller deviations compared to other points which did not contribute to the estimation result. The close-up in Figure 14b shows a comparison of the analytic result with empirical moments obtained via MC simulation. The red ellipse again represents the 95% probability region based on the analytic estimate of the homography covariance whereas the dashed blue line represent the same probability region based on $N = 10^4$ MC iterations. Both uncertainty estimates are in good agreement justifying the application of the analytic approach.

5.2 2D displacement measurement

Using the results of the previous discussion, we can now derive the uncertainty model of a 2D displacement measurement system which reflects the general structure of a vision-based metrological system as shown in Figure 4. The measurement system is part of a creep test apparatus used to obtain material parameters of polymer samples under specific conditions. The experimental setup and the measurement system are explained in more detail in Brandner et al. (2008). Figure 5a shows the practical realisation of this sensor. Care has been taken to consider environmental conditions that include the submersion of the material samples in tempered oil. Our focus in this section is to justify the particular uncertainty model applied for this measurement system.

Figure 15 depicts the geometric sketch of the displacement measurement system. A single camera is used to acquire an image of a scene comprising a planar reference target and a planar sample target. These targets each consists of circular blob features manufactured into

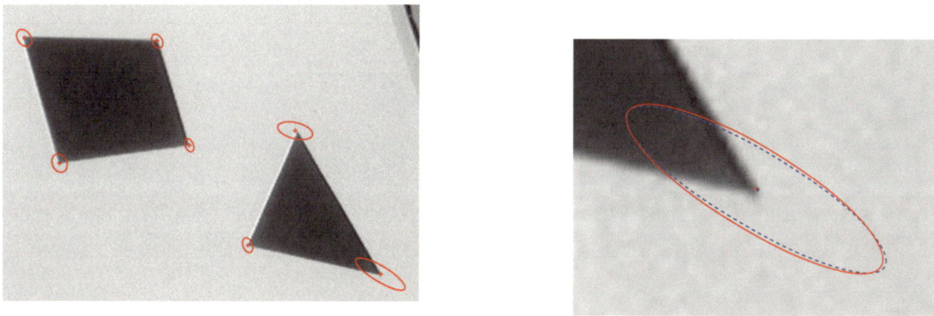

(a) (b)

Fig. 14. Direct linear estimation of the homography parameters that relate the seven corners with corresponding point positions in a model database. (a) The four corners of the rectangle and the lower-left corner of the triangle are used to estimate the homography parameters. The ellipses depict the 95% probability regions of the predicted image corners based on model-, feature detection-, and homography parameter uncertainty.
(b) Comparison of the analytic method with a Monte Carlo simulation. The close-up of the lower-right corner of the triangle shows that due to the close agreement the Monte Carlo results support our analytical estimates.

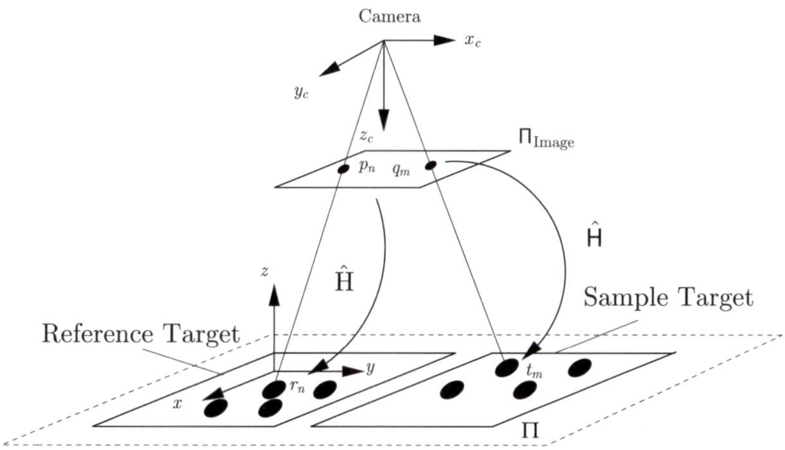

Fig. 15. Outline of the geometry of a single camera/target pair. This *single image acquisition* setup processes the same image twice: First, features on the reference target are used to estimate the transformation parameters $\hat{\text{H}}$. Second, these parameters are applied to features on the sample target in order to estimate the displacement of this target.

a stainless steel sheet by laser marking. By construction of the setup, the two targets are coplanar so that a homography $\hat{\text{H}}$ can be used to relate the image plane of the sensor Π_{Image} to the ($z = 0$)-plane which holds both targets. During the measurement process a single image is used to simultaneously obtain image points corresponding to the reference target and the sample target. Based on these image points, the sensor estimates the parameters of the homography which are then used to reconstruct the 2D displacement of the sample target with respect to the reference target.

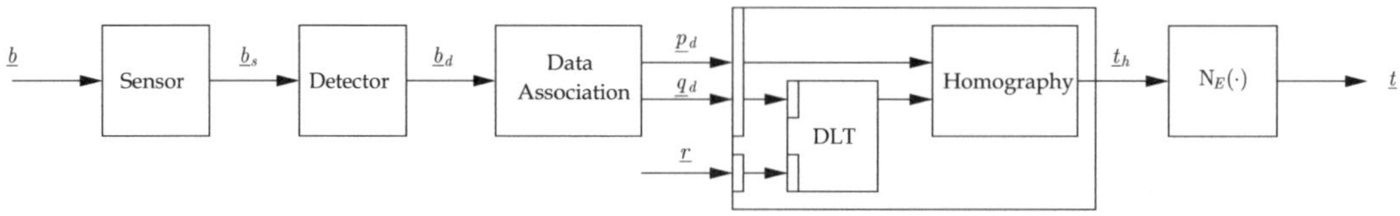

Fig. 16. Uncertainty model of the 2D displacement measurement system. The simultaneous estimation and application of the homography parameters require the proper handling of correlations.

For this specific measurement application we note that each image point is mapped by the same sensor and detected under the same illumination conditions of the scene. The common sensor calibration as well as common systematic effects such as ageing of the medium introduce a correlation between the points used to estimate the homography and the points which are transformed using the estimated homography.
Figure 16 shows the graphical model relating the input quantities (i.e. the image centres of the blobs) to the measurand (i.e. the position $\underline{t}$ in metric coordinates). This model graphically represents the measurement equation. Note that we explicitly visualise parameter correlations which is shown by the following two examples: First, the estimation of the homography parameters is performed using the direct linear transform algorithm (DLT, Hartley & Zisserman (2004)). This algorithm takes as input a sequence of image points, $\underline{q}_d$ and their corresponding model points $\underline{r}$. While the image points are correlated due to their common acquisition conditions, no dependency between the image points and their models is considered in this model. This is denoted by the two rectangles within the DLT block restricting correlations to appear *within* the rectangle only. Second, the final homography parameters are used to map the image point $\underline{p}_d$ in order to obtain $\underline{t}_h$. The common acquisition of $\underline{p}_d$ and $\underline{q}_d$ gives rise to a inter-parameter correlation between the input parameters to the homography block. The rectangle corresponding to the range of correlated input quantities is now extended to all quantities entering the block on the right - and, consequently, omitted for a clear representation. We can straight forwardly nest different layers of the model in order to better visualize relevant effects. This is shown with an aggregate model block enclosing both the DLT estimator and the homography application indicating the relevant parameter correlations at its inputs.

6. Summary

This paper addresses the problem of measurement uncertainty evaluation in vision-based measurement applications. We contribute to the state of the art by the development of a consistent frame-work for the modelling of uncertainties in vision-based applications. By combining the Gaussian representation of geometric entities in perspective spaces with the current Bayesian extensions of the Guide to the Expression of Uncertainty in Metrology (GUM) we introduce the concept of a *metrological geometry*. We identify a set of simple graphical building blocks which serve to characterise and to quantify the measurement uncertainty of the metrological application in a step-by-step approach. The presented frame-work is applicable to Gaussian quantities and transformation functions that are linear or that can be locally linearised. Using homogeneous coordinates, many constructions of entities are based on bilinear transforms which are well suited for local linearisation.

All input quantities contributing to the measurement uncertainty of the final result can be covered by the proposed frame-work. These include the calibration parameters of the sensor as well as the uncertainty introduced by transformations.

The presented work enables improvements for applications involving the analysis of measurement uncertainties in different ways: First, the presented building blocks provide an easy-to-use and intuitive way to visualise all quantities involved in the measurement process. They further explicitly highlight parameter correlations which are important to take into consideration when evaluating measurement uncertainties.

Second, the analytical derivation of the measurement uncertainty for most applications is computationally far less intensive than comparable alternatives such as Monte Carlo simulations. This allows for the construction of algorithms which determine the uncertainty of any measurement result in real-time *including* the incorporation of the best estimate. The resultant uncertainty estimates provide tighter interval boundaries which increases the usefulness of the result.

Third, correlations between quantities contributing to the measurement result are fully covered by the frame-work. As shown in the application section, the parameters of homographies can straight forwardly be estimated based on and applied to correlated features. Thus, mis-estimates of the measurement uncertainty based on false independence assumptions can be avoided. This paper extends prior work by Criminisi (2001) which targets the derivation of parameter uncertainties of 2D/2D homographies. We cover correlations within the input entities of the DLT estimator as well as correlations between the homography parameters and their respective input parameters. This allows us to tackle single image acquisition scenarios as frequently encountered in vision-based metrology.

7. References

BIPM (2006). *The International System of Units (SI)*, 8 edn, Bureau International des Poids et Mesures (BIPM).

BIPM (2008). Convention du Métre. http://www.bipm.org/en/convention (07/2008).

Brandner, M. (2006). Uncertainty estimation in a vision-based tracking system, *Proceedings of the IEEE Intl. Workshop on Advanced Methods for Uncertainty Estimation in Measurement (AMUEM 2006)*, Sardagna, Italy, pp. 40–45.

Brandner, M. (2009). *Uncertainty Evaluation in Vision-Based Measurement Systems*, PhD thesis, Graz University of Technology.

Brandner, M., Thurner, T., Kukutschki, G. & Enzinger, N. (2008). Optical 2D displacement and strain sensor for creep testing of material samples in transparent fluids, *Instrumentation and Measurement Technology Conference Proceedings - IMTC2008*, Victoria, Vancouver Island, Canada, pp. 1419–1423.

Criminisi, A. (2001). *Accurate Visual Metrology from Single and Multiple Uncalibrated Images*, Springer.

DIN1319 (1995). *Fundamentals of Metrology - Part 1: Basic Terminology*, Deutsches Institut für Normung (DIN). DIN1319-1: 1995-01.

Frstner, W. (2004). Statistics in projective geometry, Tutorial given at the European Conference on Computer Vision (ECCV).

Gelman, A., Carlin, J. B., Stern, H. S. & Rubin, D. B. (2003). *Bayesian Data Analysis*, Chapman and Hall/CRC. ISBN 1-58466-388-X.

Hartley, R. I. & Zisserman, A. (2004). *Multiple View Geometry in Computer Vision*, 2nd edn, Cambridge University Press.

Havelock, D. I. (1989). Geometric precision in noise-free digital images, *IEEE Transactions on Pattern Analysis and Machine Intelligence* 11(10): 1065–1075.

Heuel, S. (2003). *Uncertain Projective Geometry: Statistical Reasoning for Polyhedral Object Reconstruction*, number 3008 in *Lecture Notes in Computer Science*, Springer.

VIM (1993). *International vocabulary of basic and general terms in metrology*, International Organization for Standardization (ISO), Geneva, Switzerland.

Iuculano, G., Zanobini, A., Lazzari, A. & Gualtieri, G. P. (2003). Measurement uncertainty in a multivariate model: A novel approach, *IEEE Transactions on Instrumentation and Measurement* 52(5): 1573–1580.

Iversen, G. R. (1984). *Bayesian Statistical Inference, number 07-043 in Quantitative Applications in the Social Sciences*, Sage University Paper.

Jaynes, E. T. (1968). Prior probabilities, *IEEE Transactions on Systems Science and Cybernetics* 4(3): 227–241.

JCGM (2008a). Evaluation of measurement data - Guide to the expression of uncertainty in measurement, *Technical Report JCGM 100:2008*, Joint Committee for Guides in Metrology.

JCGM (2008b). Evaluation of measurement data - Supplement 1 to the Guide to the expression of uncertainty in measurement - Propagation of distributions using a Monte Carlo method, *Technical Report JCGM 101:2008*, Joint Committee for Guides in Metrology.

Kacker, R. & Jones, A. (2003). On use of Bayesian statistics to make the Guide to the Expression of Uncertainty in Measurement consistent, *Metrologia* 40: 235–248.

Kanungo, T., Jaisimha, M., Palmer, J. & Haralick, R. (1995). A methodology for quantitative performance evaluation of detection algorithms, *IEEE Transactions on Image Processing* 4(12): 1667–1674.

Lira, I. (2001). *Evaluating the Measurement Uncertainty*, Series in Measurement Science and Technology, Institute of Physics Publishing, Bristol and Philadelphia.

Ma, Y., Soatto, S., Kosecka, J. & Sastry, S. S. (2005). *An Invitation to 3-D Vision*, Springer. ISBN 0387008934.

Ochoa, B. & Belongie, S. (2006). Covariance propagation for guided matching, *Statistical Methods in Multi-Image and Video Processing*, Graz, Austria.

Papoulis, A. & Pillai, S. U. (2002). *Probability, random variables, and stochastic processes*, 4th edn, McGraw-Hill.

Sommer, K. D. & Siebert, B. R. L. (2006). Systematic approach to the modelling of measurements for uncertainty evaluation, *Metrologia* 43: 200–210.

Stuflesser, M. & Brandner, M. (2008). Vision-based control of an inverted pendulum using cascaded particle filter, *IEEE Instrumentation and Measurement Technology Conference*, Victoria, Canada, pp. 2097–2102.

Triggs, B. (2001). Joint feature distributions for image correspondence, *Proceedings of the International Conference on Computer Vision*, pp. 101–108.

Weise, K. & Wöger, W. (1999). *Meßunsicherheit und Meßdatenauswertung*, Wiley-VCH. ISBN 3-527-29610-7.

6

Real-Time Full Color Multiband Night Vision

Alexander Toet and Maarten A. Hogervorst
TNO Human Factors
The Netherlands

1. Introduction

Night vision cameras are widely used for military and law enforcement applications related to surveillance, reconnaissance, intelligence gathering, and security. The two most common night-time imaging systems are low-light-level (e.g., image-intensified) cameras, which amplify the reflected visible to near infrared (VNIR) light, and thermal infrared (IR) cameras, which convert thermal energy from the midwave (3 to 5 microns) or the long wave (8 to 12 microns) part of the spectrum into a visible image. These systems create images with a single (one-dimensional) output per pixel. As a result their ability to discriminate different materials is limited. This can be improved by combining systems that are sensitive to different parts of the electromagnetic spectrum, resulting in multiband or hyperspectral imagers. The number of different outputs increases dramatically by combining multiple sensors (e.g. up to N^2 for two sensors, when the number of different outputs for each sensor is N), which in turn leads to a significant increase in the number of materials that can be discriminated. The combination of multiple bands allows for meaningful color representation of the system output. It is therefore not surprising that the increasing availability of fused and multiband infrared and visual nightvision systems (e.g. Bandara et al., 2003; Breiter et al., 2002; Cho et al., 2003; Cohen et al., 2005; Goldberg et al., 2003) has led to a growing interest in the (false) color display of night vision imagery (Li & Wang, 2007; Shi et al., 2005a; Shi et al., 2005b; Tsagaris & Anastasopoulos, 2006; Zheng et al., 2005).
In principle, color imagery has several benefits over monochrome imagery for surveillance, reconnaissance, and security applications. The human eye can only distinguish about 100 shades of gray at any instant. As a result, grayscale nightvision images are sometimes hard to interpret and may give rise to visual illusions and loss of situational awareness. Since people can discriminate several thousands of colors defined by varying hue, saturation, and brightness, a false color representation may facilitate nightvision image recognition and interpretation. For instance, color may improve feature contrast, thus enabling better scene segmentation and object detection (Walls, 2006). This may allow an observer to construct a more complete mental representation of the perceived scene, resulting in better situational awareness. It has indeed been found that scene understanding and recognition, reaction time, and object identification are faster and more accurate with color imagery than with monochrome imagery (Cavanillas, 1999; Gegenfurtner & Rieger, 2000; Goffaux et al., 2005; Oliva & Schyns, 2000; Rousselet et al., 2005; Sampson, 1996; Spence et al., 2006; Wichmann et al., 2002). Also, observers are able to selectively attend to task-relevant color targets and to

ignore non-targets with a task-irrelevant color (Ansorge et al., 2005; Folk & Remington, 1998; Green & Anderson, 1956). As a result, simply producing a false color nightvision image by mapping multiple spectral bands into a three dimensional color space already generates an immediate benefit, and provides a method to increase the dynamic range of a sensor system (Driggers et al., 2001). However, the color mapping should be chosen with care and should be adapted to the task at hand. Although general design rules can be used to assure that the information available in the sensor image is optimally conveyed to the observer (Jacobson & Gupta, 2005), it is not trivial to derive a mapping from the various sensor bands to the three independent color channels, especially when the number of bands exceeds three (e.g. with hyperspectral imagers; Jacobson et al., 2007). In practice, many tasks may benefit from a representation that renders a nighttime scene in daytime colors. Jacobson & Gupta (Jacobson et al., 2007; Jacobson & Gupta, 2005) therefore advise to use a consistent color mapping according to a natural palette. The use of natural colors facilitates object recognition by allowing access to stored color knowledge (Joseph & Proffitt, 1996). Experimental evidence indicates that object recognition depends on stored knowledge of the object's chromatic characteristics (Joseph & Proffitt, 1996). In natural scene recognition paradigms, optimal reaction times and accuracy are obtained for normal natural (or diagnostically) colored images, followed by their grayscale version, and lastly by their (nondiagnostically) false colored version (Goffaux et al., 2005; Oliva, 2005; Oliva & Schyns, 2000; Rousselet et al., 2005; Wichmann et al., 2002). When sensors operate outside the visible waveband, artificial color mappings generally produce false color images whose chromatic characteristics do not correspond in any intuitive or obvious way to those of a scene viewed under natural photopic illumination (e.g. (Fredembach & Süsstrunk, 2008)). As a result, this type of false color imagery may disrupt the recognition process by denying access to stored knowledge. In that case observers need to rely on color contrast to segment a scene and recognize the objects therein. This may lead to a performance that is even worse compared to single band imagery alone (Sinai et al., 1999a). Experiments have indeed convincingly demonstrated that a false color rendering of night-time imagery which resembles natural color imagery significantly improves observer performance and reaction times in tasks that involve scene segmentation and classification (Essock et al., 1999; Sinai et al., 1999b; Toet & IJspeert, 2001; Vargo, 1999; White, 1998), whereas color mappings that produce counterintuitive (unnaturally looking) results are detrimental to human performance (Krebs et al., 1998; Toet & IJspeert, 2001; Vargo, 1999). One of the reasons often cited for inconsistent color mapping is a lack of physical color constancy (Vargo, 1999). Thus, the challenge is to give nightvision imagery an intuitively meaningful ("naturalistic") and stable color appearance, to improve the viewer's scene comprehension and enhance object recognition and discrimination (Scribner et al., 1999). Several techniques have been proposed to render night-time imagery in color (e.g. (Sun et al., 2005; Toet, 2003; Tsagiris & Anastassopoulos, 2005; Wang et al., 2002; Zheng et al., 2005)). Simply mapping the signals from different nighttime sensors (sensitive in different spectral wavebands) to the individual channels of a standard color display or to the individual components of perceptually decorrelated color spaces, sometimes preceded by principal component transforms or followed by a linear transformation of the color pixels to enhance color contrast, usually results in imagery with an unnatural color appearance (e.g. Howard et al., 2000; Krebs et al., 1998; Li et al., 2004; Schuler et al., 2000; Scribner et al., 2003). More intuitive color schemes may be obtained through opponent processing through feedforward center-surround shunting neural networks similar to those found in vertebrate color vision (Aguilar et al., 1998; Aguilar et al., 1999; Fay et al., 2000a; Fay et al., 2000b; Huang et al., 2007; Warren et al., 1999; Waxman et al., 1995a; Waxman et al., 1997). Although this approach produces fused nighttime images with appreciable color contrast, the resulting color schemes remain rather arbitrary and are usually not strictly related to the actual daytime color scheme of the scene that is registered. In the next section we give an overview of some recently developed color mapping schemes that can give false color multiband nightvision imagery a natural color appearance. First we present a simple false color mapping scheme that is inspired by previous color opponent processing schemes. Although this scheme produces fused false color images with large color contrast and preserves the identity of the input signals (thus making the images perceptually intuitive), the resulting color representation is not strictly natural looking (Toet & Walraven, 1996). We therefore developed a statistical extension of this coloring method which produces colorized multiband nightvision imagery with a regular daylight color appearance (Toet, 2003). This mapping transfers the first order statistics of the color distribution of a given color reference image to the multiband nighttime images, thereby giving them a similar color appearance as the reference image. In its original form this method is computationally expensive. However, computational simplicity (enabling real-time implementation) can be achieved by applying the statistical mapping approach in a lookup-table framework. Although the statistical mapping approach yields a natural color rendering, it achieves no color constancy, since the mapping depends on the relative amounts of the different materials in the scene (and will therefore change when the camera pans over or zooms in on a scene). We therefore developed a sample-based color mapping scheme that yields both color constancy and computational efficiency (Hogervorst & Toet, 2008a; Hogervorst & Toet, 2008b; Hogervorst & Toet, 2010). In contrast to the statistical color mapping method, the sample based color transfer method (for which a patent application is currently pending: Hogevorst et al., 2006) is highly specific for different types of materials in the scene and can easily be adapted for the task at hand, such as the detection of camouflaged objects. After explaining how the sample based color transformation can be derived from the combination of a given multi-band sensor image and a corresponding daytime reference image, we will dicuss how it can be deployed at night and implemented in real-time.

2. Color mapping

2.1 Center-surround opponent-color fusion

Opponent color image fusion was originally developed at the MIT Lincoln Laboratory (Gove et al., 1996; Waxman et al., 1995a; Waxman et al., 1996a; Waxman et al., 1996b; Waxman et al., 1997; Waxman et al., 1999) and derives from biological models of color vision (Schiller, 1982; Schiller, 1984; Schiller et al., 1986; Schiller, 1992) and fusion of visible light and infrared (IR) radiation (Newman & Hartline, 1981; Newman & Hartline, 1982).

In the case of color vision in monkeys and man, retinal cone sensitivities are broad and overlapping, but the images are contrast enhanced *within* bands by spatial opponent processing (via cone-horizontal-bipolar cell interactions) creating both ON and OFF center-surround response channels (Schiller, 1992). These signals are then contrast enhanced *between* bands via interactions among bipolar, sustained amacrine, and single-opponent-color ganglion cells (Gouras, 1991; Schiller & Logothetis, 1990), all within the retina. Further

color processing in the form of double-\-opponent-color cells is found in the primary visual cortex of primates (and the retinas of some fish). Opponent processing interactions form the basis of such percepts as color opponency, color constancy, and color contrast, though the exact mechanisms are not fully understood. Double-opponent-color processing has been applied to multispectral IR target enhancement (Gove et al., 1996; Waxman et al., 1995b).
Fusion of visible and thermal imagery has been observed in several classes of neurons in the optic tectum (evolutionary progenitor of the superior colliculus) of rattlesnakes (pit vipers), and pythons (boid snakes), as described by (Newman & Hartline, 1981; Newman & Hartline, 1982). These neurons display interactions in which one modality (e.g. IR) can enhance or depress the response to the other sensing modality (e.g. visible) in a strongly nonlinear fashion. Such interactions resemble opponent-processing between bands as observed in primate retina.
For opaque surfaces in thermodynamic equilibrium, spectral reflectivity ρ and emissivity ε are linearly related at each wavelength λ: $\rho(\lambda) = 1 - \varepsilon(\lambda)$. This provides a rationale for the use of both on-center and off-center channels when treating infrared imagery as characterized by thermal emissivity (Toet et al., 1997).
In the opponent-color image fusion methodology the individual input images are first enhanced by filtering them with a feedforward center-surround shunting neural network (Grossberg, 1988). This operation serves

1. to enhance spatial contrast in the individual visible and IR bands,
2. to create both positive and negative polarity IR contrast images, and
3. to create two types of single-opponent-color contrast images.

The resulting single-opponent-color contrast images represent grayscale fused images that are analogous to the IR-depressed visual and IR-enhanced visual cells of the rattlesnake (Newman & Hartline, 1981; Newman & Hartline, 1982).

2.2 Pixel based opponent-color fusion

Inspired by the opponent-color fusion approach (Waxman et al., 1995a; Waxman et al., 1996a; Waxman et al., 1996b; Waxman et al., 1997; Waxman et al., 1999), we derived a simplified (pixel based) version of this method, which fuses visible and thermal images into false color images with a relatively natural or intuitive appearance.
Let I_1 and I_2 be two input images with the same spatial resolution and dynamic range. The common component of both signals is computed as the morphological intersection:

$$I_1 \cap I_2 = \mathrm{Min}\{I_1, I_2\} \tag{1}$$

The unique or characteristic component I^* of each image modality remains after subtraction of the common component:

$$I_1^* = I_1 - I_1 \cap I_2 \quad ; \quad I_2^* = I_2 - I_1 \cap I_2 \tag{2}$$

The characteristic components are emphasized in the fused image by subtracting them from the opposite image modalities. The color fused image is then obtained by mapping these differences to respectively the red and green bands of a RGB false color image. The characteristic components of both image modalities can be further emphasized by mapping their difference to the blue band of the fused false color image, so that the final mapping is given by (Toet & Walraven, 1996):

$$\begin{pmatrix} R \\ G \\ B \end{pmatrix} = \begin{pmatrix} I_2 - I_1^* \\ I_1 - I_2^* \\ I_2^* - I_1^* \end{pmatrix} \tag{3}$$

In case of visual and thermal input images, I_1 = Vis and I_2 = *IR*. Because the method is computationally simple it can implemented in hardware or even be applied in real-time using standard processing equipment (Aguilar et al., 1998; Aguilar et al., 1999; Waxman et al., 1999). The resulting color rendering enhances the visibility of certain details and preserves the specificity of the sensor information. In addition, it has a fairly natural color appearance (Fig. 1 and Fig. 2). The resulting images agree with our natural associations of warm (red) and cool (blue). To further enhance the appearance of the fused results, the R, G, B channels can be input to a color remapping stage in which, following conversion to H, S, V (hue, saturation, value) color space, hues can be remapped to alternative "more natural'" hues, colors can be desaturated, and then reconverted back to R, G, B signals to drive a color display. Because of the enhanced color contrast and its intuitive appearance this color fused image representation is expected to improve both visual target detection and recognition performance are expected to benefit in terms of both speed and precision. Two observer studies were performed to test this hypothesis.

In the first observer study we used grayscale intensified visual and thermal images, and color fused motion sequences, depicting scenes in which a person walked across a rural scene with man-made objects (Toet et al., 1997). The reference (terrain) features were represented with high contrast in the intensified visual images (Fig. 2a) and low contrast in

Fig. 1. Visual (a) and thermal (b) input images. (c) Result of mapping (a) and (b) to respectively the green and red channels of an RGB display. (d) Result of the mapping defined by equation.

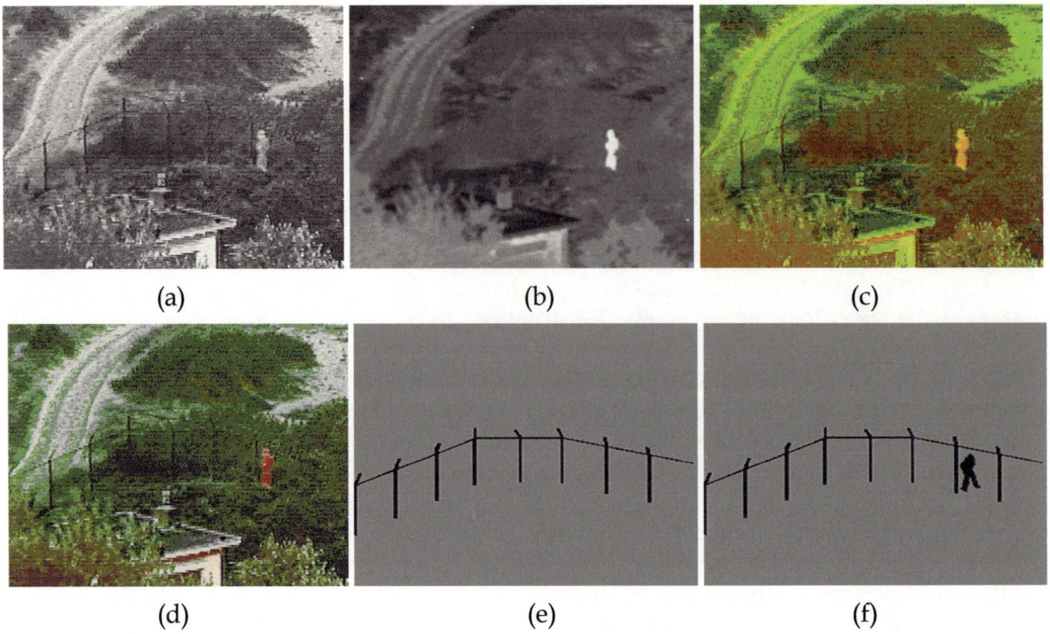

Fig. 2. Scene representing a person walking along the outside of a fence. Visual (a) and thermal (b) input images. (c) Result of mapping (a) and (b) to respectively the green and red channels of an RGB display. (d) Result of the mapping defined in equation . (e) Reference image used in the spatial localization task. (f) Image used to assess baseline localization performance.

the thermal images (Fig. 2b), while the opposite was the case for the image of the person. All details were represented in the color fused images (Fig. 2d). During the localization experiments, individual frames from the motion sequences and for each of the three image modalities (visual, thermal and color fused) were briefly (1 s) and in random order presented to human observers. After the presentation of each frame a schematic grayscale image was shown representing only the reference features on a homogeneous background (e.g. Fig. 2e). Observers were asked to indicate the perceived position of the person in the scene by placing a mouse controlled cursor at the corresponding location in the schematic reference image. The position of the reference image on the display screen was given a small random variation to prevent participants from using cues from afterimages. Baseline performance was assessed using schematic images, similar to the reference image, but with a binary image of the person at his actual location in the corresponding frames (e.g. Fig. 2f). The results show that observers can localize a person in a scene with a significantly higher accuracy and with greater confidence when they perform with color fused images, compared to the individual image modalities (visible and thermal; Toet et al., 1997).

In the second observer study we used grayscale visual and thermal (8-12 μm) motion sequences, and color fused motion sequences, depicting a mountain range in the background and grasslands in the foreground, with infantry soldiers, vehicles, and a smoke screen (Fig. 3). The visual and thermal motion sequences are a subset (images 37--93) of the MS01 Test Sequence that consists of 110 corresponding image pairs, registered at CFB Valcartier (Sévigny, 1996). Both a tow truck and a helicopter move across the scene during the registration period. The infantry soldiers are not visible in the visual images (Fig. 3a-c),

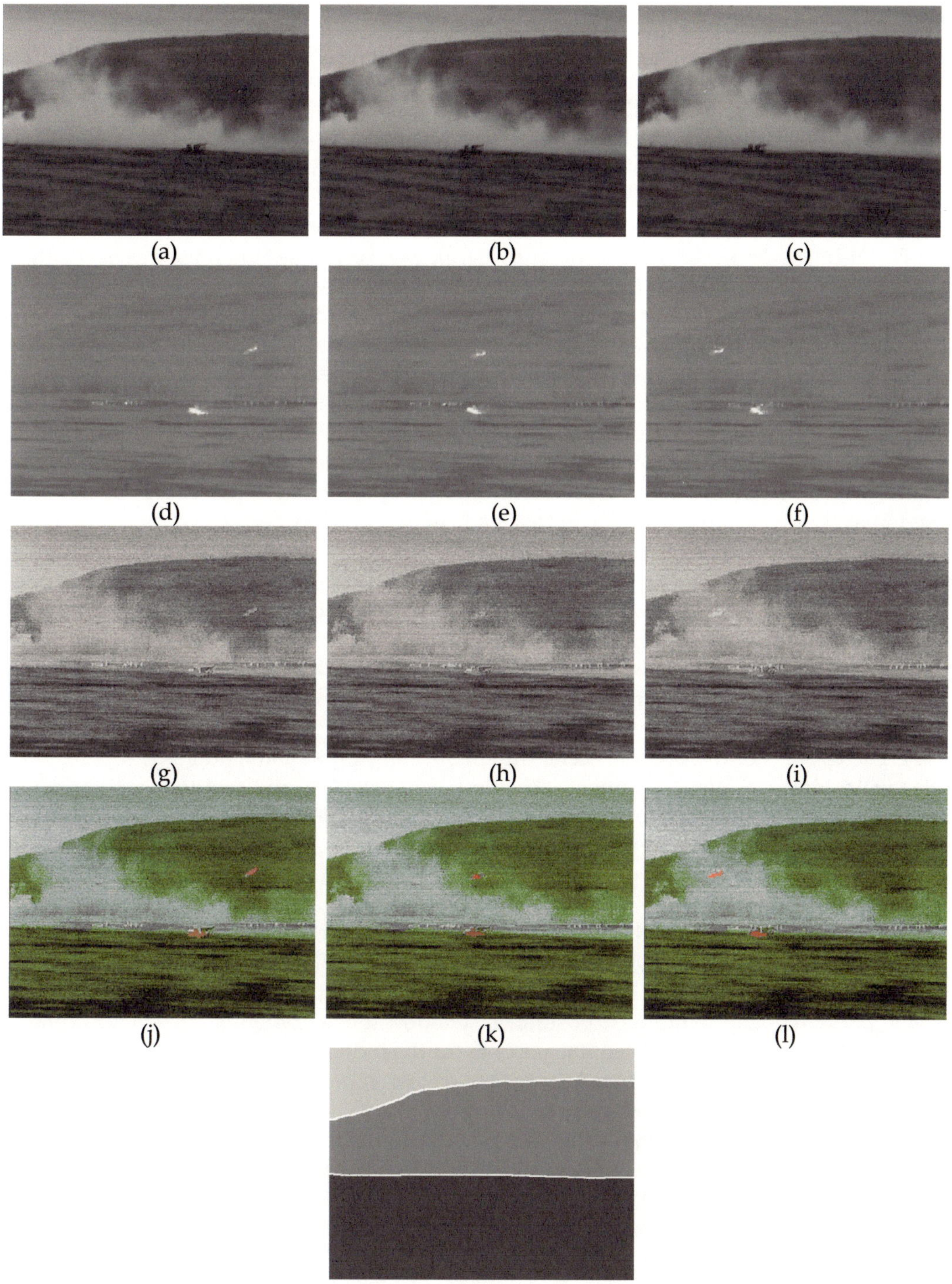

Fig. 3. Left to right: successive frames of a time sequence. Top-down: video (a-c), thermal (d-f), grayscale fused (g-i), and color fused (j-l) images. (m) Schematic reference image.

because they are obscured by the smoke screen. However, they can easily be perceived in the thermal images (Fig. 3d-f), where they appear as small hot spots. In the visual images, the visibility of the helicopter ranges from barely visible to not visible (when it flies behind the smoke screen: Fig. 3f). In the thermal images there is almost no contrast between the foreground (grassland) and the background (the mountain range). Also, the mountain range and the sky have little contrast in the thermal images (the skyline of the mountain range is barely visible). The contrast between the sky and the top of the mountain range is much larger in the CCD images. The visual and thermal images were color fused using equation 3 (see Fig. 3j-l). Fig. 3g-i shows the luminance component of Fig. 3j-l. Both the graylevel fused (Fig. 3g-i) and the color fused (Fig. 3j-l) images represent all details of interest. However, in the grayfused images, where details are represented by different shades of gray, it is sometimes hard to visually segment the scene, because there are no visible boundaries (edges) between different physical objects with the same mean luminance. For instance, in the visual images the smokescreen has a high luminance (is very bright). In the thermal images, the warmer (barren) parts of the grassland and the helicopter are represented as bright regions. As a result, there is sometimes very little contrast in the grayfused images between the smokescreen and respectively the helicopter and the grassland. In the color fused images, the additional color contrast leads to an effortless perceptual segmentation of the scene. We measured the accuracy with which observers can determine the position of the helicopter in a briefly (600 ms) presented motion sequence, for visual, thermal, and color fused image sequences. Only a limited portion (a restricted field of view) of the entire scene was displayed during each test interval. The field of view was randomly positioned on the dynamic battlefield scene. This experimental paradigm simulates a field of view search of the display of a moving camera scanning over a larger field of regard. For each individual frame a corresponding reference image was constructed, representing a segmented version of the background of the original scene (mountain range, grassland, and sky; see Fig. 3m). After watching each movie fragment, observers were asked to indicate the location where the helicopter was last seen, by placing a mouse-controlled cursor over the schematic reference image. This task requires observers to quickly determine *(a)* the location of reference contours, and *(b)* the location of the target at each stimulus presentation. This involves rapid visual scene segmentation. The performance in this relative spatial localization task depends on the accuracy with which the position of the helicopter can be perceived relative to the contours of the mountain range. The results of this experiment show that the accuracy with which observers can determine the position of a helicopter in a briefly presented and randomly positioned window on a dynamic battlefield scene is significantly higher for color fused images than for the individual visual and thermal images (Toet et al., 1997). The color fused images probably represent all relevant features at a sufficiently large perceptual contrast to allow rapid visual identification of the spatial layout of the scene, thereby enabling subjects to perform the task. We also observed that a restriction of the field of view results in a significant increase in the localization error for the visual and thermal image modalities, but not for the fused image modalities.

The false color mapping defined by equation 3 has also been successfully applied in other domains, like the fusion of retinal images (Kolar et al., 2008; Laliberté et al., 2002; Laliberté et al., 2003) and the fusion of infrared and synthetic images (Simard et al., 1999; Simard et al., 2000).

In ophthalmology, visual fundus images are often used in combination with fluorescein angiogram images. Visual images of the retina clearly represent hard exudates. Fluorescein angiogram images represent the macula, the arteries and veins at high contrast, thus allowing the detection of occluded and leaking capillaries, microaneurims, macular edema, and neovascularization. Using the mapping defined by equation 3 to fuse visual fundus images with fluorescein angiogram images provides better color contrast rendering than other opponent-color fusion methods, thus enhancing diagnostic performance and reducing visual workload (Laliberté et al., 2002; Laliberté et al., 2003). It was for instance found that this mapping clearly represents neovessels and depicts the macula at high contrast (Laliberté & Gagnon, 2006) Fig. 4. shows two examples of the fusion of grayscale visual fundus images (Fig. 4a and d) with corresponding fluorescein angiogram images (Fig. 4b and e). The fused images (Fig. 4c and f) represent the interesting details like the vascular network (purple veins) and the exudates (yellow lesions) with large color contrast. When using equation 3 to fuse thermal and autofluorescent images of the retina (Kolar et al., 2008), the resulting false color images provide higher contrast for the hyperfluent areas of the autofluorescent images (which are symptoms for glaucoma in its early stages) and clearly represent the position of the optic nerve head from the infrared image.

Simulated flight tests with fused infrared and synthetic imagery showed that the fusion technique defined by equation 3 preserves all features relevant for obstacle avoidance, and significantly improves detection distances for all simulated visibility conditions (Simard et al., 1999; Simard et al., 2000).

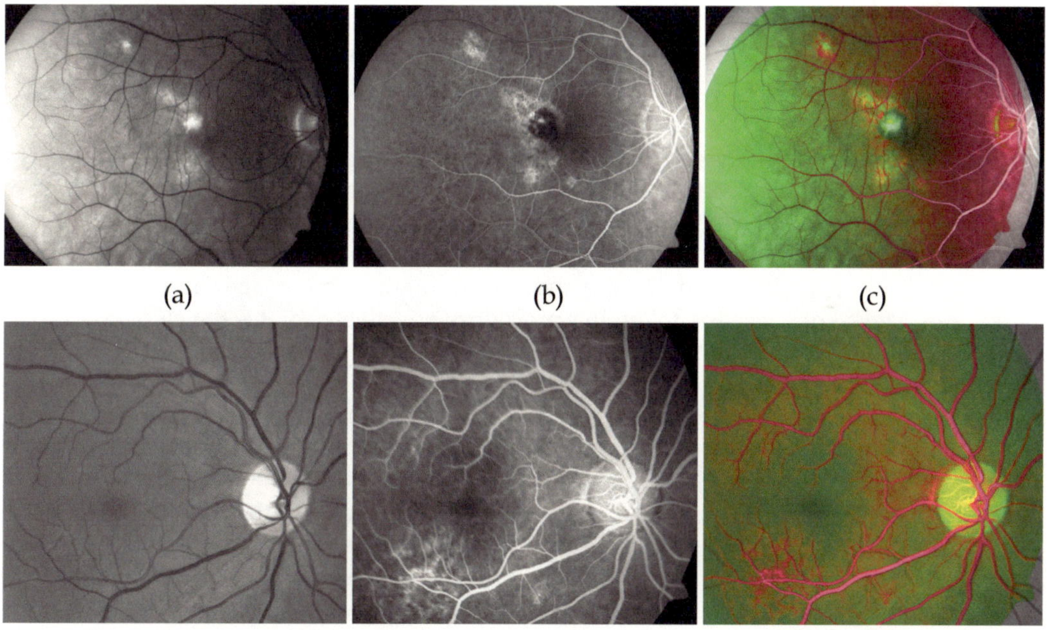

(a) (b) (c)

(d) (e) (f)

Fig. 4. Photographs (a,d) and fluorescein angiogram images (b,e) and their color fused representation (c,f).

2.3 Statistical color transform

Although the overall color appearance of images produced with the opponent-color fusion scheme is fairly intuitive, some details may still be depicted with unnatural colors. In this section we present a method that gives multiband nighttime images the appearance of regular daylight color images by transferring the first order color statistics from full color daylight imagery to the false color multiband nightvision imagery. The method is based on a technique that was developed to enhance the color representation of synthetic imagery (Reinhard et al., 2001). The outline of the method is as follows. As input the method requires a false color RGB image. This can be produced by mapping the 2 or 3 individual bands (or the first 2 or 3 principal components when the sensor system delivers more than 3 bands) of a multiband nightvision system to the respective channels of an RGB image. Next, the false color RGB nightvision image and a regular full color daylight reference image are both transformed into the perceptually decorrelated *lαβ* opponent color space (Ruderman et al., 1998). Then, the mean and standard deviation of each of the 3 color channels of the multiband nightvision image are set equal to those of the reference image:

$$\begin{aligned} l^* &= \frac{\sigma_r^l}{\sigma^l}\left(l - \langle l \rangle\right) \\ \alpha^* &= \frac{\sigma_r^\alpha}{\sigma^\alpha}\left(\alpha - \langle \alpha \rangle\right) \\ \beta^* &= \frac{\sigma_r^\beta}{\sigma^\beta}\left(\beta - \langle \beta \rangle\right) \end{aligned} \tag{4}$$

where $\langle \rangle$ denotes the mean, σ the standard deviation, and the index *r* refers to the reference image.

Finally, the multiband nightvision image is transformed back to RGB space for display. The result is a full color representation of the multiband nightvision image with a color appearance that closely resembles the color appearance of the daylight reference image. The daylight reference image should display a scene which is similar (but not necessarily identical to) the one displayed by the multiband nightvision image. The order of the mapping is irrelevant, since the following procedure effectively rotates the color coordinate axes of the false color multiband nightvision images such that these will be aligned with the axes of the referenced daylight color image in the final result.

The statistical color transform is computationally expensive and therefore not suitable for real-time implementation. Moreover, although it can give multiband nighttime imagery a natural daylight color appearance, it can not achieve color constancy for dynamic imagery (Zheng & Essock, 2008), because the actual mapping depends on the relative amounts of different materials in (i.e. the composition or statistics of) the scene. Large objects in the scene will dominate the color mapping. As a result, the color of objects and materials may change over time when the sensor system pans over (or zooms in on) a given scene. We therefore developed a fixed lookup table based version of this statistical color mapping which is *(1)* computationally efficient, so that it can easily be deployed in real time, and which *(2)* yields constant object colors.

The new lookup table based statistical color transfer approach is illustrated in Fig. 5. for a multi-band image consisting of two channels. First, the two sensor images are mapped on two of the three channels of an RGB image. In this particular example (Fig. 5c) the visual band is (arbitrarily) mapped to R (red channel) and the near-infrared band is mapped to G (green channel). The result is the red-green false-color representation of the multi-band

Fig. 5. Visible (a) and near infrared (b) image. (c) False color image obtained by assigning (a) to the green and (b) to the red channel of an RGB false color image (the blue channel is set to zero). The inset in this figure represents all possible combinations of signal values that can occur in the two sensor bands (upper left: both sensors give zero output; lower right: both sensors give maximal output). (d) Arbitrary reference daylight color image. (e) Result of mapping the first order statistics of the reference image (d) to the false color nighttime image (c). The inset in this figure represents the result of applying the same transform to the inset of (c), and shows all possible colors that can occur in the recolored sensor image (i.e. after applying the color mapping).

image shown in Fig. 5c. The statistical color transform can then be derived from the first order statistics of respectively *(a)* Fig. 5c and *(b)* a given daylight color reference image, like the one shown in square inset in Fig. 5d. The application of this statistical color transform to an input table of 2-tuples representing all possible sensor output values yields an output table containing all possible color values that can occur in the colorized nighttime image. The in- and output table pair defines the statistical color mapping and can therefore be deployed in a color lookup table transform procedure. The square inset in Fig. 5c represents the table of all possible two-band signal values as different shades of red, green and yellow. Application of the statistical color transform to the inset in Fig. 5c yields the inset shown in Fig. 5e. In a lookup table paradigm the insets in Fig. 5c and Fig. 5e together define the statistical color mapping. For any color in the false-color representation of Fig. 5c the corresponding color after application of the statistical color transform can easily be found by

(1) locating the color in the inset of Fig. 5c, and *(2)* finding the color at the corresponding location in the transformed inset in Fig. 5e. For instance, a pixel representing a high response in the visual channel and low response in the near infrared channel is represented with a red color (high value of red, low value of green) in the inset in Fig. 5c. In the inset of Fig. 5e the same pixel appears in a brownish color. The color transformation can thus be implemented by using the inset pair of Fig. 5c and Fig. 5e as color lookup tables. Then, the false color image Fig. 5c can be transformed into an indexed image using the red-green color lookup table (the inset of Fig. 5c). Replacing the color lookup table of the indexed image Fig. 5c by the transformed color lookup table (the inset of Fig. 5e) then transforms Fig. 5c into Fig. 5e. Note that the color mapping scheme is fully defined by the two color lookup tables. When all possible combinations of an 8-bit multi-band system are represented, these color lookup tables contain 256x256 entries. When a color lookup table with less entries is used (e.g. only 256), the color mapping can be achieved by determining the closest match of the table entries to the observed multi-band sensor values.

Once the color mapping has been derived from a multi-band nighttime image and its corresponding reference image, and once it has been defined as a lookup table transform, it can be applied to different and dynamic multi-band images. The advantage of this method is that the color of objects only depends on the multi-band sensor values and is independent of the image content. Therefore, objects keep the same color over time when registered with a moving camera. Another advantage of this implementation is that it requires minimal computing power. Once the color transformation has been derived and the pair of color lookup tables that defines the mapping has been created, the new color lookup table transform can be used in a (real-time) application.

2.4 Sample based color transform

In spite of all the afore-mentioned advantages of the lookup table based statistical color transform, there is still room for improvement. For instance, in this paradigm there is no strict relationship between sensor output values and object color, since the statistical approach inherently only addresses the global color characteristics of the depicted scene. In this section we will describe an alternative lookup table based method for applying natural colors to multi-band images, which alleviates this problem since it does not rely on image statistics. The color transformation is derived from a corresponding set of samples for which both the multi-band sensor values and the corresponding natural color (RGB-value) are known (Hogervorst et al., 2006). We will show that this method results in rendered multi-band images with colors that match the daytime colors more closely than the result of the statistical approach. In contrast to the statistical method, the derivation of the color mapping requires a registered image pair, consisting of a multi-band image and a daytime reference image of the same scene, sine the pixels serve as samples in this approach. Once the color mapping has been derived it can be applied to different multi-band nighttime images. Again, we will implement the color transformation using a color lookup table transformation, thus enabling real-time implementation.

The method is as follows. Given a set of samples (pixels) for which both the multi-band sensor output and the corresponding daytime colors are known, the problem of deriving the optimal color transformation is to find a transformation that optimally maps the N-dimensional (e.g. in our examples $N = 2$) multi-band sensor output vectors (one for each sample) to the 3-D vectors corresponding to the daytime colors (RGB). The mapping should minimize the difference between the modeled colors and the measured colors. Moreover, the transformation should predict the mapping of untrained samples. Several methods exist to derive a suitable mapping, such as neural networks and support vector machines. What constitutes a suitable mapping is determined by the function that is minimized. Also the statement that the difference between the modeled colors and the measured colors is minimized should be formalized. We will minimize the average perceptual color difference between the modeled color and the measured color. More precisely, we will minimize the average squared distance between the perceptual color vectors $l\alpha\beta$ (see (Ruderman et al., 1998)). We will describe a (relatively) simple implementation that is not focused towards finding the theoretical optimum mapping, but that will lead to robust and good results and can be understood intuitively. We will now describe our new method for deriving a natural color transformation using the example shown in Fig. 6. Fig. 6a depicts the full color daytime reference image, which is in this case a color photograph taken with a standard digital camera. Figs. 6b and c respectively show a visible and near-infrared image of the same scene. Fig. 6f shows the result of applying daytime colors to the two-band night-time sensor image using our new color mapping technique.

The method works as follows. First, the multi-band sensor image is transformed to a false-color image by taking the individual bands (Fig. 6b and c) as input to the R and G channels (and B when the sensor contains three bands), referred to as the RG-image (Fig. 6e). In practice any other combination of 2 channels can also be used (one could just as well use the combinations R & B or B & R). Mapping the two bands to a false color RGB-image allows us to use standard image conversion techniques, such as indexing. In the next step the resulting false color (RG-image) Fig. 6e is converted to an indexed image. Each pixel in such an image contains a single index. The index refers to an RGB-value in a color lookup table (the number of entries can be chosen by the user). In the present example of a sensor image consisting of two bands (R and G; Fig. 6e) the color lookup table contains various combinations of R and G values (the B-values are zero when the sensor or sensor pair provides only two bands). For each index representing a given R,G combination (a given false color) the corresponding natural color equivalent is obtained by locating the pixels in the target image with this index and finding the corresponding pixels in the (natural color) reference image (Fig. 6a). First, the RGB-values are converted to perceptually de-correlated $l\alpha\beta$ values (see (Ruderman et al., 1998)). Next, we calculate the average $l\alpha\beta$-vector over this ensemble of pixels. This assures that the computed average color reflects the perceptual average color. Averaging automatically takes the distribution of the pixels into account: colors that appear more frequently are attributed a greater weight. Let us for instance assume that we would like to derive the natural color associated with index 1. In that case we locate all pixels in the (indexed) false color multi-band target image with index 1. We then take all corresponding pixels in the reference daytime color image, convert them to $l\alpha\beta$, and calculate the average $l\alpha\beta$-value. Next, we transform the resulting average $l\alpha\beta$-value back to RGB. Finally, we assign this RGB-value to index 1 of the new color lookup table. These steps are successively carried out for all indices. This process yields a new color lookup table containing the natural colors associated with the various multi-band combinations in the false color (RG) color lookup table. Replacing the RG-color lookup table (left side of Fig. 6d) by the color lookup table with natural colors (right side of Fig. 6d) yields an image with a natural color appearance, in which the colors are optimized for this particular sample set (Fig. 6d). Note that the red parts in the scene in Fig. 6a do not turn out red again in the rendered night-time image Fig. 6f. This is due to the fact that other materials which occupy a larger area of the scene (and which therefore dominate the color mapping) give the same sensor output in the two bands. Also, the red flags are not apparent in the visible band (Fig. 6b). This has only a minor effect on the overall appearance of the scene as long as the parts that change between the different band recordings occupy only a relatively small area.

(a) (b) (c)

(d) (e) (f)

Fig. 6. (a) Natural daylight color reference image. Visible (b) and near-infrared (c) images of the same scene. (d) The color mapping derived from corresponding pixel pairs in a and b-c. (e) Combined RG false color representation of (b) and (c), obtained by assigning (b) to the green and (c) to the red channel of an RGB color image (the blue channel is set to zero). (f) Result of the application of the mapping scheme in (d) to the two band false color image in (e).

Fig. 7 illustrates the difference between the statistical and the sample based color transforms. In this example we determined a color mapping lookup table from a pair of images consisting of (Fig. 7a) the original version of a full color daylight photograph and (Fig. 7b) the same image from which the blue channel has been removed (B=0). Note that the sample-based color remapping (Fig. 7c), using the sample based color lookup table (inset) determined from the image pair Fig. 7a and Fig. 7b, nicely restores most of the blue hues in the scene, while the statistical color remapping procedure (Fig. 7d) is not capable to restore the missing information. This is due to the fact that the sample-based method allows for nonlinear transformations while the statistical method is a linear (affine) transformation (in CIELAB-color space).

Fig. 8a and b show respectively visual and near-infrared images of the same scene. Fig. 8c shows the red-green false color representation of Fig. 8a and b. Fig. 8d shows the daytime reference image corresponding to the multi-band sensor image. Straightforward application of the sample-base color transform results in Fig. 8e. Note that the colors of this figure closely match the daytime colors as shown in Fig. 8d (e.g. the sky is blue). However, the

(a) (b) (c) (d)

Fig. 7. (a) Full color RGB image. (b) Image from (a) after removal of the blue band (B=0). (c) Result of sample-based color remapping, using the color lookup table (inset) determined from the image pair (a,b). (d) Result of the statistical color remapping procedure.

image looks noisy and certain objects appear in the wrong color (e.g. the bench and parts of the roof). This is due to the fact that the luminance in the colorized image does not increase continuously with increasing sensor output (the luminance value in Fig. 8c). This gives an undesirable "solarizing" effect. We therefore derived from this color map (inset in Fig. 8e) another color map (inset in Fig. 8f) in which the luminance increases linearly with the distance to the top-left corner. Fig. 8f shows the result of this new color mapping. The colors in Fig. 8f closely match the daytime colors. The sky is dark instead of light-blue. This corresponds to the intuition that the sky should look dark at night, and does not affect the situational awareness. Also important is the fact that the color transformation shown in Fig. 8f is smooth, in contrast to the one shown in Fig. 8e. Intuitively a small variation in sensor output should lead to a small color change, i.e. a smooth color transformation is expected to lead to better matching colors when applied to other multi-band sensor images. Also, with smooth color transformations noise leads to less clutter. Furthermore, the color fused result provides a better impression of the depth in the scene (compare e.g. Fig. 8b and 8f).

Fig. 9a-c shows the result of applying the same lookup-table transform to multi-band sensor images of different scenes, together with the corresponding daytime full color images (Fig. 9d-f). Although the colors do not always fully match the daytime colors, they are still characteristic for the different materials displayed in the scene. Thus, the colorized fused image facilitates interpretation of the scene (situational awareness).

Dedicated color mapping schemes can be derived that are optimally tuned for different environments. When deploying the color transfer method at night an appropriate color

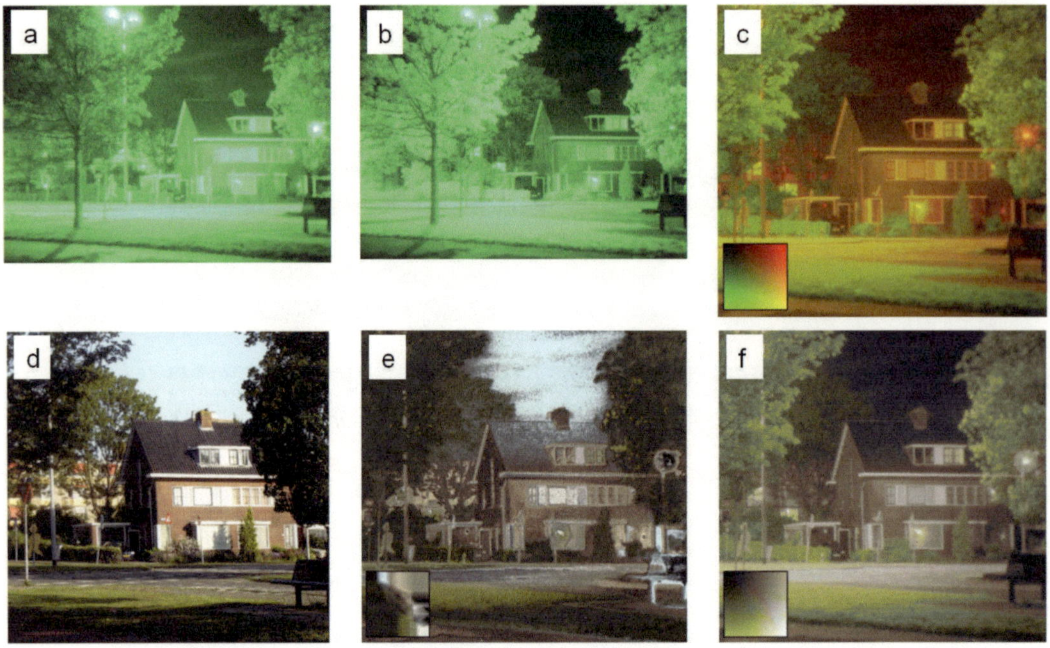

Fig. 8. Visual (a) and near-infrared (b) images of the same scene. (c) Combined red-green false color representation of (a) and (b). (d) Daytime reference color image. (e) Result of straightforward application of the sample-based transform method. (f) Result after smoothing and linearising the color lookup table.

Fig. 9. (a-c) Results of applying the coloring scheme from Fig. 8f to different multi-band sensor images. (d-f) Daylight color images corresponding to (a-c).

mapping scheme should then be selected to colorize the night-time images. The color transformation consists of *(1)* creating a false-color image (e.g. an RG-image, see Fig. 6e), *(2)* converting this image into an index image using the RG-color table, and *(3)* replacing the color lookup table with its daytime equivalent (RGB-color table, see Fig. 6d, right). The whole transformation is defined by the two color lookup tables (the RG-color table and the RGB color table). The software implementation can be very fast.

Different environments require different color mapping schemes to obtain a correct color representation. The sample images used to derive the color mapping scheme should reflect the statistics of the environment in which the mapping will be deployed.

In practice the ratio between the sensor outputs is characteristic for different materials. This becomes apparent when one inspects the color map images (e.g. Fig. 6d, right side) corresponding to the optimal color mapping of different reference and test images. In those images the hue varies little along straight lines through the top-left corner (lines for which the ratio between the two sensor outputs has a constant value). This feature can be used when deriving a color mapping from a limited number of samples. Also, the color mapping (e.g. Fig. 6d, right side) can be expected to be smooth, i.e. from point to point the color variations will be smooth. When a smooth color mapping scheme is used more subtle differences between sensor outputs will become visible.

Because the sample-based color mapping is highly specific it can effectively be used to highlight interesting image details which may otherwise go unnoticed. Camouflaged targets (e.g. persons or vehicles in military colors) are usually indistinguishable from their local background in naturally colored images. As a result, they will also have low color contrast when a natural color mapping is applied to multi-band nighttime imagery. An example of this effect is shown in Fig. 10, which presents an intensified image (Fig. 10a) and a thermal infrared (8-12 μm) image (Fig. 10b) of a person wearing a military battle dress with a camouflage pattern in a rural background. Fig. 10c shows the two-band false color image that is constructed by mapping the images from Fig. 10 (a) and (b) to respectively the R and G channels of an RGB color image (the B channel was set to zero). Fig. 10d shows the full color daytime reference image (a standard digital color photograph). Using the sample-based method we derived the color transformation that results in an optimal match between the colors in the reference image (Fig. 10d) and the multi-band sensor values (Fig. 10c). The color transformation for all sensor combinations is represented by the insets of Fig. 10c and Fig. 10e, while Fig. 10e shows the result of the color mapping. Note that the colors in the colorized multi-band image (Fig. 10e) closely match the colors in the reference image (Fig. 10d). However, since the person wears clothing in camouflage colors, he is also camouflaged in the colorized nighttime image. Although the person is clearly visible in the thermal image (Fig. 10b) he can hardly be detected in the colorized nighttime image. To make the person more salient in the colorized night-time image a color transformation can be used that depicts hot items (which usually are potential targets like vehicles or living beings) in red. For this purpose we created an alternative color mapping by manipulating the inset of Fig. 10e. The resulting lookup table is depicted in the inset of Fig. 10f. Fig. 10f shows the result of the application of this color transformation to the false color two-band nighttime image in Fig. 10c. Hot items now appear in red while the (relatively cold) background is still depicted in its natural colors. In this image representation, the naturally colored background provides the context and potential targets are highlighted by their color contrast. This color mapping may be useful for applications like surveillance and navigation, since these tasks require a correct perception of the background (terrain) for situational awareness in combination with optimal detection of targets and obstacles.

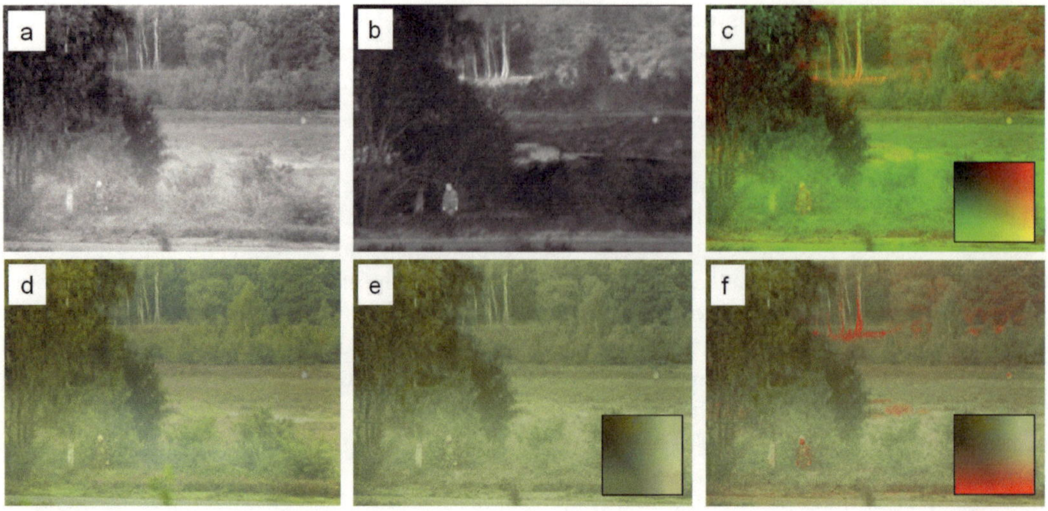

Fig. 10. Result of the application of a natural color mapping to a two-band nighttime image. (a) Intensified visual image and (b) thermal (8-12 μm) image of a rural scene with a person standing in the foreground. (c) Two-band false color image obtained by mapping (a) and (b) to respectively the G and R channels of an RGB color image (the B channel was set to zero). (d) A daylight color picture of the same scene. (e) Result of the application of the color mapping defined by inset to (c). (f) Result of the application of the color mapping defined by the inset to (c).

3. Implementation

In the next sections we describe three prototype portable dual band real-time hardware implementations of nighttime image acquisition systems that deploy the lookup-table color transform method. The first system creates a color nightvision image by fusing the visual and near-infrared bands of two identical image intensifiers. The second system presents a color fused image of the signals of an image intensifier and a longwave infrared thermal camera. The third system produces a three-band nighttime image by combining the visual and near-infrared bands of two identical image intensifiers with a longwave infrared image.

3.1 The Gecko system: combination of visual and near-infrared

The Gecko sensor module provides co-axially registered visual and NIR images. This system is named after nocturnal geckos that still have color vision at very dim light levels (Roth & Kelber, 2006). The Gecko system includes 2 image intensifiers, 2 compact EO cameras, a heat reflecting (hot) mirror, and a near-infrared reflecting mirror (Fig. 11). The image intensifiers are two GEN III type Mini N/SEAS monocular night vision goggles (NVGs) from International Technologies Lasers Ltd (ITL). They provide a 1x magnification, and have a circular field-of-view (FOV) with a diameter of 40 deg, corresponding to about 2000 pixels. They are sensitive in the visual and near infrared part of the spectrum. Both image intensifiers are placed side by side. A distinctive characteristic of the construction of our acquisition unit is the hardware registration of both NVG images. A co-aligned view is achieved through the use of a hot mirror in combination with a NIR reflecting mirror (Fig.

11a). The hot mirror is an Edmund Optics (www.edmundoptics.com) NT43-958 3.3 mm thick mirror, intended for an angle of incidence of 45°, with a multi-layer dielectric coating that reflects infrared radiation (heat), while allowing visible light to pass through. The NIR radiation is reflected by a Melles Griot 01 MFG 011 mirror (www.mellesgriot.com) that is covered with a protected aluminum coating, which has an average reflectance greater than 87% over the spectral range from 400 to 800 nm (fig. 3b). As shown in Fig. 11a, the hot mirror acts as a dichroic beam splitter, transmitting the visual part of the incoming radiation to the upper NVG, while reflecting the NIR part via the NIR reflecting mirror into the lower NVG. The image from each NVG is registered by a PixeLINK PL-A741 MV FireWire 1.3 megapixel monochrome camera with a 2/3" CMOS detector with a resolution of 1280 x 1024 pixels (www.pixelink.com). Both cameras are equipped with a 16 mm Pentax C1614A C-mount lens, yielding a horizontal FOV of 30°72'T. They operate either at 33 fps at an image size of 1k x 1k, or 105 fps at 640 x 480 pixels. After processing the two-band Gecko signals on a notebook computer the resulting colorized imagery is displayed on the screen of the notebook computer, or, alternatively, on miniature head-mounted displays

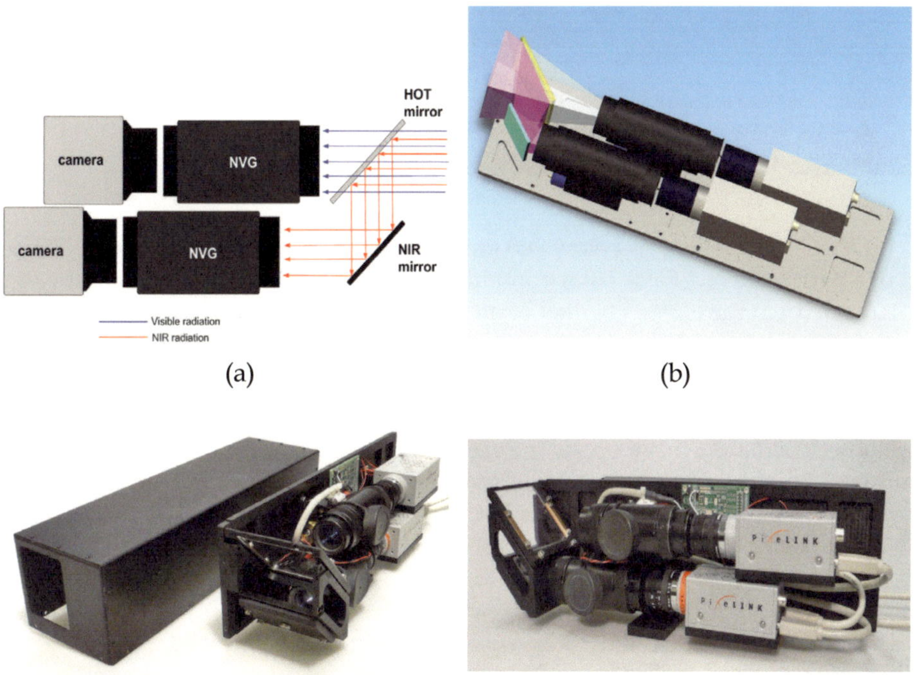

Fig. 11. The dual band Gecko system. (a) Schematic representation. (b) 3D view of the system design. (c) Front view of the system and its casing. (d) Side view.

The incoming video stream can also be stored on the hard disk of the notebook computer. The system as a whole is portable and can therefore be used to assess the benefits of color fusion in realistic surveillance and navigation scenarios.

Fig. 12d shows the Gecko image of a park scene after the application of our new color remapping technique (in this case swapping the color table of Fig. 12c by that of Fig. 12d). This multiband nightvision image closely resembles the corresponding daytime photograph

(Fig. 12e). Note that it is much easier to distinguish different materials and objects in Fig. 12d, compared to each of the individual bands (a,b) or an RG false color fused image (c).

(a) (b) (c)

(d) (e)

Fig. 12. (a) Visual (wavelengths below 700 nm) and (b) NIR (wavelengths above 700 nm) images of a park scene. (c) False color combination with the Visual image (a) in the Red and the NIR image (b) in the Green channel of an RGB color image. (d) The result of our color remapping technique. (e) A daytime color photograph of the same scene. The square insets in images (c) and (d) represent their corresponding color tables.

Fig. 13d shows the Gecko image of a road scene after the application of our new color remapping technique (in this case swapping the color table of Fig. 13c by that of Fig. 13d). This multiband nightvision image closely resembles the corresponding daytime photograph (Fig. 13f). For comparison we also show the standard intensified (NVG) image in Fig. 13e. Note that it is much easier to distinguish the borders of the road in Fig. 13d, compared to a standard NVG image Fig. 13e.

3.2 The Viper system: combination of visual and longwave infrared

The Viper sensor module provides co-axially registered visual and longwave infrared (LWIR) or thermal images. This system is named after a species of snake that fuses in its optic tectum the visual images from its eyes with thermal images from infrared sensitive organs that function like pinhole cameras (Newman & Hartline, 1982). The Viper sensor module includes a compact infrared microbolometer, a digital image intensifier, and 2 hot mirrors (Fig. 14). The FLIR Systems ThermoVision A10 infrared microbolometer has a 160 x 128 pixel focal plane array, and a spectral sensitivity range of 7.5 – 13μm, which is the range of most interest for outdoor applications. It is equipped with an 11mm (f/1.6) lens providing a 40° x 30° wide angle view. The ThermoVision A10 delivers wide dynamic range (14-bit) analog video output at 30 Hz (for RS-170) or at 25 Hz (for CCIR). It has a NETD of <85 mK. The Intevac NightVista E1100 digital image intensifier has a 1/2" sensor with a spectral

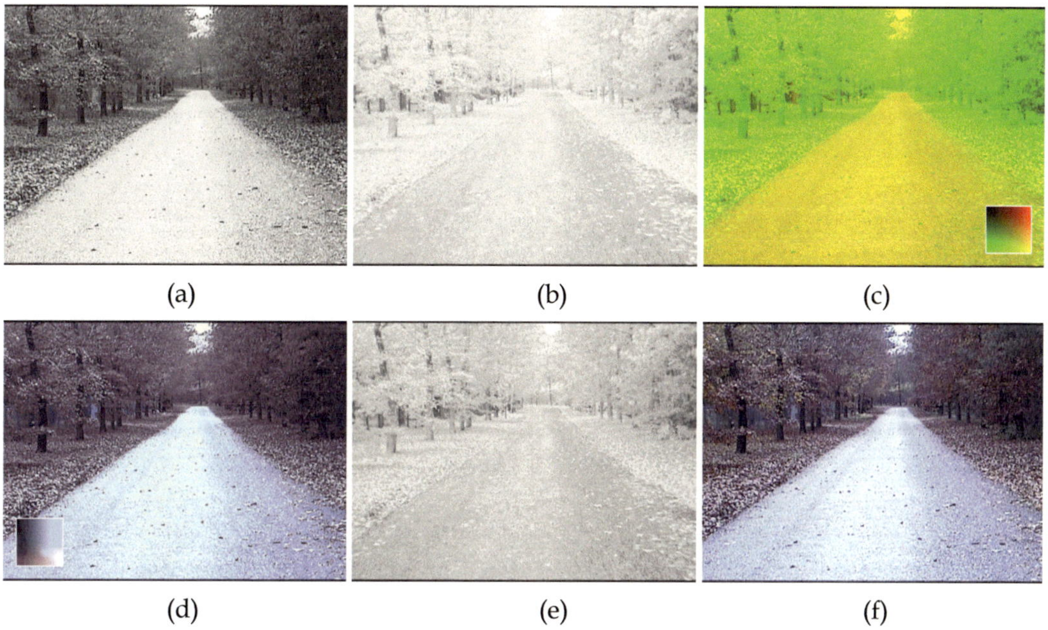

Fig. 13. (a) Visual (wavelengths below 700 nm) and (b) NIR (wavelengths above 700 nm) images of a road scene. (c) False color combination with the Visual image (a) in the Red and the NIR image (b) in the Green channel of an RGB color image. (d) The result of our color remapping technique. (e) Standard NVG image (= a+b). (f) A daytime color photograph of the same scene. The square insets in images (c) and (d) represent their corresponding color tables.

response range 400-900 nm, and delivers RS-170 VGA resolution (640x480) video signal output at 30 fps. It is equipped with an 8.5 mm C-mount Pentax C815B lens, yielding a view of 42.09° horizontally. The intensified and thermal images are co-aligned through the use of a pair of hot mirrors (Fig. 14a). The first mirror is an Edmund Optics (www.edmundoptics.com) NT43-958 3.3 mm thick mirror, intended for an angle of incidence of 45°, with a multi-layer dielectric coating that reflects infrared radiation (heat), while allowing visible light to pass through. The second mirror is a gold coated borosilicate crown optical glass plate (type BK7, CRYSTECH Inc, www.crystech.com), with a reflection coefficient larger than 99.8%.

The analog video signals of the A10 infrared microbolometer and the Intevac digital image intensifier are both converted into 8 bits digital signals by means of a DFG/1394-1e DFG/1394-1e Video-to-FireWire converter (www.theimagingsource.com) that was inserted in a Dell Inspiron 9300 notebook computer. As a result of the co-axial image registration parallax problems are eliminated and only minimal spatial alignment and image stretching (to correct for the slight difference in FOV size of both cameras) is needed before image/video exploitation. The resulting registered images are combined into an RGB format for further processing (the B channel is set to zero). The previously described color mapping is implemented as a color lookup table transform.

After processing the two-band Viper signals on a notebook computer the resulting colorized imagery is displayed on the screen of the notebook computer, or, alternatively, on miniature head-mounted displays The incoming video stream can also be stored on the hard disk of

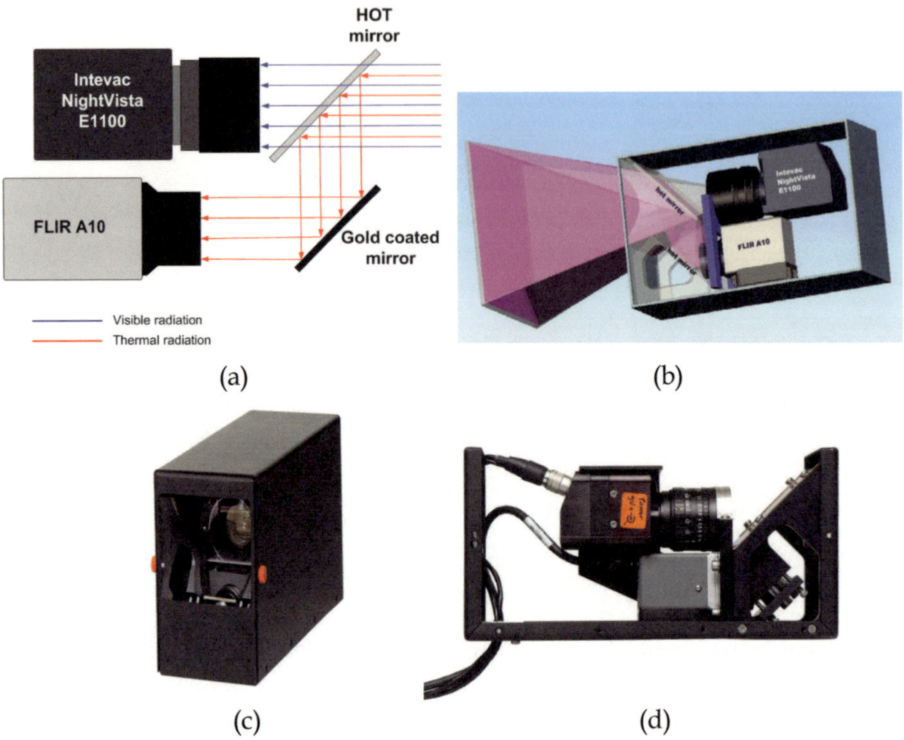

Fig. 14. The dual band Viper system. (a) Schematic representation. (b) 3D view of the system design. (c) Front view of the system and its casing. (d) Side view.

the notebook computer. The system as a whole is portable and can therefore be used to assess the benefits of color fusion in realistic surveillance and navigation scenarios.
Fig. 15d and e show the Viper image of a park scene after the application of our new color remapping technique (in this case swapping the color table of Fig. 15c by that of Fig. 15d and Fig. 15e). The results are shown for 2 different mappings. Note that objects in the scene, particularly the person, are much easier to distinguish in these color remapped images compared to each of the individual bands (Fig. 15a,b) or an RG false color fused image (Fig. 15c).
Fig. 16d shows the Viper image of a battle scene after the application of our new color remapping technique (in this case swapping the color table of c by that of d). Note that both the soldier and the smoke screen are clearly visible and represented in their correct (true) colors in the recolored Viper image (d), whereas only one of these can be seen in the individual bands (a,b).

3.3 The TRICLOBS system: combination of visual, near-infrared and longwave infrared

The TRICLOBS (TRI-band Color Low-light OBServation) system combines a three-band nightvision sensor suite, consisting of two digital image intensifiers and a thermal (LWIR) camera, in combination with a 3D digital position information system. The night vision sensor suite is sensitive in the visual (400-700 nm), the near-infrared (700-1000 nm) and the longwave infrared (8-14 μm) bands of the electromagnetic spectrum. The optical axes of all cameras are aligned.

(a) (b) (c)

(d) (e) (f)

Fig. 15. (a) Visual intensified and (b) LWIR (8-12 μm) images of a park scene. (c) False color combination with the Visual image (a) in the Red and the LWIR image (b) in the Green channel of an RGB color image. (d-e) The result of our color remapping technique for two different lookup tables. (f) A daytime color photograph of the same scene. The square insets in images (c,d,e) represent their corresponding color tables.

Fig. 17 shows a schematic representation of the layout of the sensor suite and the beam splitters that are deployed to direct the appropriate band of the incoming radiation to each of the 3 individual sensors. The incoming radiation is first split into a longwave (thermal) and a visual+NIR part by a heat reflecting (hot) mirror (a custom made Melles Griot dichroic beam splitter consisting of Schott N-BK7 Borosilicate Crown glass with an Indium Tin Oxide coating, with a reflection R > 85%). The longwave part of the spectrum is reflected into the lens of the thermal camera, while the visual+NIR light is transmitted to a combination of two digital image intensifiers that are mounted under an angle of 90 degrees. Next, a near-infrared reflecting mirror (45 deg angle of incidence, Borofloat glass, type Edmund Optics B43-958, 101x127x3.3 mm, see: www.edmundoptics.com) is used to separate the incoming light, by transmitting the visual (400–700nm) and reflecting the NIR part (700–900nm), such that one image intensifier registers the visual part and the other one only detects the NIR part of the incoming radiation. The sensor geometry is such that the optical axes of all cameras are aligned.

The two image intensifiers are high resolution (1280x960) Photonis PP3000U Intensified Camera Units (ICUs: www.photonis.com). The ICU is a low light level, intensified CMOS camera. It has a 2/3" CMOS sensor with a spectral response range of 400-900 nm, and delivers both a PAL or NTSC composite video signal output (ITU-R BT.656-4, 640x480

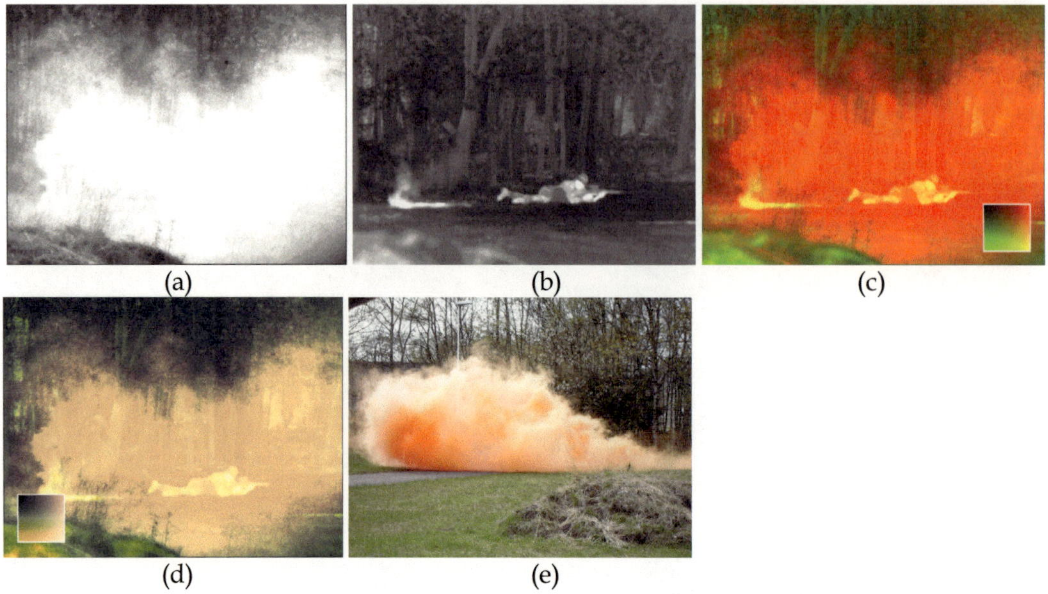

Fig. 16. (a) Visual intensified and (b) LWIR (8-12 μm) images of a battle scene. (c) False color combination with the Visual image (a) in the Red and the LWIR image (b) in the Green channel of an RGB color image. (d) The result of our color remapping technique. (e) A daytime color photograph of the same scene. The square insets in images (c,d) represent their corresponding color tables.

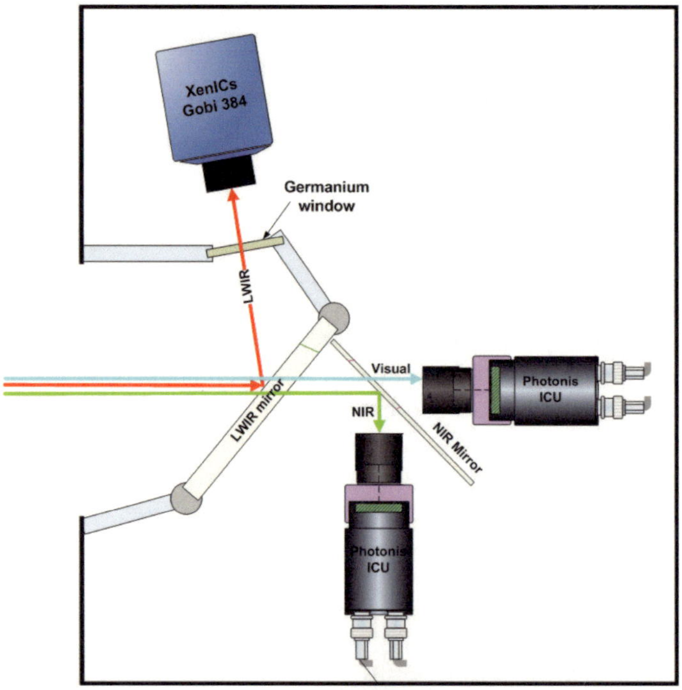

Fig. 17. Layout of the sensors and filters of the TRICLOBS sensor suite.

pixels), and an SDI - LVDS 270 Mbits/s signal. Both ICU's are equipped with Pentax C2514M CCTV lenses, with a minimal focal length of 25mm and a lens aperture of F/1.4, resulting in a FOV of 30.7° x 24.8°. The thermal camera is a XenICs Gobi 384 uncooled a-Si infrared microbolometer (www.xenics.com). It has a 384 x 288 pixel focal plane array, and a spectral sensitivity range of 8–14μm, which is the range of most interest for outdoor applications. It is equipped with an Ophir supIR18mm F/1 lens (www.ophiropt.com) providing a 29.9° x 22.6° wide angle view. The Gobi 384 has a 16-bit Ethernet and CameraLink interface.

The sensors are mounted a common metal frame, which is placed in an enclosed housing. All signal processing is done on a standard laptop. The system is mounted on a mobile all-terrain platform Fig. 18.

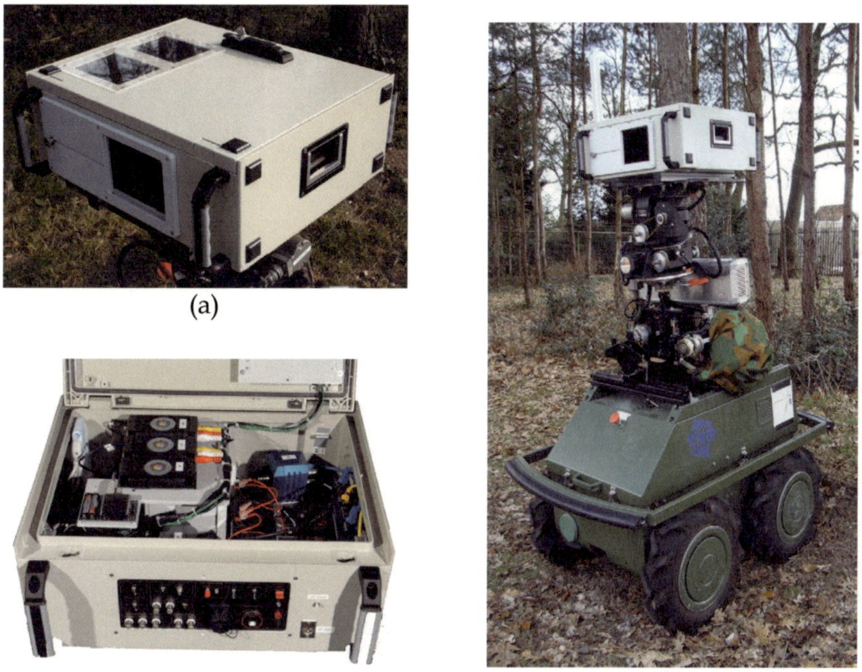

(a) (b) (c)

Fig. 18. The TRICLOBS sensor suite. (a) Top view, (b) inside , and (c) the sensor suite mounted on a mobile all-terrain platform.

4. Evaluation study

As noted before, natural color mapping schemes are not suitable for all purposes. A typical example is the task of finding a camouflaged soldier in a field, using a two-band nightvision system sensitive to the visual and thermal part of the electromagnetic spectrum. When the false color representation of the nightvision image optimally agrees with the daytime appearance of the scene, the soldier will be camouflaged, which is obviously not very helpful for the task at hand. In such cases a color mapping scheme should be deployed that represents the objects of interest with higher color contrast while still providing a color

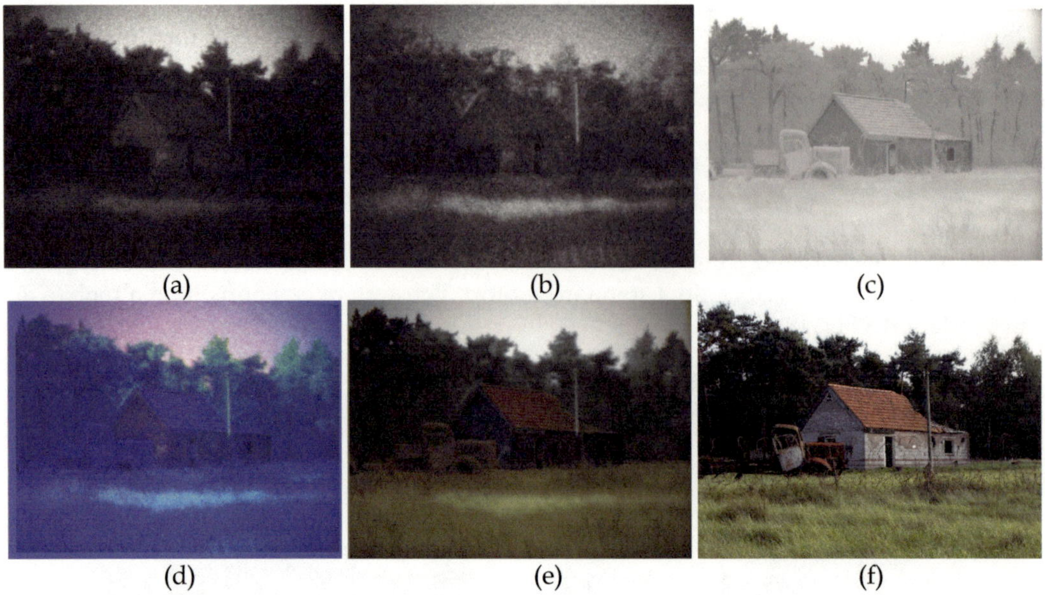

Fig. 19. Nighttime scene showing a house with a person in front, a truck and some trees. (a) Visual, (b) NIR and (c) LWIR input signals. (d) False color image obtained by mapping the three bands to respectively the R, G, and B channels. (e) Result of color remapping applied to (d). (f) Corresponding daytime image.

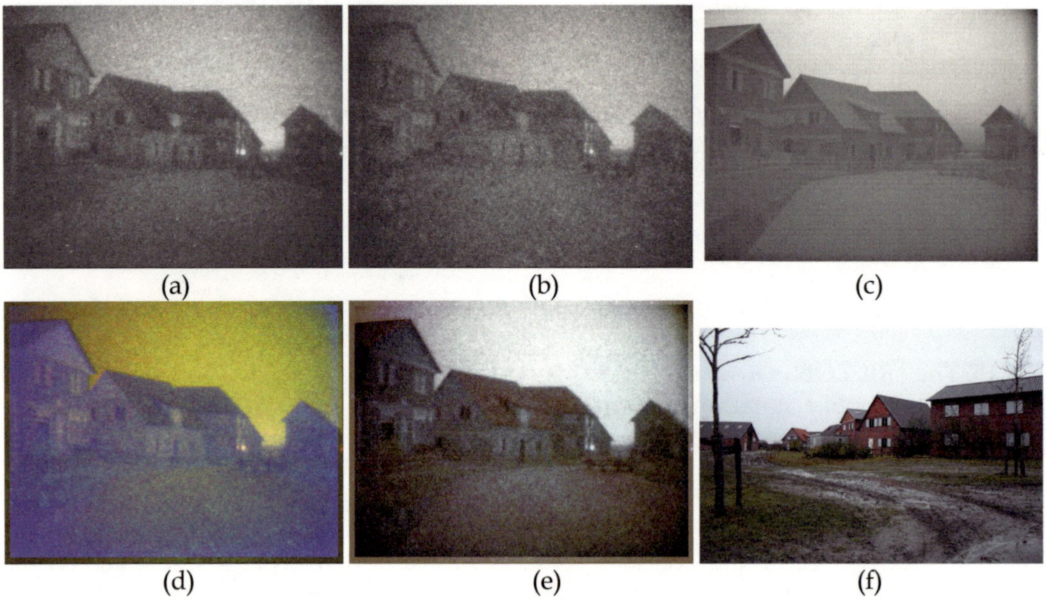

Fig. 20. Nighttime scene showing some houses, grass and a road. (a) Visual, (b) NIR and (c) LWIR input signals. (d) False color image obtained by mapping the three bands to respectively the R, G, and B channels. (e) Result of color remapping applied to (d). (f) Corresponding daytime image.

setting for the rest of the scene which is intuitively correct. We designed such a color scheme, which is targeted at optimizing the detection of (camouflaged) targets that do not contain chlorophyll, while still providing reasonably natural colors.
The dual-band Gecko system was used to register optically aligned visual (wavelengths shorter than 700 nm) and near infrared (wavelengths longer than 700 nm) images. For comparison we also created a standard intensified image of each scene containing both bands, since this is the type of image typically provided by standard night vision goggles. The visual band is represented by the Red channel of an RGB-image and the near-infrared band by the Green channel, to create a red-green representation of the dual-band sensor image (Fig. 21d). Next, for each combination of sensor outputs (represented by a shade of red, green, yellow; see inset of Fig. 21d) a color was chosen to display this sensor output. This process can be implemented by transforming the red-green image (Fig. 21d) into an indexed image in which each pixel value refers to the entry of a color lookup table. When a color lookup table is used with different colors, the colors in the indexed image are

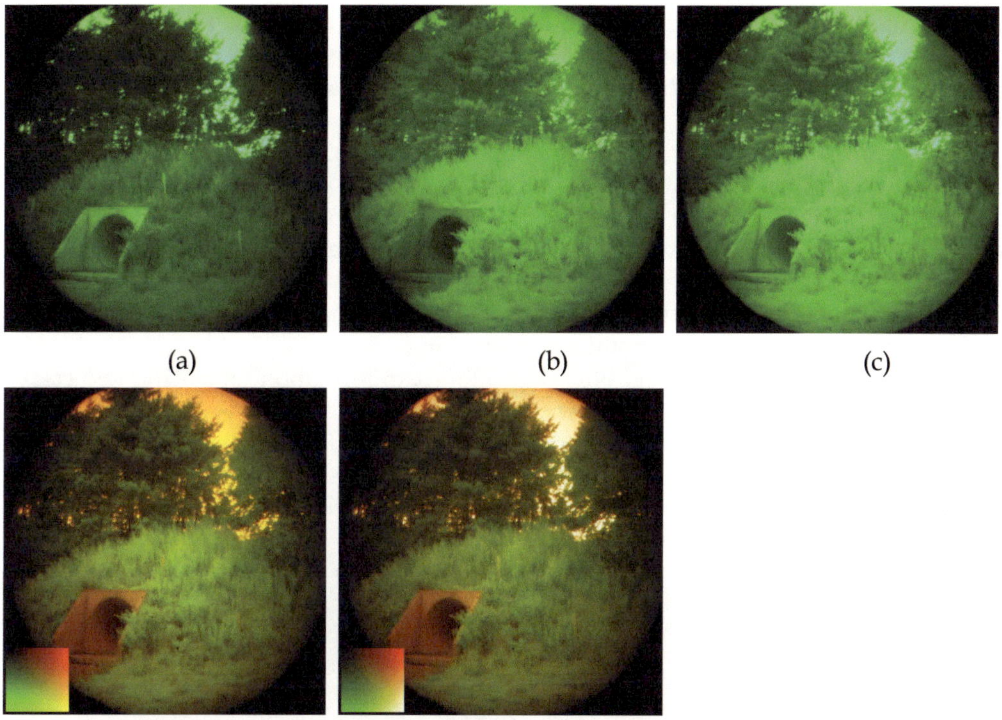

(a) (b) (c)

(d) (e)

Fig. 21. Lookup table based color remapping applied to a dual-band visual (a) and near-infrared (b) Gecko image. (c) A regular intensified image representation for comparison (e.g. a standard night vision goggle image). (d) A red-green false color representation of the dual-band image with the visual band assigned to the Red and near-infrared band assigned to the Green channel of an RGB display. The inset in (d) shows all possible dual-band outputs as shades of red (large response in band 1, small in band 2), green (small response in band 1, large in band 2) and yellow (large responses in both bands). (e) The result of the color transformation. The inset shows how the colors in the inset of (d) are transformed.

automatically transformed into other colors, in a way that all pixels with the same index will result in the same color. The method is described in detail elsewhere (Hogervorst & Toet, 2008a; Hogervorst & Toet, 2010). We tried several color transformations in our search for a color scheme that results in optimal detection of targets while preserving the natural appearance of images. The best color transformation we found for our purposes looks similar to the red-green representation, with a few modifications.

The inset of Fig. 21e shows the colors assigned to all dual-band outputs (represented by the inset of Fig. 21d) by the chosen color scheme. This color scheme emphasizes the distinction between objects containing chlorophyll (the background plants) and objects containing no chlorophyll (e.g. our targets; notable from the sharp transition between green and red at the diagonal). The Gecko sensor system separates the incoming light in a part with wavelength below 700nm and one with wavelengths above 700 nm. Since chlorophyll shows a steep rise around 700nm, this dual-band NVG system is especially suited for discriminating materials containing chlorophyll from materials containing no chlorophyll. Elements containing chlorophyll (e.g. plants) are displayed in green (i.e. in their natural color), while objects without chlorophyll are displayed in the perceptually opposite color red. To further increase the naturalness, elements with high output in both channels are displayed in white (bottom right corner of the inset of Fig. 21e). The result of our color fusion method is shown in Fig. 21e.

We evaluated the abovementioned color mapping in a target detection paradigm. We registered both nighttime dual-band (visual and near-infrared) Gecko images and daytime full color digital photographs of a scene containing grass and trees, with and without targets present. Performance for detecting targets was established for imagery of the dual-band fusion system, each of the individual NVG-bands (visual and NIR), standard NVG and daytime images (taken with a visual camera). The visual angle and display area of the daytime images was matched to that of the nighttime images.

The targets were green (Fig. 22a) and blue (Fig. 22b) foam insulation tubes. The reflectance of the tubes was such the green tubes were mostly undetectable in a standard intensified image representation and in the near infrared band (see Fig. 21), but detectable (as a bright object) in the visible band (see Fig. 21). In contrast, the blue tubes were often undetectable in the visual band while being detectable (as a dark object) in the near infrared band and in regular intensified image (see Fig. 23).

(a) (b)

Fig. 22. The green target (a) and the blue target (b) situated in a background with grass and trees.

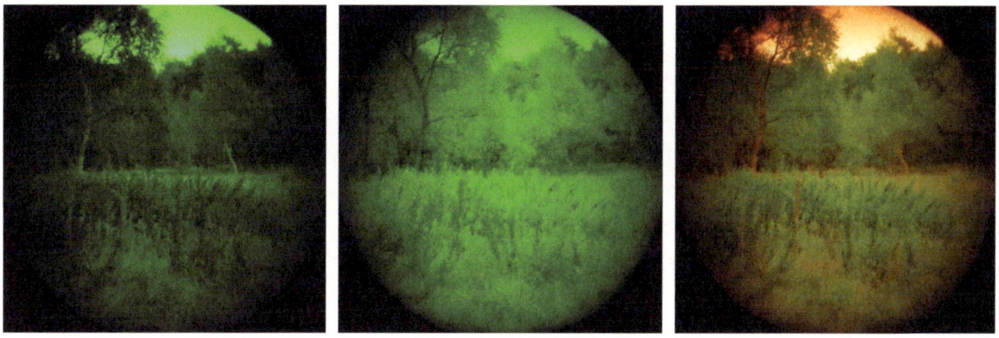

(a) (b) (c)

Fig. 23. Visual (a), near-infrared (b) and the color fused dual-band image (c) for a scene including a blue target. The target is visible in the near-infrared band as a dark tube. The dual-band image shows the target as a reddish object.

We recorded whether the subjects detected the targets when present (Hits and Misses) and whether they judged there to be a target when no target was present (False Alarms and Correct Rejections). We also recorded the response times. Since no False Alarms occurred in this experiment (i.e. the False-Alarm rate was zero), observer performance is fully characterized by the Hit-rate, i.e. the fraction of targets that was detected (ph = #Hits / (#Hits + #Misses)). Observer performance was measured for 5 different image modalities:

1. Daytime: full color daylight images (taken with a standard digital daytime camera),
2. II: grayscale intensified images, combining both visual and near-infrared
3. VIS: grayscale intensified images representing only the visual part of the spectrum,
4. NIR: grayscale intensified images representing only the near-infrared part of the spectrum,
5. FC: false color images resulting from the natural color remapping method.

For each image modality we used 56 images without a target, 26 with a green target, and 26 with a blue target. Seven subjects participated in the experiment. Each subject participated in 5 sessions in which the stimuli of each condition were shown separately. Each subject started the session with the Daylight condition to get acquainted with the procedure, the scene and the targets. The order of the remaining 4 conditions was randomized across subjects to compensate for possible training effects. The images were shown on a PC monitor with a resolution of 1600x1200 pixels (Fig. 22 gives a realistic representation of the display content).

Each experimental session started by explaining the purpose of the experiment and by showing some example stimuli of each condition. Each trial started by presenting an image. The subjects were required to decide as quickly as possible whether a target was present or not. As soon as this decision was taken the subjects clicked the mouse button. Next, the image disappeared and was replaced by a low resolution equivalent of the image, consisting of 20x15 uniformly colored squares (to prevent subjects from searching for the target after responding). We registered the time between onset of the stimulus and detection (the response time). The subject then indicated the target location or clicked on an area outside the image labeled "no target found". When the subject did not respond within 8 seconds the trial ended automatically. The indicated target location was used to check whether the subject had indeed detected the target or had seen a false target. Responses outside an ellipse with horizontal diameter of 162 and vertical diameter of 386 pixels centered on the vertically elongated target were treated as incorrect.

Fig. 24 shows the fraction of hits (hit-rate) for the various sensor conditions and target colors. Shown are the average hit-rates over subjects. Not surprisingly, performance is highest in the Daytime condition. As expected (see Fig. 21 and Fig. 23), performance for detecting the green targets is high in the visual (VIS) condition and low in the image intensified (II) and near-infrared (NIR) sensor conditions. Performance for detecting the blue targets is somewhat poorer in the single-band conditions. These targets can be detected in the NIR condition (reasonably well) and in the II condition (poorly), while they are hardly detected in the VIS condition. Detection performance for both targets is high with the false-color dual-band sensor. Optimal fusion results in performance that equals maximum performance in the individual bands. The hit-rate for the green targets is somewhat lower for the dual-band than for the visual condition. But the hit-rate for the blue targets is somewhat higher for dual-band than for NIR condition. The average hit-rate of the false color dual band sensor (0.75) is not significantly different from the average of the hit-rate for green in VIS and the hit-rate for blue in NIR (0.78). This means that this fusion scheme is (close to) optimal. The results also show that the performance with the standard intensified imagery is clearly much worse than with the false-color dual-band NVG system.

Fig. 25 shows the response times of the trials containing a target (shown are the geometric means over the response times, i.e. the exponent of the average log response times) for all conditions for the hits and misses. Note that the hits for the NIR and II modalities correspond primarily to the trials containing blue targets; the hits for the Visual modality correspond primarily to the trials containing green targets. The response times for the false color dual-band condition are comparable, but slightly larger than in the single-band Visual

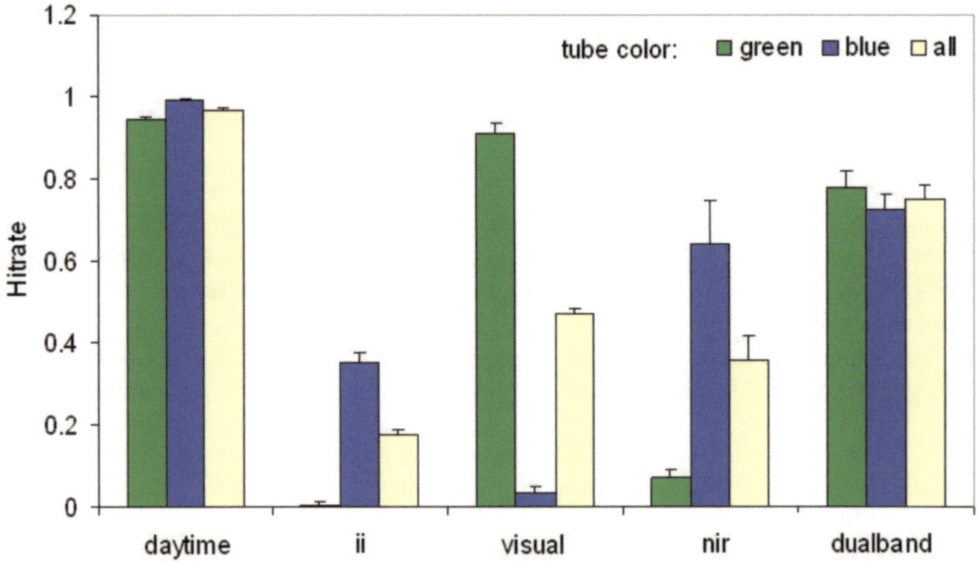

Fig. 24. Average (over all subjects) hit-rate (fraction of hits) for each of the 5 different image modalities and the 2 target colors, including the overall hit-rate ("all"). The error bars represent standard errors in the mean derived from the variance between subjects.

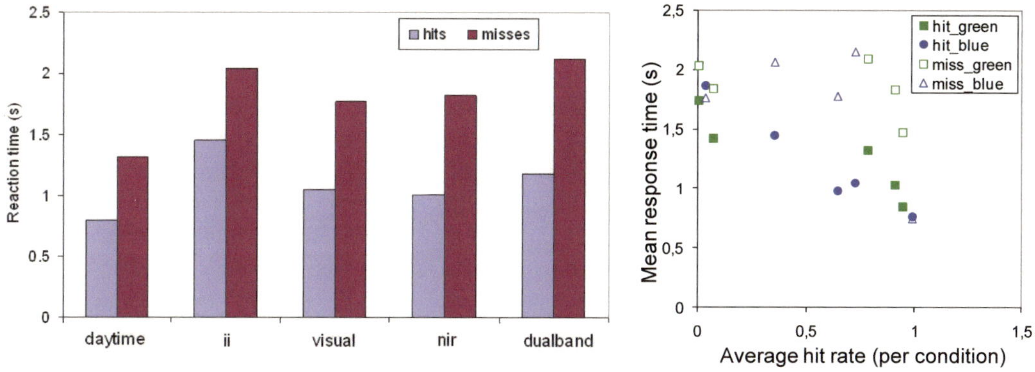

(a) (b)

Fig. 25. (a) The geometric mean (i.e. averaged in log) response times for the various image modalities, separated for hits and misses. (b) Relationship between the hit-rate for each image modality and the (geometric) mean response times for hits and misses for the two target colors.

and NIR conditions. This may be due to the fact that in this condition subjects had to attend to two types of targets, while in the single band conditions only one of the target colors was apparent.

It turns out that the response times for missed targets are comparable to the response times for stimuli in which no target is present. The average response times for missed targets do not correlate with the hit-rates (see Fig. 25b). In contrast, the average response times for hits is highly correlated with the hit-rate ($r = -0.90$, $p < 0.01$, see Fig. 25b). This indicates that when targets are more easily detected, the hit-rate goes up and the response time goes down.

Summarizing, the results show that performance of the false color dual-band system is just as good as the maximum performance that can be attained using either of its individual bands (visual and near-infrared). While the green targets can well be detected with the visual band of the system alone, the blue targets are mostly missed when subjects have to rely on this band alone. In contrast, the blue targets can well be detected with the near-infrared band, but the green targets are then largely missed in this modality. With the false color dual-band image modality both targets can be detected. The total number of targets detected in the dual band image modality is the same as the total number of targets detected in the visual and modality plus the number of targets detected in the near-infrared image modality. This indicates that the fused color representation of the two bands is (nearly) optimal from a perceptual standpoint.

5. Conclusion

In this chapter we presented three prototype portable multiband realtime night vision systems that deploy lookup table based real-time color remapping to represent nighttime imagery with a natural daylight color appearance and to enhance the detection of camouflaged targets. The systems provide respectively registered dynamic visual and near-infrared (Gecko system), visual and longwave infrared (Viper system), or visual, near-infrared and thermal images (TRICLOBS system). These co-aligned images can either be

stored on on-board harddisks, or they can be processed in real-time by a (notebook) computer. The real-time color remapping that gives the multiband signals their intuitive color appearance is implemented as a lookup table transform. The results of some laboratory experiments and preliminary field trials clearly demonstrate the benefits of these systems for surveillance, navigation and target detection tasks. The resulting false color nightvision images closely resemble daytime images (thus providing situational awareness), while thermal targets are clearly distinguishable (thus enabling target detection).
The practical value of these systems will be further evaluated in extensive field trials using realistic surveillance and navigation scenarios. Also, the systems will be used to collect a nighttime imagery in a wide range of environmental conditions and various geographical locations. This imagery will be used in laboratory observer studies and will serve as input to computational and information theoretic measures (Chen et al., 2008; Chen & Blum, 2009; Tsagaris, 2009; Tsagaris & Anastassopoulos, 2006) to assess the operational benefits of the new color mapping procedures. Further improvements of the color mapping method that will be implemented next are the optimization of color contrast (Yin et al., 2010) and image dehazing based in information from the near-infrared channels (Schaul et al., 2009).

6. Acknowledgement

Effort sponsored by the Air Force Office of Scientific Research, Air Force Material Command, USAF, under grant number FA8655-09-3095. The U.S. Government is authorized to reproduce and distribute reprints for Governmental purpose notwithstanding any copyright notation thereon.

7. References

Aguilar, M.; Fay, D.A.; Ireland, D.B.; Racamoto, J.P.; Ross, W.D. & Waxman, A.M. (1999). Field evaluations of dual-band fusion for color night vision, In: *Enhanced and Synthetic Vision 1999*, Verly, J.G. (Eds.),Vol. SPIE-3691, pp. 168-175, The International Society for Optical Engineering, Bellingham, WA.

Aguilar, M.; Fay, D.A.; Ross, W.D.; Waxman, A.M.; Ireland, D.B. & Racamoto, J.P. (1998). Real-time fusion of low-light CCD and uncooled IR imagery for color night vision, In: *Enhanced and Synthetic Vision 1998*, Verly, J.G. (Eds.),Vol. SPIE-3364, pp. 124-135, The International Society for Optical Engineering, Bellingham, WA.

Ansorge, U., Horstmann, G. & Carbone, E. (2005). Top-down contingent capture by color: evidence from RT distribution analyses in a manual choice reaction task. *Acta Psychologica*, Vol.120, No.3, 243-266.

Bandara, S.V., et al. (2003). Four-band quantum well infrared photodetector array. *Infrared Physics & Technology*, Vol.44, No.5-6, 369-375.

Breiter, R.; Cabanski, W.A.; Mauk, K.-H.; Rode, W.; Ziegler, J.; Schneider, H. & Walther, M. (2002). Multicolor and dual-band IR camera for missile warning and automatic target recognition, In: *Targets and Backgrounds: Characterization and Representation VIII*, Watkins, W.R. et al. (Eds.),Vol. SPIE-4718, pp. 280-288, The International Society for Optical Engineering, Bellingham, WA.

Cavanillas, J.A. (1999). *The role of color and false color in object recognition with degraded and non-degraded images*. (Master's thesis) Monterey, CA: Naval Postgraduate School.

Chen, Y. & Blum, R.S. (2009). A new automated quality assessment algorithm for image fusion. *Image and Vision Computing*, Vol.27, No.10, 1421-1432.
Chen, Y., Xue, Z. & Blum, R.S. (2008). Theoretical analysis of an information-based quality measure for image fusion. *Information Fusion*, Vol.9, No.2, 161-175.
Cho, E.; McQuiston, B.K.; Lim, W.; Rafol, S.B.; Hanson, C.; Nguyen, R. & Hutchinson, A. (2003). Development of a visible-NIR/LWIR QWIP sensor, In: *Infrared Technology and Applications XXIX*, Andresen, B.F. & Fulop, G.F. (Eds.),Vol. SPIE-5074, pp. 735-744, The International Society for Optical Engineering, Bellingham,WA.
Cohen, N., Mizrahni, G., Sarusi, G. & Sa'ar, A. (2005). Integrated HBT/QWIP structure for dual color imaging. *Infrared Physics & Technology*, Vol.47, No.1-2, 43-52.
Driggers, R.G.; Krapels, K.A.; Vollmerhausen, R.H.; Warren, P.R.; Scribner, D.A.; Howard, J.G.; Tsou, B.H. & Krebs, W.K. (2001). Target detection threshold in noisy color imagery, In: *Infrared Imaging Systems: Design, Analysis, Modeling, and Testing XII*, Holst, G.C. (Eds.),Vol. SPIE-4372, pp. 162-169, The International Society for Optical Engineering, Bellingham, WA.
Essock, E.A., Sinai, M.J., McCarley, J.S., Krebs, W.K. & DeFord, J.K. (1999). Perceptual ability with real-world nighttime scenes: image-intensified, infrared, and fused-color imagery. *Human Factors*, Vol.41, No.3, 438-452.
Fay, D.A.; Waxman, A.M.; Aguilar, M.; Ireland, D.B.; Racamato, J.P.; Ross, W.D.; Streilein, W. & Braun, M.I. (2000a). Fusion of 2- /3- /4-sensor imagery for visualization, target learning, and search, In: *Enhanced and Synthetic Vision 2000*, Verly, J.G. (Eds.),Vol. SPIE-4023, pp. 106-115, SPIE -The International Society for Optical Engineering, Bellingham, WA, USA.
Fay, D.A.; Waxman, A.M.; Aguilar, M.; Ireland, D.B.; Racamato, J.P.; Ross, W.D.; Streilein, W. & Braun, M.I. (2000b). Fusion of multi-sensor imagery for night vision: color visualization, target learning and search, In: *Proceedings of the 3rd International Conference on Information Fusion*, Vol. I, pp. TuD3-3-TuD3-10, ONERA, Paris, France.
Folk, C.L. & Remington, R. (1998). Selectivity in distraction by irrelevant featural singletons: evidence for two forms of attentional capture. *Journal of Experimental Psychology: Human Perception and Performance*, Vol.24, No.3, 847-858.
Fredembach, C. & Süsstrunk, S. (2008). Colouring the near-infrared, In: *Proceedings of the IS&T/SID 16th Color Imaging Conference*, pp. 176-182.
Gegenfurtner, K.R. & Rieger, J. (2000). Sensory and cognitive contributions of color to the recognition of natural scenes. *Current Biology*, Vol.10, No.13, 805-808.
Goffaux, V., Jacques, C., Mouraux, A., Oliva, A., Schyns, P. & Rossion, B. (2005). Diagnostic colours contribute to the early stages of scene categorization: Behavioural and neurophysiological evidence. *Visual Cognition*, Vol.12, No.6, 878-892.
Goldberg, A.C., Uppal, P. & Winn, M. (2003). Detection of buried land mines using a dual-band LWIR/LWIR QWIP focal plane array. *Infrared Physics & Technology*, Vol.44, No.5-6, 427-437.
Gouras,P. (1991). Color vision. In E.R.Kandel, J.H.Schwartz, & T.M.Jessel (Eds.), *Principles of Neural Science, 3rd ed.* (pp. 467-480). Oxford, UK: Elsevier.
Gove, A.N.; Cunningham, R.K. & Waxman, A.M. (1996). Opponent-color visual processing applied to multispectral infrared imagery, In: *Proceedings of 1996 Meeting of the IRIS*

Specialty Group on Passive Sensors, Vol. II, pp. 247-262, Infrared Information Analysis Center, ERIM, Ann Arbor, US.

Green, B.F. & Anderson, L.K. (1956). Colour coding in a visual search task. *Journal of Experimental Psychology*, Vol.51, No., 19-24.

Grossberg, S. (1988). *Neural networks and natural intelligence.* MIT Press, ISBN , Cambridge, MA.

Hogervorst, M.A. & Toet, A. (2008a). Method for applying daytime colors to nighttime imagery in realtime, In: *Multisensor, Multisource Information Fusion: Architectures, Algorithms, and Applications 2008*, Dasarathy, B.V. (Eds.),Vol. SPIE-6974, pp. 697403-1-697403-9, The International Society for Optical Engineering, Bellingham, WA, USA.

Hogervorst, M.A. & Toet, A. (2008b). Presenting nighttime imagery in daytime colours, In: *Proceedings of the 11th International Conference on Information Fusion*, pp. 706-713, International Society of Information Fusion, Cologne, Germany.

Hogervorst, M.A. & Toet, A. (2010). Fast natural color mapping for night-time imagery. *Information Fusion*, Vol.11, No.2, 69-77.

Hogervorst,M.A., Toet,A., & Kooi,F.L. (2006). TNO Defense Security and Safety. Method and system for converting at least one first-spectrum image into a second-spectrum image. Patent Number Patent Number PCT/NL2007050392. Patent Application Number Application Number 0780855.5-2202 .

Howard, J.G.; Warren, P.; Klien, R.; Schuler, J.; Satyshur, M.; Scribner, D. & Kruer, M.R. (2000). Real-time color fusion of E/O sensors with PC-based COTS hardware, In: *Targets and Backgrounds VI: Characterization, Visualization, and the Detection Process*, Watkins, W.R. et al. (Eds.),Vol. SPIE-4029, pp. 41-48, The International Society for Optical Engineering, Bellingham, WA.

Huang, G., Ni, G. & Zhang, B. (2007). Visual and infrared dual-band false color image fusion method motivated by Land's experiment. *Optical Engineering*, Vol.46, No.2, 027001-1-027001-10.

Jacobson, N.P. & Gupta, M.R. (2005). Design goals and solutions for display of hyperspectral images. *IEEE Transactions on Geoscience and Remote Sensing*, Vol.43, No.11, 2684-2692.

Jacobson, N.P., Gupta, M.R. & Cole, J.B. (2007). Linear fusion of image sets for display. *IEEE Transactions on Geoscience and Remote Sensing*, Vol.45, No.10, 3277-3288.

Joseph, J.E. & Proffitt, D.R. (1996). Semantic versus perceptual influences of color in object recognition. *Journal of Experimental Psychology: Learning, Memory, and Cognition*, Vol.22, No.2, 407-429.

Kolar, R., Kubecka, L. & Jan, J. (2008). Registration and fusion of the autofluorescent and infrared retinal images. *International Journal of Biomedical Imaging*, Vol.2008, No.1-513478, 1-11.

Krebs, W.K.; Scribner, D.A.; Miller, G.M.; Ogawa, J.S. & Schuler, J. (1998). Beyond third generation: a sensor-fusion targeting FLIR pod for the F/A-18, In: *Sensor Fusion: Architectures, Algorithms, and Applications II*, Dasarathy, B.V. (Eds.),Vol. SPIE-3376, pp. 129-140, International Society for Optical Engineering, Bellingham, WA, USA.

Laliberté,F., & Gagnon,L. (2006). Studies on registration and fusion of retinal images. In R.S.Blum & Z.Liu (Eds.), *Multi-Sensor Image Fusion and its Applications.* (pp. 57-106). Boca Raton, Florida, USA: Taylor & Francis CRC Press.

Laliberté, F.; Gagnon, L. & Sheng, Y. (2002). Registration and fusion of retinal images: a comparative study, In: *International Conference on Pattern Recognition 2002*, Vol. 1, pp. 715-718, IEEE Computer Society, Washington, DC, USA.

Laliberté, F., Gagnon, L. & Sheng, Y. (2003). Registration and fusion of retinal images - an evaluation study. *IEEE Transactions on Medical Imaging*, Vol.22, No.5, 661-673.

Li, G. & Wang, K. (2007). Applying daytime colors to nighttime imagery with an efficient color transfer method, In: *Enhanced and Synthetic Vision 2007*, Verly, J.G. & Guell, J.J. (Eds.),Vol. SPIE-6559, pp. 65590L-1-65590L-12, The International Society for Optical Engineering, Bellingham, MA.

Li, J.; Pan, Q.; Yang, T. & Cheng, Y. (2004). Color based grayscale-fused image enhancement algorithm for video surveillance, In: *Proceedings of the Third International Conference on Image and Graphics (ICIG'04)*, pp. 47-50, IEEE Press, Washington, USA.

Newman, E.A. & Hartline, P.H. (1981). Integration of visual and infrared information in bimodal neurons of the rattlesnake optic tectum. *Science*, Vol.213, No., 789-791.

Newman, E.A. & Hartline, P.H. (1982). The infrared "vision" of snakes. *Scientific American*, Vol.246, No.3, 116-127.

Oliva, A. (2005). Gist of a scene, In: *Neurobiology of Attention*, Itti, L. et al. (Eds.), pp. 251-256, Academic Press.

Oliva, A. & Schyns, P.G. (2000). Diagnostic colors mediate scene recognition. *Cognitive Psychology*, Vol.41, No., 176-210.

Reinhard, E., Ashikhmin, M., Gooch, B. & Shirley, P. (2001). Color transfer between images. *IEEE Computer Graphics and Applications*, Vol.21, No.5, 34-41.

Roth, L.S.V. & Kelber, A. (2006). Nocturnal colour vision in geckos. *Proceedings of the Royal Society of London B: Biological Sciences*, Vol.271, No.Biology Letters Supplement 6, S485-S487.

Rousselet, G.A., Joubert, O.R. & Fabre-Thorpe, M. (2005). How long to get the "gist" of real-world natural scenes? *Visual Cognition*, Vol.12, No.6, 852-877.

Ruderman, D.L., Cronin, T.W. & Chiao, C.-C. (1998). Statistics of cone responses to natural images: implications for visual coding. *Journal of the Optical Society of America A*, Vol.15, No.8, 2036-2045.

Sampson, M.T. (1996). *An assessment of the impact of fused monochrome and fused color night vision displays on reaction time and accuracy in target detection* (Report AD-A321226). Monterey, CA: Naval Postgraduate School.

Schaul, L.; Fredembach, C. & Süsstrunk, S. (2009). Color image dehazing using the near-infrared, In: *Procedings of the IEEE International Conference on Image Processing ICIP2009*, pp. 1629-1632, IEEE Press, Cairo, Egypt.

Schiller, P.H. (1982). Central connections of the retinal ON and OFF pathways. *Nature*, Vol.297, No.5867, 580-583.

Schiller, P.H. (1984). The connections of the retinal on and off pathways to the lateral geniculate nucleus of the monkey. *Vision Research*, Vol.24, No.9, 923-932.

Schiller, P.H. (1992). The ON and OFF channels of the visual system. *Trends in Neuroscience*, Vol.15, No.3, 86-92.

Schiller, P.H. & Logothetis, N.K. (1990). The color-opponent and broad-band channels of the primate visual system. *Trends in Neuroscience*, Vol.13, No.10, 392-398.

Schiller, P.H., Sandell, J.H. & Maunsell, J.H. (1986). Functions of the ON and OFF channels of the visual system. *Nature*, Vol.322, No.6082, 824-825.

Schuler, J.; Howard, J.G.; Warren, P.; Scribner, D.A.; Klien, R.; Satyshur, M. & Kruer, M.R. (2000). Multiband E/O color fusion with consideration of noise and registration, In: *Targets and Backgrounds VI: Characterization, Visualization, and the Detection Process*, Watkins, W.R. et al. (Eds.),Vol. SPIE-4029, pp. 32-40, The International Society for Optical Engineering, Bellingham, WA, USA.

Scribner, D.; Schuler, J.M.; Warren, P.; Klein, R. & Howard, J.G. (2003). Sensor and image fusion, In: *Encyclopedia of optical engineering*, Driggers, R.G. (Eds.), pp. 2577-2582, Marcel Dekker Inc., New York, USA.

Scribner, D.; Warren, P. & Schuler, J. (1999). Extending color vision methods to bands beyond the visible, In: *Proceedings of the IEEE Workshop on Computer Vision Beyond the Visible Spectrum: Methods and Applications*, pp. 33-40, Institute of Electrical and Electronics Engineers.

Sévigny, L. (1996). *Multisensor image fusion for detection and recognition of targets in the battlefield of the future* (Report Progress Report Canada, NATO AC/243, Panel 3, RSG.9 37th meeting). Quebec, Canada: Defense Research Establishment Valcartier.

Shi, J.; Jin, W.; Wang, L. & Chen, H. (2005a). Objective evaluation of color fusion of visual and IR imagery by measuring image contrast, In: *Infrared Components and Their Applications*, Gong, H. et al. (Eds.),Vol. SPIE-5640, pp. 594-601, The International Society for Optical Engineering, Bellingham, MA.

Shi, J.-S., Jin, W.-Q. & Wang, L.-X. (2005b). Study on perceptual evaluation of fused image quality for color night vision. *Journal of Infrared and Millimeter Waves*, Vol.24, No.3, 236-240.

Simard, P.; Link, N.K. & Kruk, R.V. (1999). Feature detection performance with fused synthetic and sensor images, In: *Proceedings of the 43rd Annual Meeting of the Human Factors and Ergonomics Society*, pp. 1108-1112, Human Factors and Ergonomics Society.

Simard, P.; Link, N.K. & Kruk, R.V. (2000). Evaluation of algorithms for fusing infrared and synthetic imagery, In: *Enhanced and Synthetic Vision 2000*, Verly, J.G. (Eds.),Vol. SPIE-4023, pp. 127-138, The International Society for Optical Engineering, Bellingham, WA.

Sinai, M.J.; McCarley, J.S. & Krebs, W.K. (1999a). Scene recognition with infra-red, low-light, and sensor fused imagery, In: *Proceedings of the IRIS Specialty Groups on Passive Sensors*, pp. 1-9, IRIS, Monterey, CA.

Sinai, M.J.; McCarley, J.S.; Krebs, W.K. & Essock, E.A. (1999b). Psychophysical comparisons of single- and dual-band fused imagery, In: *Enhanced and Synthetic Vision 1999*, Verly, J.G. (Eds.),Vol. SPIE-3691, pp. 176-183, The International Society for Optical Engineering, Bellingham, WA.

Spence, I., Wong, P., Rusan, M. & Rastegar, N. (2006). How color enhances visual memory for natural scenes. *Psychological Science*, Vol.17, No.1, 1-6.

Sun, S., Jing, Z., Li, Z. & Liu, G. (2005). Color fusion of SAR and FLIR images using a natural color transfer technique. *Chinese Optics Letters*, Vol.3, No.4, 202-204.

Toet, A. (2003). Natural colour mapping for multiband nightvision imagery. *Information Fusion*, Vol.4, No.3, 155-166.

Toet, A. & IJspeert, J.K. (2001). Perceptual evaluation of different image fusion schemes, In: *Signal Processing, Sensor Fusion, and Target Recognition X*, Kadar, I. (Eds.),Vol. SPIE-

4380, pp. 436-441, The International Society for Optical Engineering, Bellingham, WA.

Toet, A., IJspeert, J.K., Waxman, A.M. & Aguilar, M. (1997). Fusion of visible and thermal imagery improves situational awareness. *Displays*, Vol.18, No.2, 85-95.

Toet, A. & Walraven, J. (1996). New false colour mapping for image fusion. *Optical Engineering*, Vol.35, No.3, 650-658.

Tsagaris, V. (2009). Objective evaluation of color image fusion methods. *Optical Engineering*, Vol.48, No.066201.

Tsagaris, V. & Anastasopoulos, D. (2006). Multispectral image fusion for improved RGB representation based on perceptual attributes. *International Journal of Remote Sensing*, Vol.26, No.15, 3241-3254.

Tsagaris, V. & Anastassopoulos, V. (2006). Assessing information content in color images. *Journal of Electronic Imaging*, Vol.14, No.4, 043007-1-043007-10.

Tsagiris, V. & Anastassopoulos, V. (2005). Fusion of visible and infrared imagery for night color vision. *Displays*, Vol.26, No.4-5, 191-196.

Vargo, J.T. (1999). *Evaluation of operator performance using true color and artificial color in natural scene perception* (Report AD-A363036). Monterey, CA: Naval Postgraduate School.

Walls, G.L. (2006). *The vertebrate eye and its adaptive radiation.* Cranbrook Institute of Science, ISBN , Bloomfield Hills, Michigan.

Wang, L.; Jin, W.; Gao, Z. & Liu, G. (2002). Color fusion schemes for low-light CCD and infrared images of different properties, In: *Electronic Imaging and Multimedia Technology III*, Zhou, L. et al. (Eds.),Vol. SPIE-4925, pp. 459-466, The International Society for Optical Engineering, Bellingham, WA.

Warren, P., Howard, J.G., Waterman, J., Scribner, D.A. & Schuler, J. (1999). *Real-time, PC-based color fusion displays* (Report A073093). Washington, DC: Naval Research Lab.

Waxman, A.M., et al. (1999). Solid-state color night vision: fusion of low-light visible and thermal infrared imagery. *MIT Lincoln Laboratory Journal*, Vol.11, No., 41-60.

Waxman, A.M.; Carrick, J.E.; Fay, D.A.; Racamato, J.P.; Augilar, M. & Savoye, E.D. (1996a). Electronic imaging aids for night driving: low-light CCD, thermal IR, and color fused visible/IR, In: *Proceedings of the SPIE Conference on Transportation Sensors and Controls*, Vol. SPIE-2902, The International Society for Optical Engineering, Bellingham, WA.

Waxman, A.M.; Fay, D.A.; Gove, A.N.; Seibert, M.C.; Racamato, J.P.; Carrick, J.E. & Savoye, E.D. (1995a). Color night vision: fusion of intensified visible and thermal IR imagery, In: *Synthetic Vision for Vehicle Guidance and Control*, Verly, J.G. (Eds.),Vol. SPIE-2463, pp. 58-68, The International Society for Optical Engineering, Bellingham, WA.

Waxman, A.M., Gove, A.N., Fay, D.A., Racamoto, J.P., Carrick, J.E., Seibert, M.C. & Savoye, E.D. (1997). Color night vision: opponent processing in the fusion of visible and IR imagery. *Neural Networks*, Vol.10, No.1, 1-6.

Waxman, A.M.; Gove, A.N.; Seibert, M.C.; Fay, D.A.; Carrick, J.E.; Racamato, J.P.; Savoye, E.D.; Burke, B.E.; Reich, R.K. et al. (1996b). Progress on color night vision: visible/IR fusion, perception and search, and low-light CCD imaging, In: *Enhanced and Synthetic Vision 1996*, Verly, J.G. (Eds.),Vol. SPIE-2736, pp. 96-107, The International Society for Optical Engineering, Bellingham, WA.

Waxman, A.M., Seibert, M.C., Gove, A.N., Fay, D.A., Bernardon, A.M., Lazott, C., Steele, W.R. & Cunningham, R.K. (1995b). Neural processing of targets in visible, multispectral IR and SAR imagery. *Neural Networks*, Vol.8, No.7/8, 1029-1051.

White, B.L. (1998). *Evaluation of the impact of multispectral image fusion on human performance in global scene processing*. (M.Sc.) Monterey, CA: Naval Postgraduate School.

Wichmann, F.A., Sharpe, L.T. & Gegenfurtner, K.R. (2002). The contributions of color to recognition memory for natural scenes. *Journal of Experimental Psychology: Learning, Memory, and Cognition*, Vol.28, No.3, 509-520.

Yin, S., Cao, L., Ling, Y. & Jin, G. (2010). One color contrast enhanced infrared and visible image fusion method. *Infrared Physics & Technology*, Vol.53, No.2, 146-150.

Zheng, Y. & Essock, E.A. (2008). A local-coloring method for night-vision colorization utilizing image analysis and fusion. *Information Fusion*, Vol.9, No.2, 186-199.

Zheng, Y.; Hansen, B.C.; Haun, A.M. & Essock, E.A. (2005). Coloring night-vision imagery with statistical properties of natural colors by using image segmentation and histogram matching, In: *Color imaging X: processing, hardcopy and applications*, Eschbach, R. & Marcu, G.G. (Eds.),Vol. SPIE-5667, pp. 107-117, The International Society for Optical Engineering, Bellingham, WA.

7

Quality Map Generation in Two-Dimensional Phase Unwrapping Process by Using Edge Detection Techniques

Yuangang Lu, Wancheng Zhao and Xuping Zhang
Nanjing University
China

1. Introduction

Two-dimensional phase unwrapping is the task of recovering the true phase values, given the wrapped phase values in an image. Phase unwrapping arises in several branches of applied optics, physics, medicine and engineering, such as homomorphic signal processing, solid-state physics, optical interferometry, adaptive or compensated optics, magnetic resonance imaging, synthetic aperture radar interferometry, and optical and electron holography (Volkov & Zhu, 2003). In these applications, the measured information is denoted by a two-dimensional phase distribution called the wrapped phase image. In wrapped phase images, the phase is the interval $(-\pi, \pi]$ or $(0, 2\pi]$ due to the use of the mathematical arctangent function (Bone, 1991). Since this wrapped phase suffers from $2\text{-}\pi$ phase jumps, it is unusable until the phase discontinuities are removed. In order to recovering the true continuous phase values to denote real physical quantity, a phase unwrapping process is needed to recovering the true phase values. The procedure of phase unwrapping is performed by either adding or subtracting integer multiples of 2π to all successive pixels when a phase discontinuity encounters, which are based on some kind of threshold mechanism (Ghiglia et al., 1987).

However, many factors, such as surface discontinuities, noise, under-sampling, or shadow, would produce unreliable phase data, which make the recovery of the wrapped phase challenging. To solve the problem, many phase unwrapping algorithms have been developed during the last three decades. These phase unwrapping algorithms can be found in a very good reference book (Ghigli & Pritt, 1998) and review papers such as (Baldi et al., 2002; Jenkinson, 2003; Su & Chen, 2004; Zappa & Busca, 2008). In many phase unwrapping algorithms, a quality map, which evaluated the quality or the reliability of the phase data, is used for completing the phase unwrapping process. In wrapped phase images, the quality of a pixel is low if it is located in areas where the surface discontinuities, noise or under-sampling exists. On the contrary, the quality of a pixel is high if it is located in areas where the variation of phase value is low. From the mathematical point of view, quality map is a matrix of the same size of phase image that assign a quality value to each pixel. The quality values are usually normalized in the range [0, 1], where a large value means high reliability of the corresponding pixel. In most phase unwrapping algorithms, a quality map is necessary to guide the phase unwrapping process for achieving desire results. Furthermore, whether the unwrapping result is satisfied, to a large extent, depends on whether the quality map can truly reflect the phase data quality.

Until now there are more than ten quality maps proposed to guide the two-dimensional phase unwrapping. As we will see, most quality maps are based on the phase gradients or phase derivatives of the wrapped phase images, and thus can be obtained by edge detection techniques. It is well known that gradient estimation is the first step in the widely used three-step edge detection procedure (Meer & Georgescu, 2001). Therefore, edge detection techniques, which aim at identifying points at which the image brightness changes sharply, play important roles in two-dimensional phase unwrapping process. By means of edge detection techniques, new quality maps based on weighted phase gradients can be generated to effectively guide phase unwrapping process.

This chapter will review the existing literature related to quality map, enlarge the family of quality map by using edge detection techniques. In the following Section 2, the existing quality maps will be reviewed, and the performance of some widely used quality maps on phase unwrapping will be evaluated by unwrapping three typical intractable wrapped phase images. Then, in Section 3, some new quality maps, which are based on existing methods, will be developed from a perspective of edge detection techniques. Finally, conclusions are drawn and directions for further research on quality maps are outlined in Section 4.

2. Existing quality maps

In this section we review existing quality maps that are used in phase unwrapping process. Some quality maps widely used in phase unwrapping process will be evaluated by unwrapping three typical intractable wrapped phase images.

Most quality maps can be directly derived from wrapped phase image that is generated from the original measurement data, but there are some kinds of quality maps that can only be derived from the original measurement data, such as intensity of fringe pattern. According to their origin, quality maps can be divided into two categories: quality map derived from wrapped phase image and quality map derived from original measurement data.

2.1 Quality map derived from wrapped phase image

The wrapped phase images can be obtained from most of the phase measurements such as magnetic resonance imaging, synthetic aperture radar, adaptive optics, and optical interferometry. Fig. 1 shows three examples of the wrapped phase images. The first one is obtained by computer simulation and its corresponding real phase image is shown in Fig. 1(a), which is 256×256 pixels in size. The image is defined by two spiral plane surfaces that have been tilted relative to one another (Ghigli & Pritt, 1998). The wrapped phase image of the Fig. 1(a) is shown in Fig. 1(b), where the phase of each pixel is wrapped into the interval $(-\pi, \pi]$. In the figure, wrapped phase image is scaled between black and white to cover the full dynamic range. The real phase discontinuities between the two spiral surfaces make the phase unwrapping intractable. Fig. 1(c) shows the wrapped phase image of an optical fiber connector endface, which is also 256×256 pixels in size. It is the measurement data by use of four step phase shifted optical interferometry (Kwon, 1984). Unlike the phase data obtained by computer simulation, the original real phase data cannot be given because it is unknown before the wrapped image is unwrapped. As we can see, the wrapped phase image is corrupted by salt-and-pepper noise, especially in the center of image. In addition, in this area the dense fringe may cause under-sampling problem. The last example shown in Fig.

1(d) is a curved surface with a rectangle hole obtained by computer simulation, and the wrapped phase image of Fig. 1(d) is shown in Fig. 1(e). The wrapped image is 100×100 pixels in size. It is suffered from the surface discontinuities and shadow in a closed rectangle hole below the center of the image, and the phase along the vertical direction of image changes more complicated than that of image shown in Fig. 1(b). These factors make its phase unwrapping difficult.

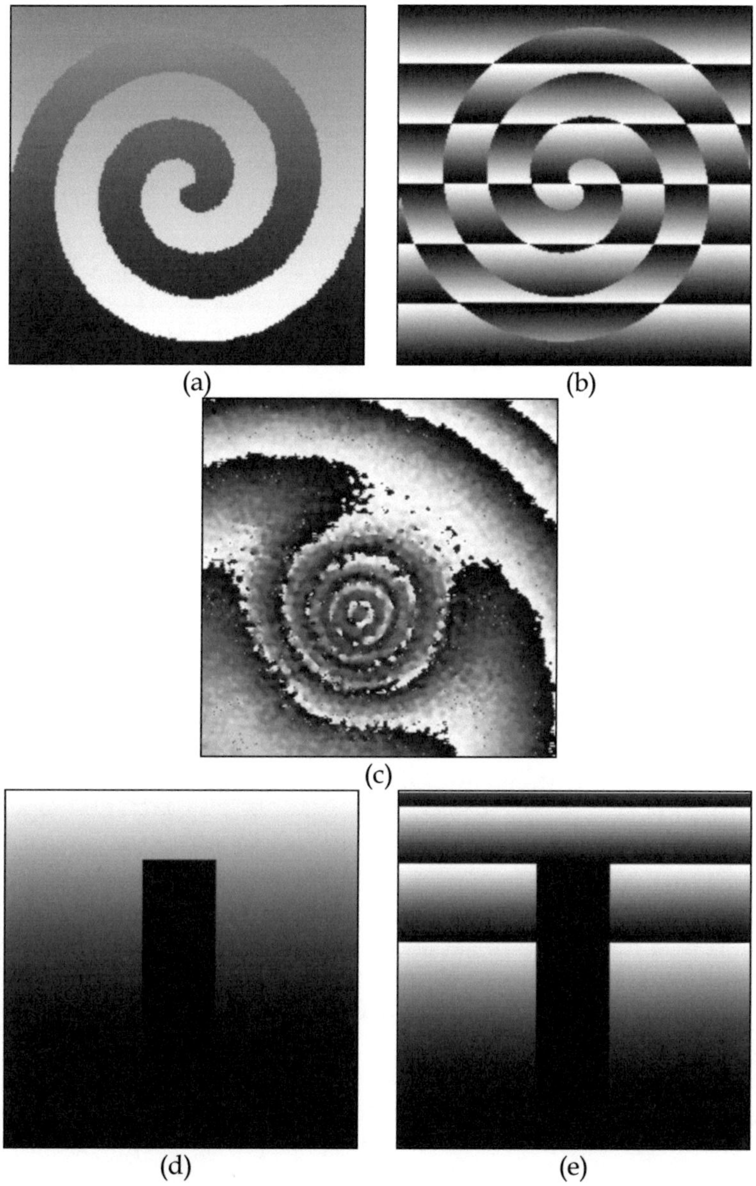

Fig. 1. (a) The spiral shear surface. (b) The wrapped phase image of Fig. 1(a). (c) The wrapped phase image of the optical fiber connector endface. (d) The curved surface with a rectangle hole. (e) The wrapped phase image of figure 1(d).

In this and the following sections, the three wrapped phase images will be unwrapped by a quality guide phase unwrapping algorithm (Flynn, 1996) using some quality maps that can be derived from the wrapped phase images.

2.1.1 Pseudo-correlation map

The pseudo-correlation map (Ghiglia & Pritt, 1998) is designed to measure the correlation of the wrapped phase images. The value of the quality map for pixel (m, n) is calculated according to

$$q_{m,n} = \frac{\sqrt{(\sum \cos\psi_{i,j})^2 + (\sum \sin\psi_{i,j})^2}}{k^2}, \tag{1}$$

where $\psi_{i,j}$ is the wrapped phase value and the sums are evaluated in the k×k neighborhood centered at each pixel (m, n). Normally, k is 3 or 5 in practice.

The pseudo-correlation map is based on the correlation of the wrapped phase image. It is sensitive to the noisy phase data, since the noisy regions of wrapped phase image are normally the low correlation regions. However, the pseudo-correlation map may mark the reliable regions with steep slopes as low quality regions. This is due to the low correlation of phase data in these regions. In this sense, a conservative strategy is chosen in this quality map. It is unreasonable to presume that all the low correlation areas should be marked as low quality. Therefore, the unwrapping results obtained by use of pseudo-correlation map are not always correct, especially when the wrapped phase image contains reliable regions with steep slopes.

The pseudo-correlation maps of the three wrapped phase images are shown in Fig. 2(a), 2(c) and 2(e), respectively. 3×3 window is chosen to compute the correlation of wrapped phase images. The values of quality maps are normalized into [0, 1] and the low quality values are shown as dark pixels and the high quality values as light pixels. Fig. 2(b), 2(d) and 2(f), respectively, show the unwrapping results by use of quality guide algorithm and the pseudo-correlation maps shown respectively in Fig. 2(a), 2(c) and 2(e). The result of the optical fiber connector endface, which shown in Fig. 2(d), is satisfactory. The pseudo-correlation map copes well with the intractable wrapped phase image, producing a correct unwrapping result. However, the other two unwrapping results, Fig. 2(b) and 2(f), are incorrect. The pseudo-correlation map incorrectly marks the steep surfaces of the spiral shear and curved surface, which are shown in Fig. 1(a) and 1(d) respectively, as low quality regions. Furthermore, and more importantly, the map fails to isolate the sheared planes from one another in spiral shear surface, and fails to isolate the closed area from other areas in the curved surface. These factors result in some degree of phase-unwrapping error. So we can say that the pseudo-correlation map is not a very good estimator of phase quality.

2.1.2 Phase derivatives variance map

The phase derivatives variance map (Ghiglia & Pritt, 1998) measures the statistical variance of the phase derivatives. The value of this map for pixel (m, n) is expressed as

$$q_{m,n} = \frac{\sqrt{\sum(\Delta^x_{i,j} - \overline{\Delta^x_{m,n}})^2} + \sqrt{\sum(\Delta^y_{i,j} - \overline{\Delta^y_{m,n}})^2}}{k^2}, \tag{2}$$

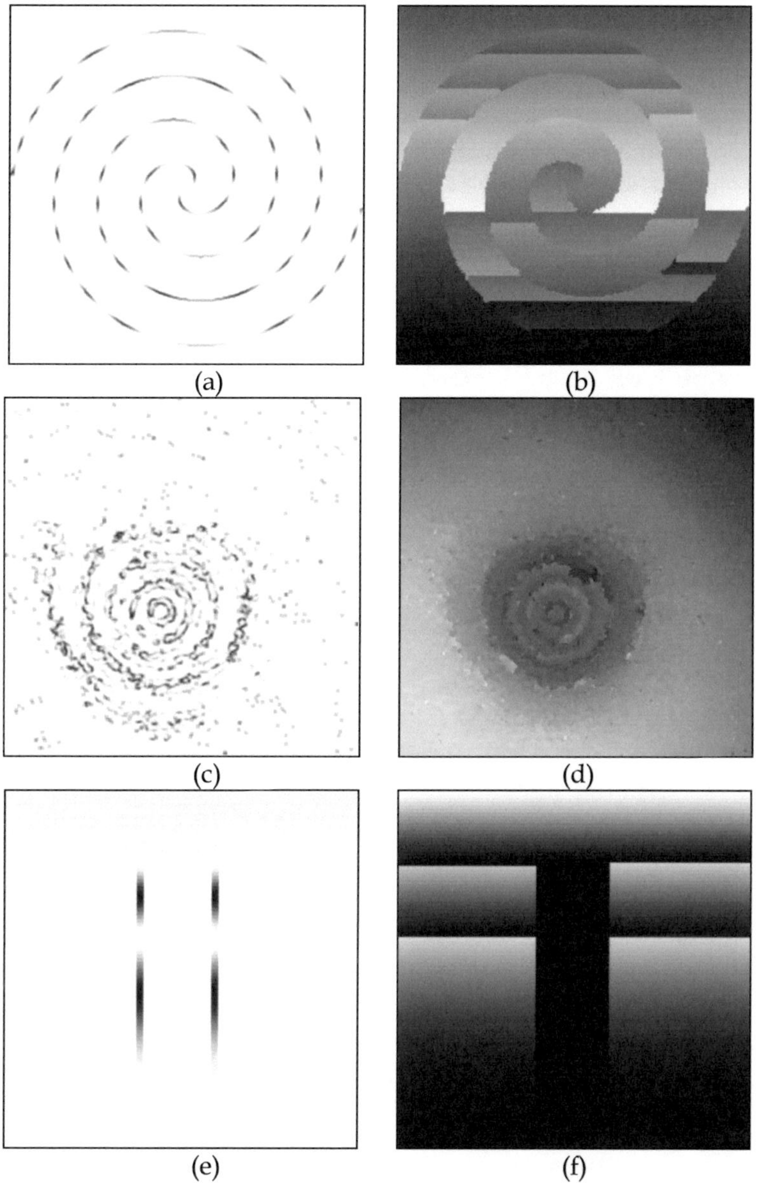

Fig. 2. (a) Pseudo-correlation map of Fig. 1(b). (b) Unwrapping result by use of Fig. 2(a). (c) Pseudo-correlation map of Fig. 1(c). (d) Unwrapping result by use of Fig. 2(c). (e) Pseudo-correlation map of Fig. 1(e). (f) Unwrapping result by use of Fig. 2(e).

where the terms $\Delta_{i,j}^{x}$ and $\Delta_{i,j}^{y}$ are the partial derivatives of the phase, the terms $\overline{\Delta_{m,n}^{x}}$ and $\overline{\Delta_{m,n}^{y}}$ are the averages of these partial derivatives in the k×k windows, and the sums evaluated in the k×k neighborhood centered at the pixel (m, n).

The phase derivatives variance map can be estimated as the local sample variance of the phase derivatives. The map indicates the badness of the phase data. In other words, the more unreliable the phase data is, the higher the phase derivatives variance is. So it should be negated to represent goodness of the phase data. Unlike the conservative strategy used in the pseudo-correlation map, an aggressive strategy is adopted in the phase derivatives variance map. For example, in regions where the isolated noise points are located, the phase variation is large, but the phase derivatives variance is low. Therefore, the phase derivatives variance map may mark the noisy regions as high quality area, especially when the size of window k is large.

The phase derivatives variance map is based on the phase derivatives of the wrapped phase image. However, if the phase gradients or derivatives are used directly to the construction of quality map, that will result in error quality map. Taking the wrapped spiral shear surface for example, its phase derivatives variance map is shown in Fig. 3. As it can be seen, the 2π phase jumps lines, i.e. the horizontal lines, in the wrapped phase are detected and marked as low quality. Actually, the phase jump lines are not unreliable regions, so the quality map shown in Fig. 3 does not reflect the real quality of the wrapped phase, which will result in an incorrect unwrapping result.

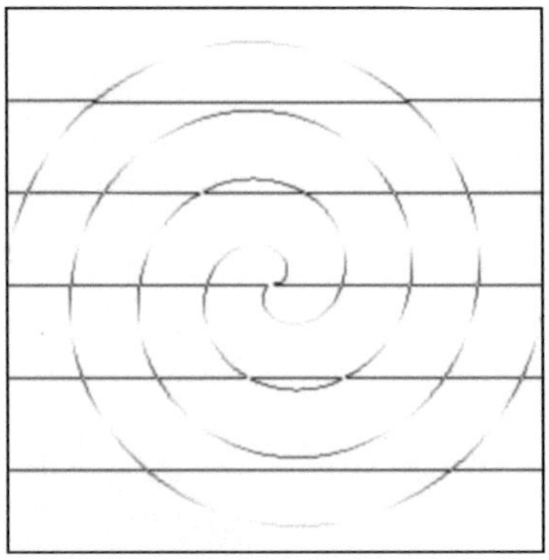

Fig. 3. Phase derivatives variance map of wrapped spiral shear surface without removing 2π phase jumps.

Therefore, before phase derivatives are obtained, a pre-processing is needed to remove the 2π phase jump lines. When the phase jump lines are detected, 2π is added or subtracted to remove the phase jumps. Then the phase derivatives can be extracted, and thus the quality map can be obtained. For all quality maps based on the phase derivatives, the pre-processing is need to avoid the influence of 2π phase jumps

The phase derivatives variance maps of the three wrapped phase images are shown in Fig. 4(a), 4(c) and 4(e), respectively. A 3×3 window is chosen to compute the variance of the phase derivatives. These quality maps are different from the pseudo-correlation maps shown in Fig. 2(a), 2(c), and 2(e). For example, where the phase exhibits a constant variation, such as that induced by the spiral shear surface, the phase derivative variance is zero while the pseudo-correlation is nonzero. The variance operation to phase gradient makes the quality map more reliable.

Fig. 4(b), 4(d) and 4(f) respectively, show the unwrapping results by means of quality guide algorithm and the phase derivatives variance maps shown respectively in Fig. 4(a), 4(c) and 4(e). The unwrapping result of the spiral shear surface shown in Fig. 4(b) is just the same as the phase data shown in Fig. 1(a). The unwrapping result is quite good. The unwrapping result of the optical fiber connector endface shown in Fig. 4(d) is defective since there is some mistake in the center of the map. This may result from the salt- and-pepper noise. Fig. 4(f) shows the unwrapping result of the curved surface wrapped phase. The result is also unsatisfactory, since the quality map fails to strictly differentiate the reliable and unreliable areas due to the presence of the real phase discontinuities and shadow.

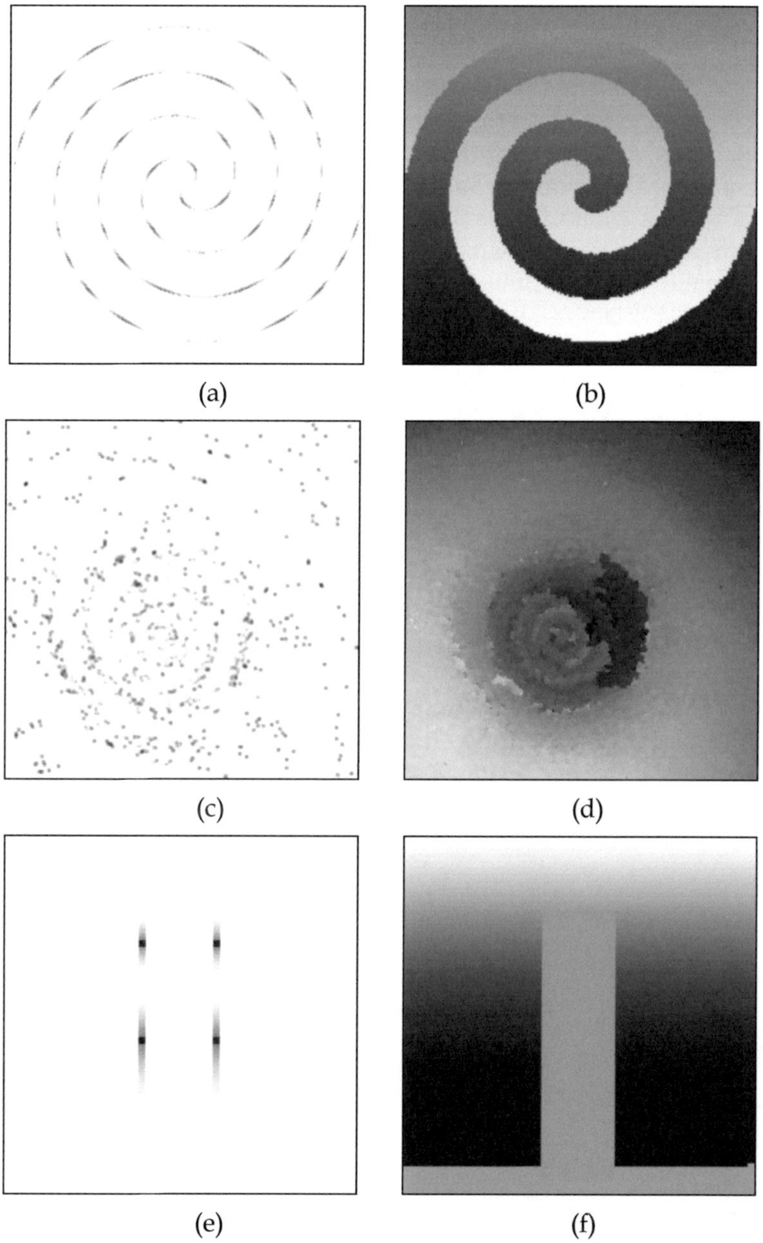

Fig. 4. (a) Phase derivatives variance map of Fig. 1(b). (b) Unwrapping result by use of Fig. 4(a). (c) Phase derivatives variance map of Fig. 1(c). (d) Unwrapping result by use of Fig. 4(c). (e) Phase derivatives variance map of Fig. 1(e). (f). Unwrapping result by use of Fig. 4(e).

2.1.3 Maximum phase gradient map

The maximum phase gradient map (Ghiglia & Pritt, 1998) is defined as the largest phase gradient value in the k×k neighborhood of each pixel. The value of the quality map for pixel (m, n) is calculated according to

$$z_{m,n} = \max\{\max\{|\Delta^x_{i,j}|\}, \max\{|\Delta^y_{i,j}|\}\}, \tag{3}$$

where the terms $\Delta^x_{i,j}$ and $\Delta^y_{i,j}$ are the partial derivatives of the phase and the *max* are evaluated in k×k neighborhoods of the given pixel.

The maximum phase gradient map takes the largest phase gradient value in the k×k neighborhood of each pixel as quality value. Therefore, it also denotes the badness rather than the goodness of the phase data, just as the phase derivatives variance map. The disadvantage of the maximum phase gradient map is that the reliable regions with steep slopes will be masked as low quality, which is similar to that of pseudo-correlation map. However, the map has an advantage that it is sensitive to the noisy phase data. In the regions where the noisy phase is present, the gradients tend to be large and thus the quality values are low.

The maximum phase gradient map of the three wrapped phase data are shown respectively in Fig. 5(a), 5(c) and 5(e). A 3×3 window is chosen to compute the maximum phase gradient. Fig. 5(b), 5(d) and 5(f) respectively show unwrapping results by use of quality guide algorithm and the maximum phase gradient maps shown respectively in Fig. 5(a), 5(c) and 5(e). Because the quality maps fail to mark the quality of reliable regions with steep slopes as high values, the unwrapping results of the spiral shear surface and curved phase are defective, as that shown in Fig. 5(b) and 5(f). The unwrapping result of the optical fiber connector endface shown in Fig. 5(d) is correct, due to the maximum phase gradient map's high sensitivity on the noisy phase area.

2.1.4 Derivative variance correlation map

The derivative variance correlation map (Lu et al., 2005; Lu et al., 2006; Lu et al., 2007) is a hybrid from two commonly used quality maps, the pseudo-correlation map and the derivative variance map. The value of the quality map for pixel (m, n) is calculated according to

$$q_{m,n} = \frac{\dfrac{\sqrt{\sum(\Delta^x_{i,j} - \overline{\Delta^x_{m,n}})^2} + \sqrt{\sum(\Delta^y_{i,j} - \overline{\Delta^y_{m,n}})^2}}{k^2}}{(1 - \dfrac{\sqrt{(\sum\cos\psi_{i,j})^2 + (\sum\sin\psi_{i,j})^2}}{k^2})}, \tag{4}$$

where $\psi_{i,j}$ is the wrapped phase values , the terms $\Delta^x_{i,j}$ and $\Delta^y_{i,j}$ are the partial derivatives of the phase, the term $\overline{\Delta^x_{m,n}}$ and $\overline{\Delta^y_{m,n}}$ are the averages of these partial derivatives in the k×k windows, and the sums evaluated in the k×k neighborhood centered at each pixel (m, n). Normally k is 3 or 5 in practice.

Because the derivative variance correlation map is a hybrid from the pseudo-correlation map and the derivative variance map, it has advantages of both of the latter two maps. For example, it is sensitive to the noisy phase data like the pseudo-correlation map, and works well in steep areas.

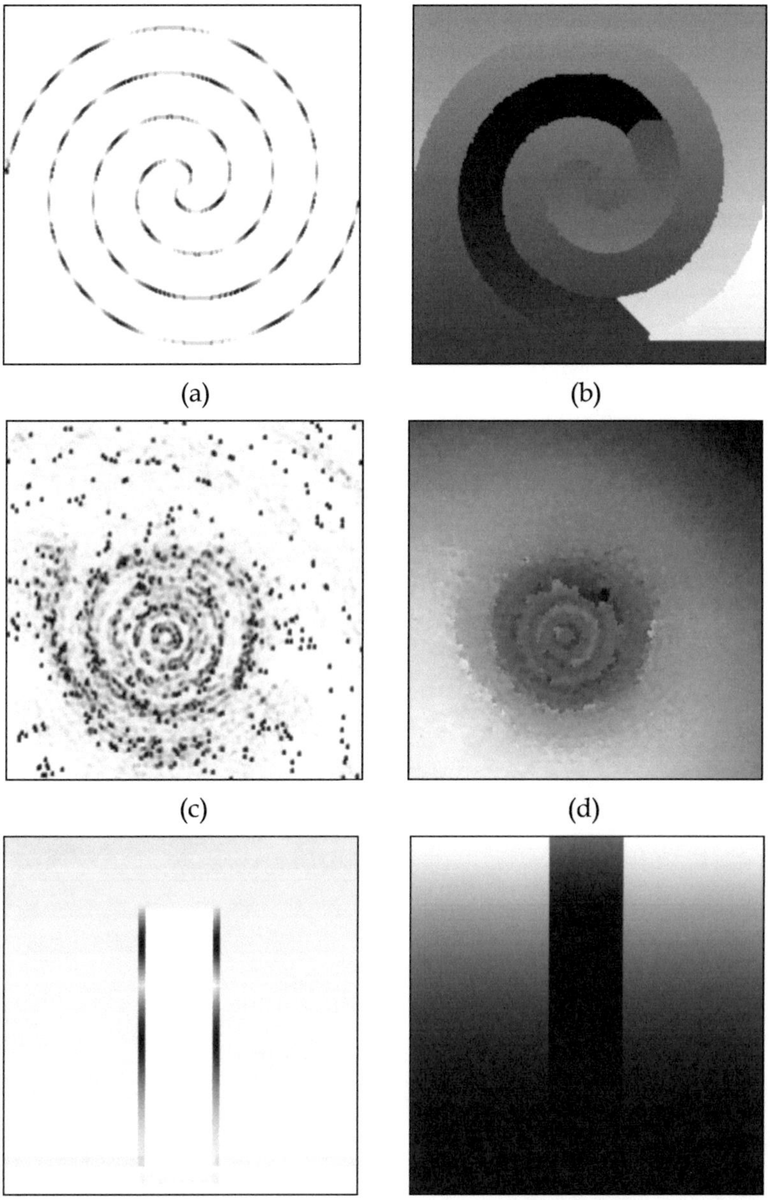

(a) (b)
(c) (d)
(e) (f)

Fig. 5. (a) Maximum phase gradient map of Fig. 1(b). (b) Unwrapping result by use of Fig. 5(a). (c) Maximum phase gradient map of Fig. 1(c). (d) Unwrapping result by use of Fig. 5 (c). (e) Maximum phase gradient map of Fig. 1(e). (f) Unwrapping result by use of Fig. 5 (e).

The derivative variance correlation maps of the three wrapped phase data are shown in Fig. 6(a), 6(c) and 6(e), respectively. A 3×3 window is chosen to compute the value of quality map. Fig. 6(b), 6(d) and 6(f) respectively show the unwrapping results by means of quality guide algorithm and the derivative variance correlation maps shown respectively in Fig.

6(a), 6(c) and 6(e). The unwrapping results are satisfactory. So we can see that the map can truly reflect wrapped phase quality, ensuring a more reliable unwrapping result. However, it is more complicated than some other maps.

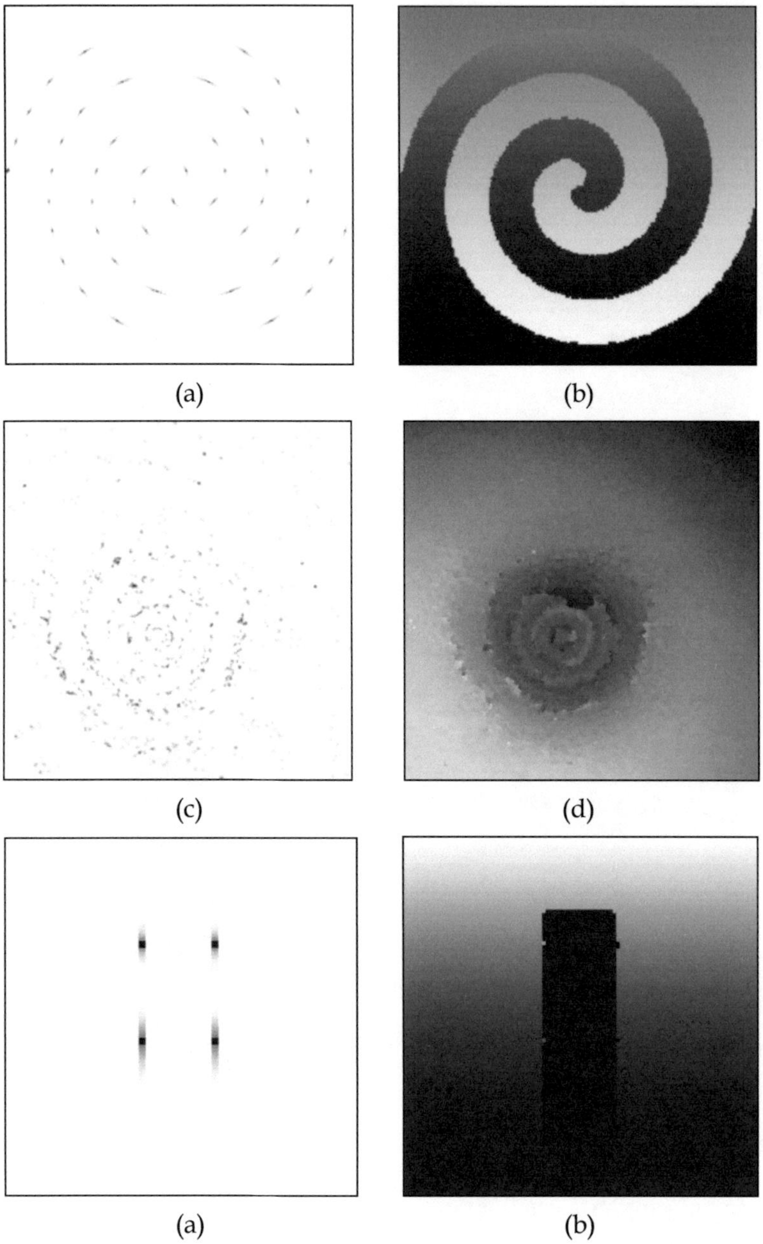

Fig. 6. (a) Derivative variance correlation map of Fig. 1(b). (b) Unwrapping result by use of Fig. 6(a). (c) Derivative variance correlation map of Fig. 1(c). (d) Unwrapping result by use of Fig. 6(c). (e) Derivative variance correlation map of Fig. 1(e). (f). Unwrapping result by use of Fig. 6(e).

2.1.5 Some other quality maps

There are also a few quality maps derived from wrapped phase data other than the quality maps mentioned above. The residue-vector map (Karout et al., 2007) is a quality map which combines both the concept of the quality maps and the knowledge of the residues and their branch cuts. The windowed Fourier filtering quality map (Qian et al., 2008) is based on the filtered amplitude derived by the windowed Fourier filtering. There are also hybrid quality maps which are combination of the existing two maps. For example, the quality map combined by pseudo-correlation map and maximum phase gradient map (Lu et al., 2004), and the second differences of the phase data can also be used to construct quality maps (Bone, 1991).

2.2 Quality maps derived from original measurement data

2.2.1 Correlation map

The correlation map (Ghiglia & Pritt, 1998) is defined by the correlation coefficients of the interferometric synthetic aperture radar (IFSAR) data. The value of the quality map for pixel (m, n) is calculated according to

$$q_{m,n} = \frac{\sum u_{i,j}\overline{v_{i,j}}}{\sqrt{\sum |u_{i,j}|^2 \sum |v_{i,j}|^2}}, \tag{5}$$

where $\overline{v_{i,j}}$ is the complex conjugate of $v_{i,j}$, $u_{i,j}$ and $v_{i,j}$ are the corresponding complex values from the two images after interpolation. The sum is performed in the k×k neighborhood centered at each pixel (m, n).

The correlation map is the best estimator of the quality of the phase data extracted from the IFSAR. However, it cannot be derived from the wrapped phase data, which is the most commonly used phase data in the phase unwrapping algorithms.

2.2.2 Fringe modulation map

The fringe modulation map is based on the intensity modulation of the fringe pattern, which is the original measurement data in optical interferometry. Therefore, the quality map can be extracted from the phase shifted interferogram. The value of the fringe modulation quality map for pixel (m, n) is calculated according to

$$q_{m,n} = \sqrt{(\sum_{i=1}^{N} I_i(m,n)\sin(2\pi n / N))^2 + (\sum_{i=1}^{N} I_i(m,n)\cos(2\pi n / N))^2}, \tag{6}$$

where N is the number of phase shifts employed in the measurement processing, and I_i is the intensity distribution of the *i*th phase shifting fringe pattern.

The fringe modulation map can be derived by the phase shifted interferogram or a single fringe pattern from which the wrapped phase can be obtained. In phase-shift interferometry, at least 3 fringe patterns are needed to obtain the quality map. That is to say, in equation (6) N is required no less than 3. In this case, the corresponding quality map is called as the temporal fringe modulation map (Su et al., 1993). However, when the fringe pattern projected on an object surface is sinusoidal, a quality map can be derived from a single fringe pattern. The value of the quality can be obtained by using equation (6) where N equals 1. Accordingly, the quality map is named as the spatial fringe modulation map (Quan et al., 2003).

The fringe modulation map is regarded as a kind of reliable and robust map. However, like the correlation map, it cannot be directly extracted from the wrapped phase data. Therefore, it cannot be used to guide phase unwrapping when the original measurement data are not available.

3. Quality maps derived by the edge detecting techniques

As we can see, several kinds of quality maps are based on the phase derivatives, such as the phase derivative variance map, the maximum phase gradient map and the derivative variance correlation map. The phase derivatives reflect the phase qualities to some extent and play important roles in the construction of quality maps. As that mentioned in section 1, the phase derivatives can be obtained by edge detection techniques. Some new quality maps based on weighted phase gradients can be generated by means of edge detection techniques. Strictly speaking, the process of obtaining the quality map based on phase derivatives or gradients in section 2 also contains the edge detection techniques. The edge detection masks are the first order phase derivatives, which are shown in Fig. 7. They are the simplest masks in edge detection techniques. In this figure, "X" denotes the horizontal direction and "Y" the vertical direction, and the underlined elements indicates the origin of the mask. Beyond that, there are some other commonly used edge detection masks(Gonzalez, 2002). Masks of size 2×2 are shown in Fig. 8(a), which are very simple masks in edge detection named as Roberts

$$\underset{X}{\begin{pmatrix} \underline{-1} & 1 \\ 0 & 0 \end{pmatrix}} \quad \underset{Y}{\begin{pmatrix} \underline{-1} & 0 \\ 1 & 0 \end{pmatrix}}$$

Fig. 7. The masks of first-order differential operator. The underlined elements in the two masks indicate the location of origin.

$$\text{(a)}\quad \underset{X}{\begin{pmatrix} \underline{-1} & 0 \\ 0 & 1 \end{pmatrix}} \underset{Y}{\begin{pmatrix} \underline{0} & -1 \\ 1 & 0 \end{pmatrix}}$$

$$\text{(b)}\quad \underset{X}{\begin{pmatrix} -1 & -1 & -1 \\ 0 & \underline{0} & 0 \\ 1 & 1 & 1 \end{pmatrix}} \underset{Y}{\begin{pmatrix} -1 & 0 & 1 \\ -1 & \underline{0} & 1 \\ -1 & 0 & 1 \end{pmatrix}}$$

$$\text{(c)}\quad \underset{X}{\begin{pmatrix} 0 & 1 & 1 \\ -1 & \underline{0} & 1 \\ -1 & -1 & 0 \end{pmatrix}} \underset{Y}{\begin{pmatrix} -1 & -1 & 0 \\ -1 & \underline{0} & 1 \\ 0 & 1 & 1 \end{pmatrix}}$$

$$\text{(d)}\quad \underset{X}{\begin{pmatrix} -1 & -2 & -1 \\ 0 & \underline{0} & 0 \\ 1 & 2 & 1 \end{pmatrix}} \underset{Y}{\begin{pmatrix} -1 & 0 & 1 \\ -2 & \underline{0} & 2 \\ -1 & 0 & 1 \end{pmatrix}}$$

$$\text{(e)}\quad \underset{X}{\begin{pmatrix} 0 & 1 & 2 \\ -1 & \underline{0} & 1 \\ -2 & -1 & 0 \end{pmatrix}} \underset{Y}{\begin{pmatrix} -2 & -1 & 0 \\ -1 & \underline{0} & 1 \\ 0 & 1 & 2 \end{pmatrix}}$$

Fig. 8. (a) The masks of Roberts operators. (b) The masks of Prewitt operators. (c) The masks of modified Prewitt operators. (d) The masks of Sobel operators. (e) The masks of modified Sobel operators. The underlined elements in these masks indicate the location of origin.

operators. The masks of Prewitt operators and its modified form are shown in Fig. 8(b) and Fig. 8(c), respectively. The Prewitt operators have the strongest responses along the Fig. 8(c), respectively. The Prewitt operators have the strongest responses along the horizontal and vertical direction, but the modified Prewitt operators are more suitable for detecting diagonal edges. The masks of Sobel operators and its modified form are shown in Fig. 8(d) and Fig. 8(e), respectively. Because the masks shown in Fig. 8 can be seen as the weighted forms of the masks shown in Fig. 7, new weighted quality maps can be developed by means of these edge detection operators. In this section, two weighted quality maps derived by the edge detecting techniques will be presented.

3.1 Weighted phase derivatives variance maps

Weighted phase derivatives variance maps can be generated from the equation (2), in which the value of $\Delta_{i,j}^{x}$ and $\Delta_{i,j}^{y}$ and is obtained by use of the operators shown in Fig. 8. As that mentioned in section 2, a pre-processing is needed to remove the 2π phase jump lines before the weighted versions of $\Delta_{i,j}^{x}$ and $\Delta_{i,j}^{y}$ can be obtained.

The masks of Prewitt operators are chosen to generate the weighted phase derivatives variance map. The quality maps of the wrapped phase images shown in Fig. 1(b), 1(c) and 1(e), are shown in Fig. 9(a), 9(c) and 9(e), respectively. The corresponding unwrapping result by use of the quality guide algorithm and the weighted phase derivatives variance map, are shown in Fig. 9(b), 9(d) and 9(f) respectively. The unwrapping results of the optical fiber connector endface and the curved surface is quite right though there may be a little defective in some regions. The unwrapping result of the spiral shear surface is also correct, although it looks different from the original phase data shown in Fig. 1(a). This is because that the two surfaces of the spiral shear surface, which are tilted relative to one another, are unwrapped separately in the process of phase unwrapping. There may be 2kπ phase difference between the two unwrapped surfaces, but it can be eliminated by add the known phase difference to one of the unwrapped surface. In Fig. 9(b), the two surfaces are both unwrapped correctly, so it can be thought as a good unwrapping result. When compare the results with the unwrapping results shown in Fig. 4(b), 4(d) and 4(f), we can find that the results of the spiral shear surface are correct, while the results of the optical fiber connector endface and the curved phase in Fig. 9 are much better than that shown in Fig. 4(d) and 4(f). Therefore, suitable masks of edge detection operators can be utilized to improve the quality of the unwrapping results.

3.2 Weighted maximum phase gradient map

Another new quality map generated by means of edge detection techniques is the weighted maximum phase gradient map. Like the phase derivatives variance map, the maximum phase gradient map is based on the phase derivatives. Thus the edge detection techniques can be utilized to enlarge its family. Weighted maximum phase gradient maps can be generated from the equation (3), in which the value of $\Delta_{i,j}^{x}$ and $\Delta_{i,j}^{y}$ is obtained by use of the operators shown in Fig. 8. A pre-processing is also needed to remove the 2π phase jump lines before the weighted versions of $\Delta_{i,j}^{x}$ and $\Delta_{i,j}^{y}$ can be obtained.

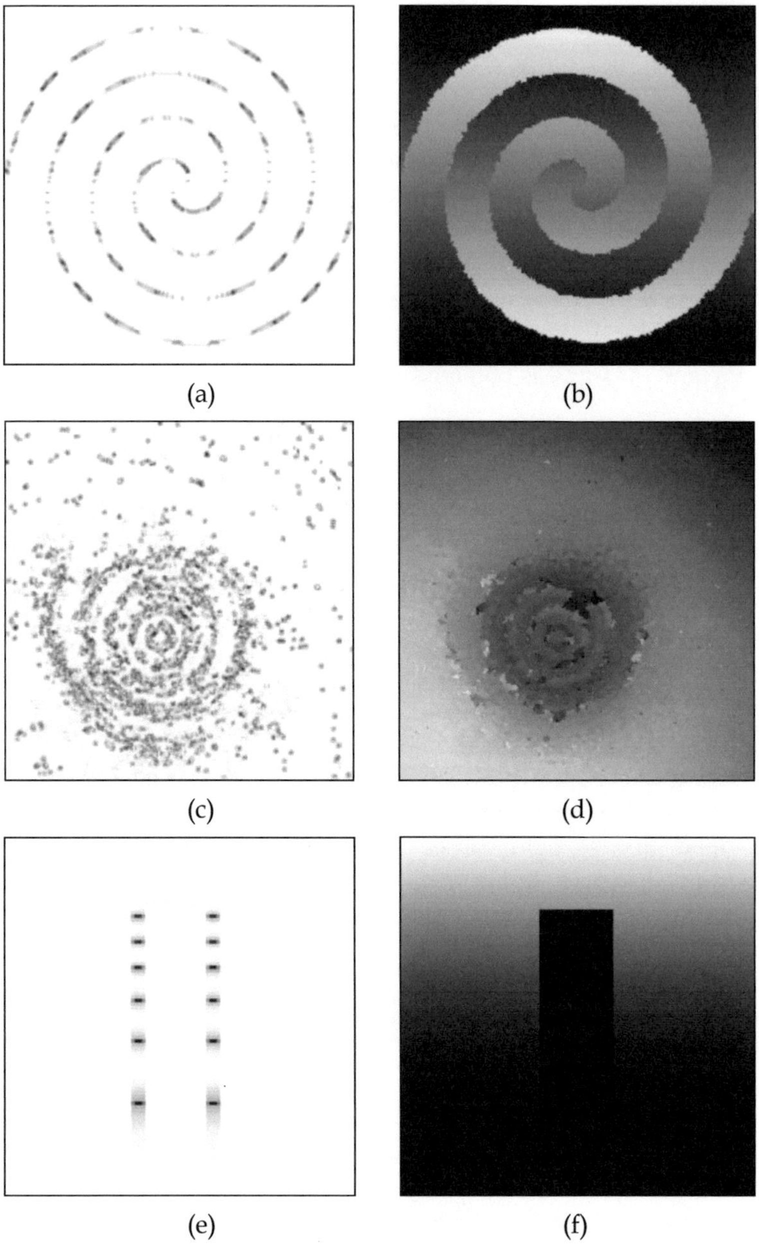

Fig. 9. (a) Weighted phase derivatives variance map of Fig. 1(b) generated by use of Prewitt operators. (b) Unwrapping result by use of Fig. 9(a). (c) Weighted phase derivatives variance map of Fig. 1(c) generated by use of Prewitt operators. (d) Unwrapping result by use of Fig. 9 (c). (e) Weighted phase derivatives variance map of Fig. 1(e) generated by use of Prewitt operators. (f) Unwrapping result by use of Fig. 9(e).

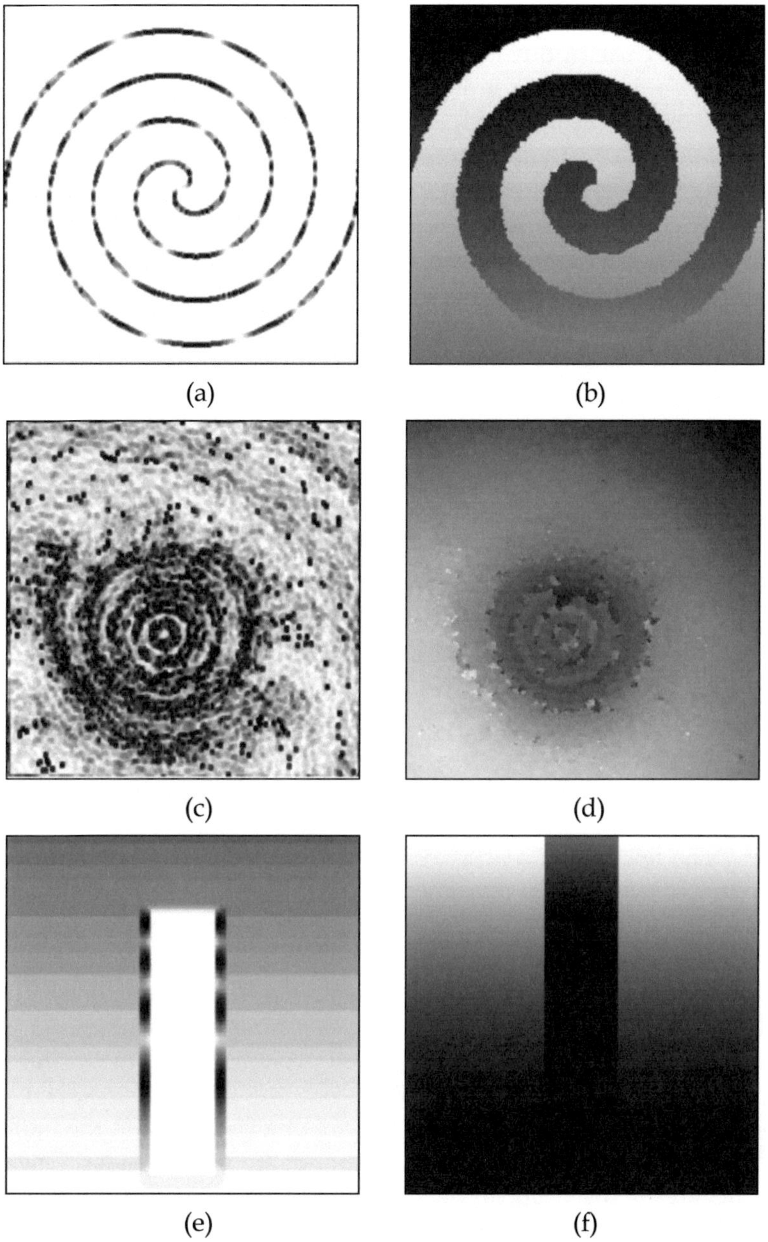

Fig. 10. (a) The weighted maximum phase gradient map of Fig. 1(b) generated by use of diagonal versions of Prewitt operators. (b) Unwrapping result by use of Fig. 10(a). (c) The weighted maximum phase gradient map of Fig. 1(c) generated by use of diagonal versions of Prewitt operators. (d) Unwrapping result by use of Fig. 10(c). (e) The weighted maximum phase gradient map of Fig. 1(e) generated by use of diagonal versions of Prewitt operators. (f). Unwrapping result by use of Fig. 10(e).

In this section, the masks in Fig. 8(c), i.e. the diagonal version of Prewitt operators, are chosen. The weighted maximum phase gradient map of the three wrapped phase data are shown in Fig. 10(a), 10(c) and 10(e), respectively. Fig. 10(b), 10(d) and 10(f) show the unwrapping results by use of quality guide algorithm and the weighted maximum phase gradient maps shown respectively in Fig. 10(a), 10(c) and 10(e). Compare the unwrapping results with that shown in Fig. 5(b), 5(d) and 5(f) respectively. The unwrapping results of the optical fiber connector endface and the curved phase are just the same as that shown in Fig. 5(d) and 5(f), where the result of curved surface is defective. The unwrapping result of the spiral shear surface is quite good and much better than the result shown in Fig. 5(b), though there exist $2k\pi$ phase difference between the two surfaces, which makes the unwrapping result looks different from the original phase data as that shown in Fig. 9(b). Therefore, because the diagonal versions of Prewitt operators have strong responses along the diagonal directions, the operators are the suitable masks that can be used in the case of the spiral shear surface unwrapping.

4. Conclusion and future work

Quality maps play very important role in two-dimensional phase unwrapping process. In this chapter we have introduced the quality map generation method using the edge detection techniques. Existing quality maps which are commonly used in phase unwrapping process have been reviewed, and we find that each quality map has its advantages and disadvantages. Edge detection techniques are utilized to enlarge the family of quality maps due to the fact that most quality maps are based on the phase gradients or phase derivatives of the wrapped phase images. Some new quality maps, which are weighted versions of existing quality maps, are developed by means of edge detection operators. The unwrapping results show that appropriate edge detection operator can make the quality map more reliable.

Although more than ten quality maps have been proposed and we enlarge their family by constructing a few of new quality maps in this work, there are still some challenges related to the quality maps in future work. For example, although we can use edge detection techniques to obtain a new quality map, we still need to evaluate its reliability. Until now, there are no recognized standards in this important area. The common evaluation method is evaluating the unwrapping results of some kinds of intractable wrapped phase images. However, the wrapped phase images are chosen arbitrarily and the visual evaluation of unwrapping results may not be accurate. Therefore, the standard wrapped phase images should be identified for evaluating the reliability of quality map, and the uniform standard should be developed for judging the reliability of quality map. Besides, new quality maps based on new features of the wrapped phase image, such as phase correlation or the entropy of phase data, should be developed to make up for the deficiencies of the existing quality maps.

5. Acknowledgments

It is gratefully noted that the work was supported by the National Natural Science Foundation of China under Grant No. 60607007.

6. References

Baldi, A.; Bertolino, F. & Ginesu, F. (2002). On the performance of some unwrapping algorithms, *Opt Laser Eng*, Vol. 37, pp. 313–330

Bone, D. J. (1991). Fourier fringe analysis: the two-dimensional phase unwrapping problem, *Appl. Opt*, Vol. 30, pp. 3627-3632

Flynn, T. J. (1996). Consistent 2-D phase unwrapping guided by a quality map, *Proceedings of the 1996 International Geoscience and Remote Sensing Symposium*, pp. 2057–2059, Lincoln, NE, May 1996

Ghiglia, D.; Mastin, G. & Romero, L. (1987). Cellular-automata method for phase unwrapping, *J. Opt. Soc. Am.A*, Vol. 4, No. 1, pp. 267- 280

Ghiglia, D. C. & Pritt, M. (1998). *Two-dimensional phase unwrapping: theory, algorithms, and software*, Wiley-Interscience publication, New York

Gonzalez, R. C. & Woods, R. E. (2002). *Digital Image Processing Second Edition,* Pearson Education, Inc., Prentice Hall

Jenkinson, M. (2003). Fast, automated, N-dimensional phase-unwrapping algorithm, *Magnetic Resonance in Medicine,* Vol. 49, pp. 93–197

Karout, S. A.; Gdeisat, M. A.; Burton, D. R. & Lalor, M. J. (2007). Residue vector, an approach to branch-cut placement in phase unwrapping: theoretical study. *Appl. Opt.*, Vol. 46, No. 21, pp. 4712-4727

Kwon, O. Y. (1984). Multichannel phase-shifted interferometer, *Opt. Lett.*, Vol. 9, No. 2, pp. 59–61

Lu, Y.; Wang, X.; Zhong, X.; He, G.; Liu, Y. & Zheng, D. (2004). A new quality map for quality-guided phase unwrapping, *Chinese optics letters*, Vol. 2, No. 12, pp. 698-700

Lu, Y.; Wang, X. & He, G. (2005). Phase unwrapping based on branch cut placing and reliability ordering, *Optical Engineering*, Vol. 44, No. 5, 055601

Lu, Y. & Zhang, X. (2006). Minimum L^0-norm two-dimensional phase unwrapping algorithm Based on the derivative variance correlation map, *Journal of Physics: Conference Series,* Vol. 48, pp. 308–312

Lu, Y.; Wang, X. & Zhang, X. (2007). Weighted least-squares phase unwrapping algorithm based on derivative variance correlation map, *Optik*, Vol. 118, pp. 62-66

Meer, P. & Georgescu, B. (2001). Edge detection with embedded confidence, *IEEE Transactions on pattern analysis and machine intelligence*, Vol. 23, No. 12, pp. 1351-1365

Qian, K.; Gao, W. & Wang, H. (2008). Windowed Fourier-filtered and quality-guided phase-unwrapping algorithm, *Applied optics*, Vol. 47, No. 29, pp. 5420-5428

Quan, C.; Tay, C. J.; Chen, L. & Fu, Y. (2003). Spatial-fringe-modulation-based quality map for phase unwrapping, *Appl. Opt.*Vol. 42, No. 35, pp. 7060-7065

Su, X.; von Bally, G. & Vukicevic, D. (1993). Phase-stepping grating profilometry: utilization of intensity modulation analysis in complex object evaluation, *Opt. Comm.*, Vol. 98, pp. 141-150

Su, X. & Chen, W. (2004). Reliability-guided phase unwrapping algorithm: a review, *Opt. Lasers Eng*, Vol. 42, pp. 245-261

Volkov, V. V. & Zhu, Y. (2003). Deterministic phase unwrapping in the presence of noise, *Opt. Lett,* Vol. 28, No. 22, pp. 2156–2158

Zappa, E. & Busca, G. (2008). Comparison of eight unwrapping algorithms applied to Fourier transform profilometry, *Opt. Lasers Eng,* Vol. 46, pp. 106-116

8

Video Colour Denoising using Fuzzy and Directional Techniques

Francisco J. Gallegos-Funes, Alberto J. Rosales-Silva,
Jose M. De-la-Rosa-Vazquez and Jose H. Espina-Hernandez
National Polytechnic Institute of Mexico
Mexico

1. Introduction

Different classes of filters have been proposed for removing noise from gray scale and colour images (Astola & Kuosmanen, 1997; Bovik, 2000; Kotropoulos & Pitas, 2001). They are classified into several categories depending on specific applications. Linear filters are efficient for Gaussian noise removal but often distort edges and have poor performance against impulsive noise. Nonlinear filters are designed to suppress noise of different nature, they can remove impulsive noise and guarantee detail preservation. Rank order based filters have received considerable attention due to their inherent outlier rejection and detail preservation properties (Astola & Kuosmanen, 1997; Bovik, 2000; Kotropoulos & Pitas, 2001, Plataniotis & Venetsanopoulos, 2000).

In the last decade, many useful colour processing techniques based on vector processing have been investigated due to the inherent correlation that exists between the image channels compared to traditional component-wise approaches (Plataniotis & Venetsanopoulos, 2000). The fuzzy filters are designed by fuzzy rules to remove noise and to provide edge and fine detail preservation (Russo & Ramponi, 1994). The fuzzy filter depends on the fuzzy rules and the defuzzification process, which combines the effects of applied rules to produce an only output value (Russo & Ramponi, 2004, Schulte et al., 2007). The vector directional filters employ the directional processing taking pixels as vectors, and obtaining the output vector that shows a less deviation of its angles under ordering criteria in respect to the other vectors (Trahanias & Venetsanopoulos, 1996).

This chapter presents the capability features of Fuzzy Directional (FD) filter to remove impulse noise from corrupted colour images (Ponomaryov, et al., 2010). The FD filter uses directional processing, where vectorial order statistics are employed, and fuzzy rules that are based on gradient values and angle deviations to determine, if the central pixel is noisy or present local movement. Simulation results in colour images and video sequences have shown that the restoration performance is better in comparison with other known filters. In Addition, we present the Median M-Type L- (MML) filter for the removal of impulsive noise in gray-scale and colour image processing applications (Gallegos-Funes et al., 2008, Toledo-Lopez et al., 2008). The proposed scheme is based on modification of L- filter that uses the MM (Median M-type) -estimator to calculate the robust point estimate of the pixels within the filtering window. The proposed filter uses the value of the central pixel within the filtering window to provide the preservation of fine details and the redescending *M*-

estimators combined with the calculation of the median estimator to obtain the sufficient impulsive noise rejection. Influence functions into the *M*-estimator can be used to provide better impulsive noise suppression. Simulation results in gray-scale and colour images have demonstrated that the proposed filters consistently outperform other filters by balancing the tradeoff between noise suppression, fine detail preservation, and color retention.

2. Proposed filters

2.1 Fuzzy Directional filter

In the proposed Fuzzy Directional filter, a 3x3 sliding window is used in the centre of a bigger one of size 5x5. Last window is employed to calculate values in different directions with respect to neighbour pixels in the initial 3x3 window. Each a neighbour of a central pixel $x_c^{\beta} = (x_c^R, x_c^G, x_c^B)$ (in the RGB colour space) corresponds to one of the eight directions, as it is illustrated in Figure 1. We introduce the basic gradient values $\nabla_{(k,l)}^{\beta} x(i,j)$ for central pixel and its neighbours as follows (Ponomaryov, et al., 2010),

$$\nabla_{(k,l)}^{\beta} x(i,j) = \nabla\left[x_C^{\beta}(i,j), x^{\beta}(i+k,j+l)\right] = \left|x_C^{\beta}(i,j) - x^{\beta}(i+k,j+l)\right| \quad (1)$$

where each one of the (*k,l*) pairs corresponds to each one of eight directions of (*i,j*) point, $k,l \in (-1,0,+1)$, and $\beta = (R,G,B)$.

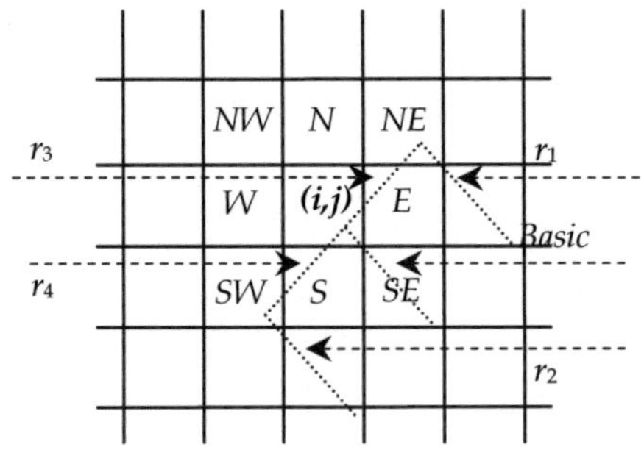

Fig. 1. Basic and related (r_1, r_2, r_3, r_4) gradient values.

We introduce subindex $\gamma = (N,E,S,W,NW,NE,SE,SW)$ the related gradient values can be calculated in relation to the basic gradient direction. According with Figure 1, the basic gradient value for *SE* direction is written as,

$$\nabla_{(1,1)}^{\beta} x(i,j) = \nabla_{SE}^{\beta} \quad (2)$$

and its four related gradients values are given by,

$$\nabla_{(0,2)}^{\beta} x(i-1,j+1) = \nabla_{SE(r_1)}^{\beta},\ \nabla_{(2,0)}^{\beta} x(i+1,j-1) = \nabla_{SE(r_2)}^{\beta},\ \nabla_{(-1,1)}^{\beta} x(i-1,j+1) = \nabla_{SE(r_3)}^{\beta}, \text{ and } \nabla_{(1,-1)}^{\beta} x(i+1,j-1) = \nabla_{SE(r_4)}^{\beta} \quad (3)$$

We propose two fuzzy sets: the fuzzy set SMALL that characterizes the membership level for a gradient value when it is sufficiently small, this infers in membership value as a big value. So, if a membership level is ≈1 this implies that there is *no movement* and/or *noise*

presence in a sample to be processed. In opposite case, we use the fuzzy set BIG. We also introduce the fuzzy angular deviation for a single component leaving another two out of the calculus.
For example, for R component in SE direction, the basic angular deviation is written as,

$$\theta^R_{(1,1)}x(i,j) = \theta^R_{SE} \tag{4}$$

and its related angular deviations are given by,

$$\theta^R_{(0,2)}x(i-1,j+1) = \theta^R_{SE(r_1)},\ \theta^R_{(0,2)}x(i+1,j-1) = \theta^R_{SE(r_2)},\ \theta^R_{(-1,1)}x(i-1,j+1) = \theta^R_{SE(r_3)},\ \theta^R_{(1,-1)}x(i+1,j-1) = \theta^R_{SE(r_4)} \tag{5}$$

To characterize the fuzzy gradients and fuzzy angular deviation values, the following Gaussian membership functions are employed (Ponomaryov, et al., 2007)

$$G(F^\beta_\gamma \text{SMALL}) = \begin{cases} 1, & F^\beta_\gamma < med_F \\ \exp\left\{-\left[(F^\beta_\gamma - med_F)^2 / 2\sigma^2_F\right]\right\}, & \text{otherwise} \end{cases} \tag{6}$$

$$G(F^\beta_\gamma \text{BIG}) = \begin{cases} 1, & F^\beta_\gamma > med_F \\ \exp\left\{-\left[(F^\beta_\gamma - med_F)^2 / 2\sigma^2_F\right]\right\}, & \text{otherwise} \end{cases} \tag{7}$$

We propose fuzzy rules that are based on gradient values and angle deviations to determine: if the central component is noisy or present local movement. Table 1 presents the proposed fuzzy rules employ in the FD filter (Ponomaryov, et al., 2010).

Fuzzy Rule 1 defines the fuzzy angular-gradient value $\nabla^{\beta F}_\gamma \theta^{\beta F}_\gamma$.
By other words, the membership level of central pixel x^β_c in fuzzy set BIG in γ direction: **IF**(∇^β_γ B⊗ $\nabla^\beta_{\gamma(r_1)}$ S⊗ $\nabla^\beta_{\gamma(r_2)}$ S⊗ $\nabla^\beta_{\gamma(r_3)}$ B⊗ $\nabla^\beta_{\gamma(r_4)}$ B) $\otimes_1$ (θ^β_γ B⊗ $\theta^\beta_{\gamma(r_1)}$ S⊗ $\theta^\beta_{\gamma(r_2)}$ S⊗ $\theta^\beta_{\gamma(r_3)}$ B⊗ $\theta^\beta_{\gamma(r_4)}$ B) **THEN** $\nabla^{\beta F}_\gamma \theta^{\beta F}_\gamma$ B
Fuzzy rule 2 defines the fuzzy *noise* factor as r^β.
IF $\nabla^{\beta F}_N \theta^{\beta F}_N$ B ⊕ $\nabla^{\beta F}_S \theta^{\beta F}_S$ B ⊕ $\nabla^{\beta F}_E \theta^{\beta F}_E$ B ⊕ $\nabla^{\beta F}_W \theta^{\beta F}_W$ B ⊕ $\nabla^{\beta F}_{SW} \theta^{\beta F}_{SW}$ B ⊕ $\nabla^{\beta F}_{NE} \theta^{\beta F}_{NE}$ B ⊕ $\nabla^{\beta F}_{NW} \theta^{\beta F}_{NW}$ B ⊕ $\nabla^{\beta F}_{SE} \theta^{\beta F}_{SE}$ B **THEN** r^β B.

Table 1. Fuzzy rules used in the proposed FD filter.

From Fuzzy rule 1, a central pixel is considered *noisy* or belongs to fuzzy set BIG if its basic values with respect to related values satisfy to:

$$\begin{gathered} G(\nabla^\beta_\gamma) \approx G(\nabla^\beta_{\gamma(r_3)}) \approx G(\nabla^\beta_{\gamma(r_4)}),\ G(\theta^\beta_\gamma) \approx G(\theta^\beta_{\gamma(r_3)}) \approx G(\theta^\beta_{\gamma(r_4)}), \\ G(\nabla^\beta_\gamma) \neq G(\nabla^\beta_{\gamma(r_1)}) \neq G(\nabla^\beta_{\gamma(r_2)}),\ \text{and}\ G(\theta^\beta_\gamma) \neq G(\theta^\beta_{\gamma(r_1)}) \neq G(\theta^\beta_{\gamma(r_2)}) \end{gathered} \tag{8}$$

The value r^β in Fuzzy rule 2 denotes the noise level of central pixel formed with the neighbour components. The big membership levels are given in the fuzzy set BIG, so, this rule shows when a noisy or fine detail pixel is present. If $r^\beta \geq R_0$ the filtering is realized using fuzzy membership levels obtained for the fuzzy set BIG, otherwise output filtered pixel is: $y_o^\beta = x_C^\beta$. In these Fuzzy rules $A \otimes B = A \text{ AND } B$, $A \otimes_1 B = \min(A,B)$, $A \oplus B = \max(A,B)$, and PB and QS denote that value P is BIG and value Q is SMALL, respectively.

The fuzzy values are the weights for each a neighbour component and should be taken in consideration before using fuzzy membership levels. To obtain the fuzzy weights in the filtering algorithm, we propose to determine the membership level for the fuzzy set FREE (free noise) as: $\upsilon_\gamma^{\beta F} = 1 - \nabla_\gamma^{\beta F} \theta_\gamma^{\beta F}$. The weight value for central component in fuzzy set FREE is chosen as: $\upsilon_\gamma^{\beta F} = 3\sqrt{1 - r^\beta}$.

The filtering procedure is performed selecting one of the neighbour components to avoid the detail and edge smoothing. Besides, it is proposed the filtering of a sample using their fuzzy weights and according to their ordering properties. The component values of the 3x3 sample are ordered as follows:

$$x_\gamma^{\beta(1)} \le x_\gamma^{\beta(2)} \le \cdots \le x_\gamma^{\beta(9)} \text{ and } \upsilon_\gamma^{\beta(1)} \le \upsilon_\gamma^{\beta(2)} \le \cdots \le \upsilon_\gamma^{\beta(9)} \tag{9}$$

Equation (9) permits to withdraw the components that are sufficiently far with respect to a central value. For this reason, we define $sum^\beta = \upsilon_\gamma^{\beta(j)}$, where j decreases from 9 to 1; decreasing of j is valid until $sum^\beta > \left(\sum_\gamma \upsilon_\gamma^{\beta F} + 3\sqrt{1 - r^\beta}\right)/2$. When j satisfies this condition, the j-th ordered value is selected as the output filtered value,

$$x_\gamma^{\beta(j)} = y_o^\beta \tag{10}$$

Finally, the values for Gaussian membership functions were found according to optimal values of PSNR and MAE criteria, these values are given by: σ_1^2=1000, med_1=60 and med_2=10 for fuzzy gradient sets BIG and SMALL, respectively, σ_2^2=0.8, med_3=0.1 and med_4=0.8 for fuzzy angular deviation sets BIG and SMALL, respectively, and R_0=0.3.

2.2 Median M-type L-filter

To improve the robustness of L-filter, we propose to use the Median M-type (MM) – estimator (Gallegos-Funes et al., 2008),

$$\varepsilon_{\text{medM}} = MED\left\{X_i\tilde{\psi}\left(X_i - MED\{\vec{\mathbf{X}}\}\right),\ i = 1,\ldots,N\right\} \tag{11}$$

where X_k is data sample, $\tilde{\psi}$ is the normalized influence function ψ : $\psi(X) = X\tilde{\psi}(X)$, and X_N is the primary data sample. The Median estimator provides good properties of impulsive noise suppression and the M-estimator uses different influence functions to provide better robustness, for these reasons it can be expected that the properties of combined MM-estimator could be better in comparison with Median and M- estimators.

The representation of L-filter is $F_L = \sum_{i=1}^{N} a_i \cdot X_{(i)}$ where $X_{(i)}$ is the ordered data sample, i=1,…,N, $a_i = \int_{i-1/N}^{i/N} h(\lambda)d\lambda \Big/ \int_0^1 h(\lambda)d\lambda$ are the weight coefficients, and $h(\lambda)$ is a probability density function (Kotropoulos & Pitas, 2001).

To introduce the MM-estimator (11) in the scheme of L-filter, we present the ordered data sample of L-filter as function of an influence function (Gallegos-Funes et al., 2008),

$$\hat{F}_L = \sum_{i=1}^{N} a_i \cdot \psi(X_i) \cdot X_i \tag{12}$$

where $N = (2L+1)^2$ is the filtering window size, $\psi(X_i) \cdot X_i$ is the ordered data sample, $\psi(u) = \begin{cases} c, & |u| \le r \\ 0, & \text{otherwise} \end{cases}$ is the influence function, c is a constant, and r is connected with the range of $\psi(u)$.

Therefore, the MML filter can be obtained by the combination of L-filter (12) and the MM-estimator (11) (Gallegos-Funes et al., 2008),

$$\hat{F}_{MML} = \frac{MED\left\{a_i \cdot \left[X_i \cdot \psi\left(X_i - MED\{\vec{X}\}\right)\right]\right\}}{a_{MED}} \tag{13}$$

where $X_i\psi\left(X_i - \text{MED}\{\vec{X}\}\right)$ are the selected pixels in accordance with the influence function used in a sliding filter window and a_{MED} is the median of coefficients a_i used as a scale constant.

To improve the properties of noise suppression of MML filter we use an impulsive noise detector (IND) (Aizenberg et al., 2003),

$$\text{IND} = \begin{cases} \hat{F}_{\text{MML}}, & \text{if } \left[(D \le s) \vee (D \ge N - s)\right] \wedge \left(\left|X_c - \text{MED}(\vec{X})\right| \ge U\right) \\ X_c, & \text{otherwise} \end{cases} \tag{14}$$

where X_c is the central pixel in the filtering window, s>0 and U≥0 are thresholds, N is the length of the data, and $D=rank(X_c)$ is the rank of element X_c.

The coefficients a_i are computed using the Laplacian and Uniform distribution functions in $h(\lambda)$ and the simple cut $\psi_{\text{cut}(r)}(X) = X \cdot 1_{[-r,r]}(X) = \begin{cases} X, & |X| \le r \\ 0, & \text{otherwise} \end{cases}$ and Andrew's sine $\psi_{\sin(r)}(X) = \begin{cases} \sin(X/r), & |X| \le r\pi \\ 0, & \text{otherwise} \end{cases}$ influence functions are used in the filtering scheme, where the parameter r is connected with restrictions on the range of $\psi(X)$.

3. Experimental results

To compare the performance of noise suppression of various filters the *peak signal to noise ratio* (PSNR) was used, and for the evaluation of fine detail preservation the *mean absolute error* (MAE) was computed (Astola & Kuosmanen, 1997; Bovik 2000),

$$\text{PSNR} = 10 \cdot \log\left[\frac{(255)^2}{\text{MSE}}\right] \text{ dB} \tag{15}$$

$$\mathrm{MAE} = \frac{1}{MN}\sum_{i=0}^{M-1}\sum_{j=0}^{N-1}\left|f(i,j) - \hat{F}(i,j)\right| \tag{16}$$

where $\mathrm{MSE} = \frac{1}{MN}\sum_{i=0}^{M-1}\sum_{j=0}^{N-1}\left[f(i,j) - \hat{F}(i,j)\right]^2$ is the *mean square error*, $f(i,j)$ is the original image; $\hat{F}(i,j)$ is the restored image; and *M*, *N* is the size of the image.

We also compute the *mean chromaticity error* (MCRE) for evaluation of chromaticity retention, and the *normalized color difference* (NCD) for quantification of color perceptual error (Plataniotis & Venetsanopoulos, 2000):

$$\mathrm{MCRE} = \sum_{i=1}^{M_1}\sum_{j=1}^{M_2}\left\|p_{i,j} - \hat{p}_{i,j}\right\|_{L_2}^{2} \Big/ M_1 M_2 \tag{17}$$

$$\mathrm{NCD} = \sum_{i=1}^{M_1}\sum_{j=1}^{M_2}\left\|\Delta E_{Luv}(i,j)\right\|_{L_2} \Big/ \sum_{i=1}^{M_1}\sum_{j=1}^{M_2}\left\|E_{Luv}^{*}(i,j)\right\|_{L_2} \tag{18}$$

where $p_{i,j}$ and $\hat{p}_{i,j}$ are the intersection points of $f(i,j)$ and $\hat{F}(i,j)$ with the plane defined by the Maxwell triangle, respectively, $\left\|\Delta E_{Luv}(i,j)\right\|_{L_2} = \left[\left(\Delta L^{*}(i,j)\right)^2 + \left(\Delta u^{*}\right)^2 + \left(\Delta v^{*}\right)^2\right]^{1/2}$ is the norm of color error, ΔL^*, Δu^*, and Δv^* are the difference in the L^*, u^*, and v^* components, respectively, between the two color vectors that present the filtered image and uncorrupted original one for each a pixel (*i,j*) of an image, $\left\|E_{Luv}^{*}(i,j)\right\|_{L_2} = \left[\left(L^{*}\right)^2 + \left(u^{*}\right)^2 + \left(v^{*}\right)^2\right]^{1/2}$ is the norm or magnitude of the uncorrupted original image pixel vector in the $L^*u^*v^*$ space, and $\left\| \cdot \right\|_{L_2}$ is the L_2-vector norm.

3.1 Noise suppression in colour images using the FD filter

The FD filter has been evaluated, and its performance has been compared with INR (Schulte, et al., 2007), MMKNN (Ponomaryov, et al., 2007), AMNF, WMKNN, and ABSTMKNN (Ponomaryov, et al., 2005b), VMF_SAR (Smolka, et al., 2003), WVDF1 (Lukac, 2003) and AVMF (Lukac, et al., 2004) filters.

The 320x320 colour images Lena and Mandrill, were corrupted by impulsive noise in wide range of intensity, from 5% to 30%. Tables 2 and 3 expose the criteria NCD and MAE, respectively. From these tables one can see that FD filter has the best chromaticity and fine details preservation performance in low and middle impulsive noise levels.

Figure 2 presents the processed images for image Mandrill illustrating visual filtering performance. Fig. 2b-c exhibit the filtered images produced by the VMF_SAR and INR filters, respectively. Fig. 2d shows the proposed FD filtered image, where it appears to have a very good subjective quality in comparison with Fig. 2b-c.

3.2 Noise suppression in video colour sequences using the FD filter

Proposed 3D-FD filter uses two colour frames of a video sequence (past and present) which are processed agree to the movement and noise levels present by central sample pixel in

Algorithm	5%	15%	20%	30%
INR filter	1.66	1.76	1.84	2.14
MMKNN filter	1.68	1.91	2.06	2.51
AMNF filter	1.95	2.12	2.22	2.52
WMKNN filter	0.96	1.66	2.07	3.02
ABSTMKNN filter	2.03	2.26	2.40	2.83
VMF_SAR filter	0.44	1.34	1.78	2.78
LWVDF filter	1.87	2.34	2.65	3.62
WVDF1 filter	1.56	2.13	2.50	3.67
AVMF filter	0.96	1.40	1.65	2.35
Proposed FD filter	0.37	0.84	1.15	2.06

Table 2. NCDx10^2 criteria in colour image "Lena" for different impulsive noise intensity.

Algorithm	5%	15%	20%	30%
INR filter	4.41	4.70	4.98	5.98
MMKNN filter	4.41	5.06	5.54	6.92
AMNF filter	5.03	5.45	5.74	6.69
WMKNN filter	2.55	4.75	6.12	9.23
ABSTMKNN filter	5.15	5.78	6.22	7.49
VMF_SAR filter	1.19	3.69	5.00	8.09
LWVDF filter	5.10	6.36	7.34	10.5
WVDF1 filter	4.27	5.82	7.03	10.9
AVMF filter	2.39	3.62	4.40	6.53
Proposed FD filter	0.91	2.17	3.11	5.96

Table 3. MAE criteria in colour image "Lena" for different impulsive noise intensity.

present frame. It is employed a 5x5x2 sliding window processing formed by past and present frames. Difference magnitude values between these frames are computed to obtain a parameter indicating pixel magnitude differences in central pixel respect to neighbouring pixels (Ponomaryov et al., 2009).

The same procedure developed in Section 2.1 should be repeated to compute the basic and four related values in any direction. As in 2D Fuzzy Directional Filter (Sec. 2.1), calculate the absolute difference directional values of a central pixel with respect to its neighbours as an angle variance value between present and past frames. Using angle variance value, we can present the absolute variance directional values to the *SE* (basic) direction only.

Let employ the same Gaussian membership functions for fuzzy values as in the equations 6 and 7, introducing the fuzzy gradient-directional difference values. Numerical experiments realized in this case have given the values used for the functions described in equations 6 and 7: with *med3=0.1*, *med4=0.01* according to the best *PSNR* and *MAE* criteria results.

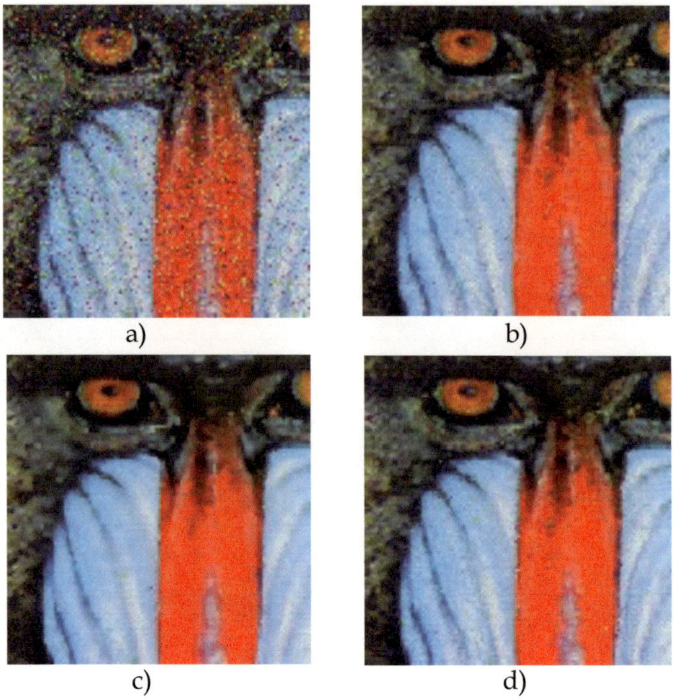

Fig. 2. Filtered images with 15% of impulsive noise: a) Degraded image, b) VMF_SAR, c) INR, d) FD.

Designed fuzzy rules in processing video sequences are oriented to detect the movement and noise levels presence in central component pixel. First fuzzy rule characterizes the confidence in the movement and noise in a central component pixel due to neighbouring fuzzy values in any γ direction. Second fuzzy rule characterizes the confidence in the no movement and no noise in a central pixel in any γ direction. So, the distinctness of the different area (uniform region, edge or fine detail), where a current central pixel component belongs, can be realized using this rule. Third fuzzy rule characterizes the movement-noisy factor and estimate the movement and noise levels presence in a central pixel component using fuzzy values determined for all directions. Finally the fourth fuzzy rule is designed to characterize no movement-no noisy factor, allowing the estimation of no movement and no noise levels presence in a central component pixel using fuzzy values determined for all directions (Ponomaryov et al., 2009).

The parameters obtained using fuzzy rules can be applied efficiently in a decision scheme (Ponomaryov et al., 2009), where decisions if a central component pixel is noisy, or is in movement, or is a free one of both mentioned events, are treated in the denoising scheme. Fuzzy Rules from the first to the fourth determine the novel algorithm based on the fuzzy parameters. Filtering output of the scheme proposed consists of the *j-th* component pixel, which satisfies to the proposed conditions, guaranteeing that edges and fine details should be preserved according to the sort ordering criterion sketched in the scheme by the past and present frames.

Non-stationary noise left by this algorithm, should be processed with the application of the Proposed FD filter developed in Section 2.1. This application permits decreasing the influence of the non-stationary noise left by the video processing scheme. As we are processing a video frame that is free from noise, the Proposed FD filter parameters changes slightly (Ponomaryov et al., 2009).

Algorithms used as comparative are robust and were obtained in literature presenting good results; the 3D-MF is an adaptation to process video sequences of the Median Filter, 3D-VMF is an adaptation of the Vector Median Filter (Astola et al., 1990). 3D-GVDF is a directional algorithm designed to process colour images; we present an adaptation of this filter in 3D environment (Trahanias et al., 1996). Finally the 3D-ATM is an adaptation of the Alpha-trimmed-mean algorithm in video colour sequence processing (Zlokolica et al., 2002).

In Table 4 is shown the results of the proposed 3D filter, the best results are given for our design in MAE criterion for all noise level percentages, and in PSNR criterion the best results are present until 30% of impulsive noise. Video sequence used is the well known Flowers, and results are the averaging for 100 video frames forming Flowers video colour sequence. In Table 5, for Flowers video colour sequence in the averaging results, the best performance was obtained for our methodology. This criterion characterizes colour chromaticity properties preservation. For all noise levels is achieved the best results.

(%) noise	3D-FD filter		3D-MF		3D-VMF		3D-GVDF		3D-ATM	
	MAE	PSNR	MAE	PSNR	MAE	PSNR	MAE	PSNR	MAE	PSNR
5	2,13	29,52	6,65	26,83	6,63	26,78	7,44	25,56	6,80	26,85
15	3,37	27,76	7,19	26,22	7,14	26,20	7,71	25,29	7,35	26,27
30	6,08	25,04	8,59	24,77	8,49	24,69	9,74	23,24	8,88	24,79
40	9,15	22,82	10,8	22,82	10,6	22,70	11,4	22,08	11,5	22,85

Table 4. Averaging Criteria Results for Flowers sequence

(%)Noise	3D-FD filter	3D-MF	3D-VMF	3D-GVDF	3D-ATM
5	0,004	0,014	0,014	0,016	0,014
15	0,007	0,015	0,015	0,016	0,015
25	0,010	0,017	0,017	0,018	0,017
30	0,012	0,018	0,018	0,020	0,018

Table 5. Averaging NCD Criterion Results for Flowers sequence

In Figure 3, for 10th Miss America video frame, the best subjective results are perceived for our proposal, showing better chromaticity properties preservation as well as edge and fine details, against the other ones as can be perceived in zoomed face regions of the Miss America colour frame.

3.3 Noise suppression in gray scale images using the MML filter

The described MML filter was implemented with Simple cut (S) and Andrew's sine (A) influence functions, Laplacian (L) and Uniform (U) distribution functions, and with (D) and without (ND) impulsive noise detector and its performance has been compared with *adaptive center weighted median* (ACWM) (Chen & Wu, 2001), *rank order mean* (ROM) (Abreu

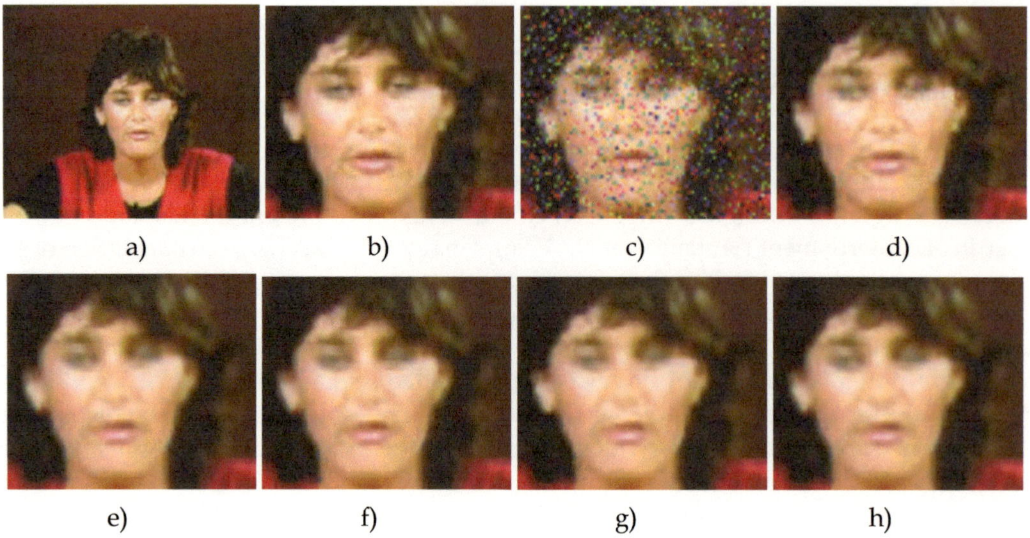

Fig. 3. a) 10th Miss America original image, b) Zoomed region analyzed, c) 15% of impulsive noise, d) Proposal 3D-FD filter, e) 3D-MF; f) 3D-VMF, g) 3D-GVDF, h) 3D-VATM.

Filters	Impulsive noise = 20%		Speckle noise = 0.1	
	PSNR	MAE	PSNR	MAE
ACWM	25.56	8.75	17.73	26.42
ROM	25.20	9.11	21.67	15.78
MFrost	21.62	15.80	22.52	12.82
NLMS-L	22.03	12.83	20.45	14.68
SFWO	23.01	10.24	22.07	14.20
MML (S,L,ND)	24.79	9.11	21.14	17.19
MML (S,U,ND)	25.59	7.38	22.84	13.48
MML (A,L,ND)	24.68	9.33	21.05	17.46
MML (A,U,ND)	25.59	7.40	22.82	13.49
MML (SA,L,D)	24.97	8.05	21.16	17.04
MML (S,U,D)	25.47	7.02	22.68	13.71
MML (A,L,D)	24.40	7.85	21.57	16.21
MML (A,U,D)	25.94	6.96	22.70	13.87

Table 6. Performance results in image "Lena" obtained by different filters.

et al., 1996), *Normalized Least Mean Squares L* (NLMS-L) (Kotropoulos & Pitas, 1996), *Sampled-Function Weighted Order* (SFWO) (Öten & De Figueiredo, 2002), and *Modified Frost* (MFrost) (Lukin et al., 1998) filters.

Table 6 shows the performance results for "Lena" image degraded with 20% of impulsive noise and σ^2=0.1 of speckle noise. From Table 6, the proposed MML filter provides better noise suppression and detail preservation than other filters in the most of cases. Figure 4 exhibits the filtered images in the case of 20% of impulsive noise. The restored image by proposed MML filter appears to have better subjective quality in comparison with other filters.

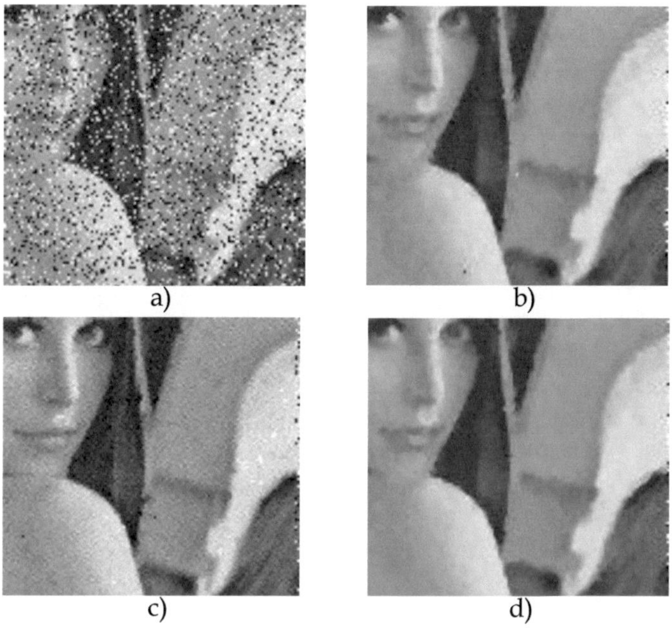

Fig. 4. Filtered images with 20% of impulsive noise: a) Degraded image, b) ROM, c) ACWM, d) MML (A,L,ND).

3.4 Noise suppression in colour images using the MML filter

The described MML filter was adapted to work in colour imaging (Toledo-Lopez et al., 2008). The proposed filter is called as Vector Median M-type L (VMML) -filter and its performance has been compared with *vector median* (VM), *basic vector directional* (BVD), *generalized vector directional* (GVD), *adaptive* GVD (AGVD), *double window* GVD (GVD_DW), *multiple non-parametric* (MAMNFE) (Plataniotis et al., 1997) (Trahanias et al., 1996), *vector median M-type K-nearest neighbor* (VMMKNN) (Ponomaryov, et al., 2005), and *fast adaptive similarity* VM (FASVM) (Smolka et al., 2003) filters.

The 320x320 "Lena" color image was corrupted by 20% of impulsive noise. Table 7 shows that the performance criteria are often better for the proposed VMML filter in comparison when other filters in the most of cases. The visual results are given in Figure 5.

3.5 Noise suppression in colour SAR images using the MML filter

To demonstrate the performance of the proposed filtering scheme we applied it for filtering of SAR images, which naturally have speckle noise. The filtering results are presented in Figure 6 for "Rio Grande" SAR image. It is possible to see analyzing the filtering images that speckle noise can be efficiently suppressed, while the sharpness and fine feature are preserved using the proposed filter with and without noise detector.

Algorithm	PSNR	MAE	MCRE	NCD
VM	21.15	10.73	0.035	0.038
BVD	20.41	12.72	0.043	0.045
GVD	20.67	11.18	0.038	0.040
AGVD	22.01	11.18	0.028	0.036
GVDF_DW	22.59	10.09	0.028	0.039
MAMNFE	22.67	9.64	0.027	0.035
VMMKNN (S)	23.15	10.00	0.033	0.034
VMMKNN (A)	23.07	10.01	0.033	0.035
FASVM	24.80	5.00	0.025	0.017
VMML (S,L,ND)	25.81	6.49	0.026	0.016
VMML (S,U,ND)	25.88	5.53	0.026	0.026
VMML (A,L,ND)	25.88	7.00	0.026	0.015
VMML (A,U,ND)	26.52	5.36	0.022	0.015
VMML (S,L,D)	26.46	2.90	0.023	0.027
VMML (S,U,D)	26.47	2.79	0.023	0.025
VMML (A,L,D)	26.59	3.00	0.022	0.029
VMML (A,U,D)	26.73	2.74	0.021	0.025

Table 7. Comparative restoration results for 20% impulsive noise for colour image "Lena"

a) b) c)

d) e) f)

Fig. 5. Subjective visual qualities of restored colour image "Lena", (a) Original test image "Lena", (b) Input noisy image (with 20% of impulsive noise), (c) FASVM filtering image, (d) VMMKNN filtered image, (e) Proposed VMML filtering image (S,E,ND), and (f) Proposed VMML filtering image (S,E,D).

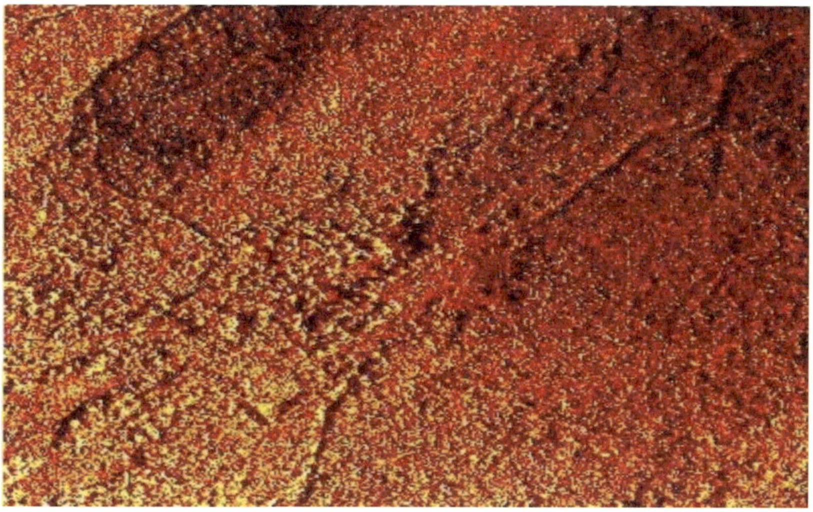

(a)

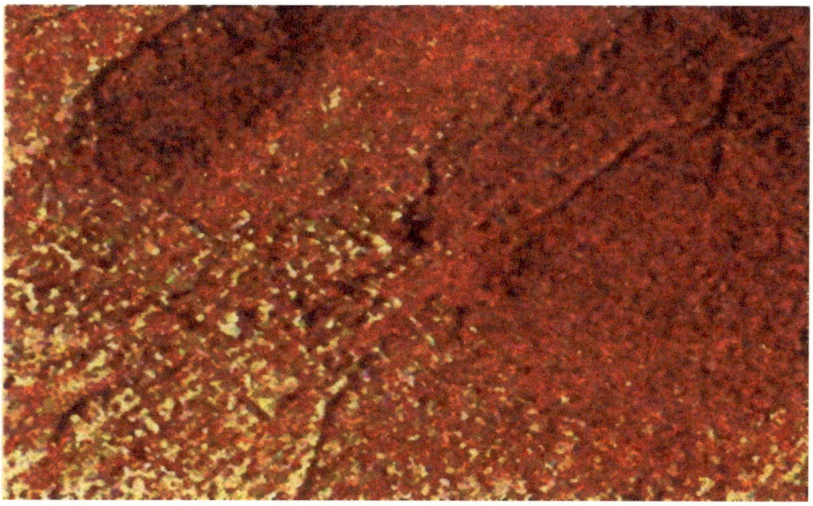

(b)

Fig. 6. Visual results of despeckled SAR image. a) Original image "Manzano", 2m resolution, Ku Band SAR, 15GHz, vertical polarization, source Sandia National Lab., b) Despeckled image from (a) with the proposed VMML filter (S,U,D).

4. Conclusions

The proposed FD filter connects two commonly used in colour imaging techniques: directional processing where vector order statistics are employed, and fuzzy logic procedures that applied membership values found for pixels to be processed. FD filter has presented good performance in terms of noise suppression, edge and fine detail preservation, and chromaticity preservation properties, as well in visual subjective analysis. The proposed MML filter is able to remove impulsive noise and preserve the edges and details in gray scale and colour imaging. The proposed MML filter uses the robust MM-estimator and utilizes an impulsive noise detector to provide better noise suppression, detail preservation, and in the case of colour imaging, provides better color retention. The VMML filter has demonstrated better quality of image processing, both in visual and analytical sense in comparison with different known colour image processing algorithms.

5. Acknowledgement

The authors would thank National Polytechnic Institute of Mexico for their support to realize this work.

6. References

Abreu, E., Lightstone, M., Mitra, S. K. & Arakawa, K. (1996). A new efficient approach for the removal of impulse noise from highly corrupted images. *IEEE Trans. Image Process.*, Vol.5, No.6, 1012-1025, ISSN:1057-7149

Aizenberg, I., Astola, J., Bregin, T., Butakoff, C., Egiazarian, K., & Paily, D. (2003). Detectors of the impulsive noise and new effective filters for the impulsive noise reduction, *Proc. SPIE Image Process., Algorithms and Syst. II*, Vol. 5014, ISBN: 9780819448149, pp. 419-428, San Jose, Ca, USA

Astola, J., Haavisto, P., Neuvo, Y. (1990). Vector Median Filters. *Proceedings of the IEEE*, Vol. 78, 678-689.

Astola, J. & Kuosmanen, P. (1997). *Fundamentals of Nonlinear Digital Filtering*, CRC Press. ISBN:0-8493-2570-6, Boca Raton-New York, USA

Bovik, A. (2000). *Handbook of Image and Video Processing*, Academic Press., ISBN:0121197921, San Diego CA

Chen, T. & Wu, H. R. (2001). Adaptive impulse detection using center-weighted median filters. *IEEE Signal Processing Letters*, Vol.8, No.1, 1-3, ISSN:1070-9908

Gallegos-Funes, F., Varela-Benitez, J., & Ponomaryov, V. (2008). Rank M-Type L (RM L)-Filter for image denoising, *IEICE Trans. Funds. Electronics, Comms. Computer Sciences*, Vol.E91A, No.12, 3817-3819, ISSN:0916-8508

Kotropoulos, C., & Pitas, I. (1996). Adaptive LMS *L*-filters for noise suppression in images. *IEEE Trans. Image Process.*, Vol.5, No.12, 1596-1609, ISSN:1057-7149

Kotropoulos, C. & Pitas, I. (2001). *Nonlinear Model-Based Image/Video Processing and Analysis*, John Wiley & Sons, ISBN:0-471-37735-X, New York

Lukac, R. (2003). Adaptive vector median filtering. Pattern Recognition Letters, Vol. 24, 1889-1899, ISSN:0167-8655

Lukac, R., Smolka, B., Plataniotis, K.N., Venetsanopoulos, A.N. (2004). Selection weighted vector directional filters. *Comput. Vision and Image Unders.*, Vol. 94, 140-167, ISSN:1077-3142

Lukin, V., Melnik, V., Chemerovsky, V., Astola, J., Saarinen, K. (1998). Hard-switching adaptive filter for speckle image processing, *Proc. SPIE Mathematical Modeling and Estimation Techniques in Computer Vision,* Vol. 3457, pp. 31-42, San Diego, USA

Öten, R., De Figueiredo, R.J.P. (2002). Sampled-Function weighted order filters. *IEEE Trans. Circuits and Systems-II,* Vol.49, No.1, 1-10, ISSN:1057-7130

Plataniotis, K. N., Androutsos, D., Vinayagamoorthy, S. & Venetsanopoulos, A. N. (1997). Color image processing using adaptive multichannel filters. *IEEE Trans. Image Process.*, Vol.6, No.7, 933-949,. ISSN:1057-7149

Plataniotis, K. N., & Venetsanopoulos, A. N. (2000). *Color Image Processing and Applications,* Springer-Verlag, Berlin Heidelberg, ISBN:3-540-66953-1

Ponomaryov, V., Gallegos-Funes, F., Rosales-Silva, A. (2005a). Real-Time color image processing using order statistics filters. *Journal of Mathematical Imaging and Vision,* Vol. 23, No. 3, 315–319, ISSN:0924-9907

Ponomaryov, V.I., Gallegos-Funes, F.J., Rosales-Silva, A. (2005b). Real-time color imaging based on RM-filters for impulsive noise reduction. *Journal of Imaging Science and Technology,* Vol. 49, No. 3, 205-219, ISSN:1062-3701.

Ponomaryov, V., Gallegos, F., Rosales, A., Loboda, I. (2006). 3D Vector Directional Filters to Process Video Sequences. *Lecture Notes in Computer Science Springer,* Vol. 4225/2006, ISBN: 978-3-540-46556-0.

Ponomaryov, V., Rosales, A., Gallegos, F., Loboda, I. (2007). Adaptive Vector Directional Filters to Process Multichannel Images. *IEICE Trans. Funds. Electronics Comms. Computer Science,* Vol. E90B, No. 2, 429-430, ISSN: 0916-8508.

Ponomaryov V, Rosales-Silva A., Gallegos-Funes F (2009) 3D Filtering of Colour Video Sequences Using Fuzzy Logic and Vector Order Statistics, Lect. Not. in Artif. Intell., Vol. LNAI 5807, pp.210-221. ISSN:0302-9743.

Ponomaryov, V., Rosales-Silva, A., Gallegos-Funes, F., Perez-Meana H. (2010). Fuzzy Directional (FD) Filter to Remove Impulse Noise from Colour Images. *IEICE Trans. Funds. Electronics Comms. Computer Science,* Vol. E93A, No. 2, 570-572, ISSN: 0916-8508.

Russo, F., & Ramponi, G. (1994). Nonlinear fuzzy operators for image processing. *Signal Process. Lett.*, Vol. 38, No. 4, 429-440, ISSN:1000-9000

Schulte, S., Morillas, S., Gregori, V., Kerre, E. (2007). A new fuzzy color correlated impulse oise reduction method. *IEEE Trans. Image Process.,* Vol. 16, No. 10, 2565-2575, ISSN:1057-7149

Smolka, B., Lukac, R., Chydzinski, A., Plataniotis, K.N., Wojciechowski W. (2003). Fast adaptive similarity based impulsive noise reduction filter. *Real-Time Imaging,* 261-276, ISSN:1077-2014

Toledo-Lopez, A., Gallegos-Funes, F.J., Ponomaryov, V. (2008). Vector Median M-Type L Filter to process multichannel images. *Lecture Notes in Computer Science,* Vol.5197, 54-61, ISSN 0302-9743

Trahanias, P. E., Karakos, D. G., & Venetsanopoulos, A. N. (1996). Directional processing of color images: Theory and experimental results. *IEEE Trans. Image Process.*, Vol.5, No.6, 868-880, ISSN:1057-7149.

Zlokolica, V., Philips, W., Van De Ville, D. (2002). A new non-linear filter for video processing. *Proceedings of the third IEEE Benelux Signal Processing Symposium*, 221-224.

9

Three-Dimensional Ultrasound Imaging Utilizing Hardware Accelerator Based on FPGA

Keiichi Satoh[1], Jubee Tada[2], Gensuke Goto[2], Toshio Koga[2],
Kazuhiro Kondo[2] and Yasutaka Tamura[2]
[1]*Yamagata university of Graduate School (current affiliation is Fujitsu. Ltd.),*
[2]*Yamagata University of Graduate School*
Japan

1. Introduction

We have developed a 3D ultrasound imaging system involving computations for use in medical diagnostic applications [1,2]. This system enables us to observe 3D images of moving objects for each transmission. Therefore, we can acquire a 3D image sequence at a high frame rate. Fig. 1 shows a 3D image reconstructed by our 3D ultrasound imaging system. In the pork block, a needle is inserted as a marker.
In the present system, a 3D image reconstruction algorithm is implemented by using the C language software (SW). When processing is performed by a personal computer (PC) with Pentium 4 2.53 [GHz] CPU and DDR512 [MB] memory, the latency for generating a 3D image is approximately 40 s. As apparent from the above latency value, it would be difficult to realize high-speed image reconstruction by employing a SW implementation approach.
Reduction in the processing time is one of the most important issues in practical applications. As a solution to this issue, we have investigated the HW implementation of the algorithm.

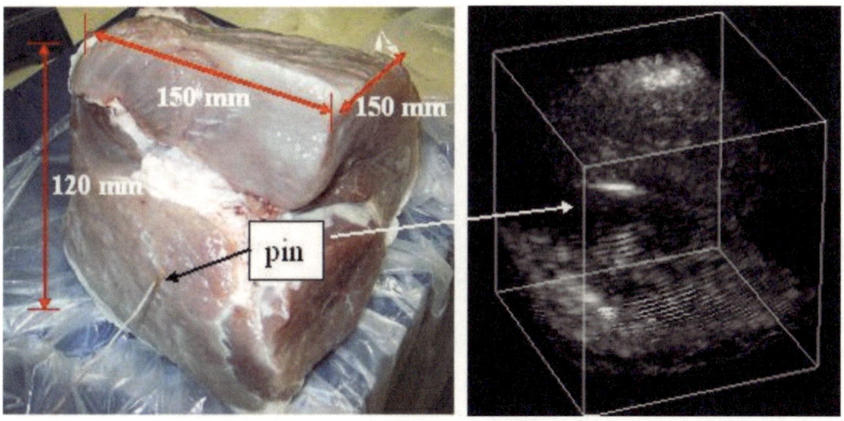

(a) Pork block (b) Reconstructed 3D image

(Image size: a cube of dimensions 70 × 70 × 70 mm)

Fig. 1. Three-dimensional image reconstructed by our system.

Presently, FPGA is mainly utilized to implement algorithms in various applications such as radio telescopes [3], streaming computations [4], and neurocomputing [5]. The reason for using FPGA is that it enables us to design flexible HW at a low cost by using a reconfiguration function. Thus, we decided to employ the HW implementation approach and used FPGA as the target device.

In this paper, we first present the 3D image reconstruction algorithm and then describe the processing system and HW architecture. Next, we search critical path delay in the HW and the modify the path to accelerate raising the maximum frequency. Finally, we evaluate the performance (latency required for a 3D image output) and the scale of the synthesized HW.

2. Principle of ultrasound transmission and reception

Ultrasound waves are simultaneously transmitted from N_T (must be in powers of 2) transmitters and the reflected echo waveforms are detected by N_R receivers from two-dimensional (2D) transducer arrays. We use sinusoidal waves of frequency f_0 modulated by a system of Walsh functions synchronized by a clock signal.

The period of the clock signal Δt is equal to an integral multiple of the sine wave period $1/f_0$. The transmitting and receiving processes are repeated at a constant period. The transmission codes corresponding to the transmitters are changed in every transmission and reception cycle. At the p-th transmission and reception cycle, the transmission signal corresponding to the i-th (i = 0, 1, 2, ... , N_T-1) transmitter at $\boldsymbol{x}_{Tj}$ and the waveform detected by the j-th (j = 0, 1, 2, ... , N_R-1) receiver at $\boldsymbol{x}_{Ri}$ are denoted by $u_j^{(p)}(t)$ and $r_i^{(p)}(t)$, respectively. In order to simplify the discussion, the origins (t = 0) of these functions are fixed at the starting positions of each transmitting pulse.

The pulse transmitted from the i-th transmitter in the p-th cycle is given as

$$u_i^{(p)}(t) = \begin{cases} \sum_{k=0}^{N_T-1} w_{(i\oplus p)k} \cdot f(t - k \cdot \Delta t) \cdots 0 \le t \le N_T \Delta t \\ 0 \qquad \cdots \ t < 0,\ t > N_T \Delta t \end{cases} \tag{1}$$

where

$$f(t) = \begin{cases} \sin(2\pi f_0 t) & 0 \le t \le \Delta t \\ 0 & t < 0, t > \Delta t \end{cases} \tag{2}$$

is a single sinusoidal pulse of frequency f_0, w_{nm} denotes the (n, m) component of the $N_T \times N_T$ Hadamard matrix (to simplify the equation, the column and row numbers are indexed from 0 to N–1), and $\oplus$ denotes the dyadic sum, i.e., the modulo 2 addition for every corresponding bit of binary numbers. Fig. 2 shows a schematic diagram of ultrasound transmission and reception in which the coded *wavefront* generated by Walsh functions is employed.

3. Principle of image reconstruction

The equations given below represent a mathematical model that can be used for image reconstruction. A sequence of complex pixel values, $s^{(p)}(\boldsymbol{x})$, corresponding to the position vector $\boldsymbol{x}$ is given by

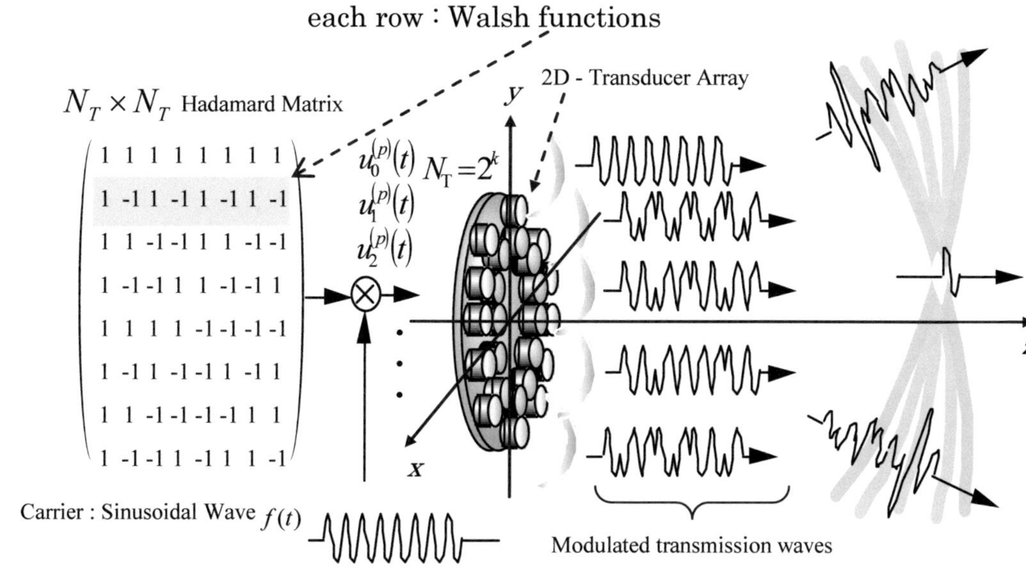

Fig. 2. Schematic drawing of the coded *wavefront* generated by Walsh functions.

$$s^{(p)}(\boldsymbol{x}) = \int \sum_{j=0}^{N_R-1} r_j^{(p)}(t+\tau_j) \sum_{i=0}^{N_T-1} u_i^{(p)}(\text{t-}\tau_i)^* dt$$

$$= \int \sum_{j=0}^{N_R-1} r_j^{(p)}\left(t+\frac{|\boldsymbol{x}-\boldsymbol{x}_{Rj}|}{c}\right) \sum_{i=0}^{N_T-1} u_i^{(p)}\left(\text{t-}\frac{|\boldsymbol{x}-\boldsymbol{x}_{Ti}|}{c}\right)^* dt, \tag{3}$$

where $\boldsymbol{\tau}_i$ and $\boldsymbol{\tau}_j$ denote the sound propagation delays between the position $\boldsymbol{x}$ and the transducers, the symbol * indicates complex conjugate, x_i and x_j represent the position vectors of the i-th transmitter and j-th receiver, respectively, and c is the speed of sound. Fig. 3 shows the concept of image reconstruction.
The delay between positions $\boldsymbol{x}$ and $\boldsymbol{x}_i$ is given by

$$\tau_i = \frac{|\boldsymbol{x}-\boldsymbol{x}_i|}{c}, \tag{4}$$

and is computed according to the following approximation:

$$\tau = \frac{\sqrt{(x-x_i)^2+(y-y_i)^2+z^2}}{c} \tag{5}$$

$$\approx \frac{R - r_i\cos(\varphi-\varphi_i)\sin\theta + r_i^2/(2R)}{c}, \tag{6}$$

$$\text{where} \quad R = |\boldsymbol{x}| = \sqrt{x^2+y^2+z^2}, \tag{7}$$

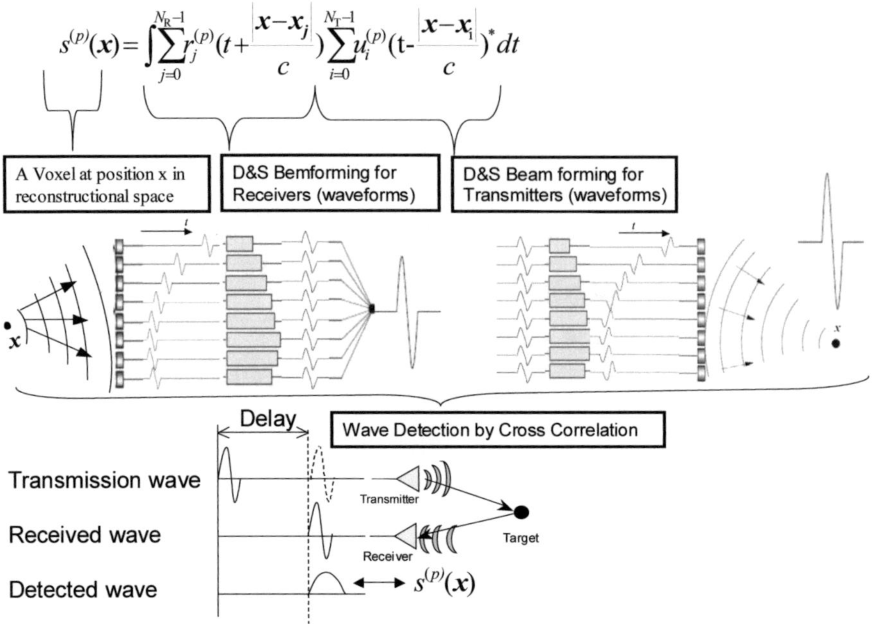

Fig. 3. Concept of image reconstruction.

$$\theta = \sin^{-1}(\sqrt{x^2 + y^2} / R), \tag{8}$$

and

$$\varphi = \tan^{-1}(y / x) \tag{9}$$

represent the polar coordinate of a position in 3D space, $r_i = \sqrt{x_i^2 + y_i^2}$ and φ_i gives the polar coordinate of the *i*-th element in the array plane. Fig. 4 shows the geometry of the transducer array and the image space.

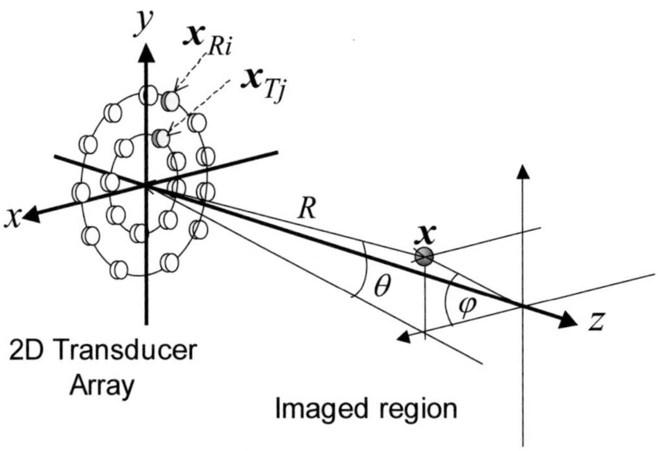

Fig. 4. Geometry of the array and imaged region.

When it is known that the object is stationary, a single image can be obtained as an accumulation of the complex image sequence:

$$I(\boldsymbol{x}) = \left| \sum_p s^{(p)}(\boldsymbol{x}) \right|^2 . \tag{10}$$

4. Image reconstruction algorithm

The image reconstruction algorithm [6] involves the use of matched filter banks; it is generally composed of the following operations: a beamforming operation by delay and sum (D&S) and a matching operation by cross-correlation. The operations are performed in the frequency domain. Cross-correlation is performed by FFT, complex multiplications, and IFFT [7]. Frequency domain beamforming is computationally efficient [8,9]. Additionally, it is advantageous for HW implementation [9]. First, beamforming and cross-correlation in the frequency domain are performed by simple multiplications. Consequently, these computations can be performed with lesser computational complexity than that in the time domain. Second, the implementation of the frequency domain beamformer requires lesser hardware resource than that required in the time domain. The frequency domain beamformer requires few complex multipliers, while the time domain beamformer requires FIR filters by MACs (Multiply and ACcumulation). The time domain beamformer requires more HW resources because the FIR filter must contain more taps to achieve high throughput. Further, for HW implementation on an FPGA it is difficult to obtain a large number of taps with the limited FPGA resources. On the other hand, the frequency domain beamformer requires few complex multipliers for high throughput. Thus, the resource utilization is lesser than that in the time domain. Consequently, the HW architecture can provide high cost performance. Fortunately, the FPGA selected as the target device provides many high-performance dedicated multipliers; it is suitable for the HW implementation on the FPGA to utilize the multipliers for frequency domain image reconstruction.

From the above discussion, it is efficient for the HW to perform the operation in the frequency domain.

A schematic diagram of the operation is shown in Fig. 5. The filters compute the cross-correlations between the outputs of the received beamformer and the reference waveforms. Each signal is obtained by performing the D&S operation on the reference and received beamformer waveforms.

We have introduced a paraxial approximation [6] to compute the delays for the D&S operation in order to reduce the computational complexity. The procedure of the algorithm is as follows:

i. The reference and received waveforms are transformed by using FFT into those in the frequency domain. The components within a given frequency band are processed. Consequently, the computational complexity is reduced. Let $H_i^{(p)}(f)$ ($i = 0,\ldots, N_T - 1$) and $R_j^{(p)}(f)$ ($j = 0,\ldots, N_R - 1$) denote the frequency-domain description of the transmitted waveform related to the i-th transmitter and the received waveform related to the j-th receiver for a frequency f in the p-th transmission, respectively.

ii. The reference waveform $B_H^{(p)}(\theta,\varphi,f)$ corresponding to the direction (θ,φ) is computed by the D&S operation using $H_i^{(p)}(f)$ and phase rotations ($e^{-j2\pi f \tau_{\theta,\varphi,i}}$) that

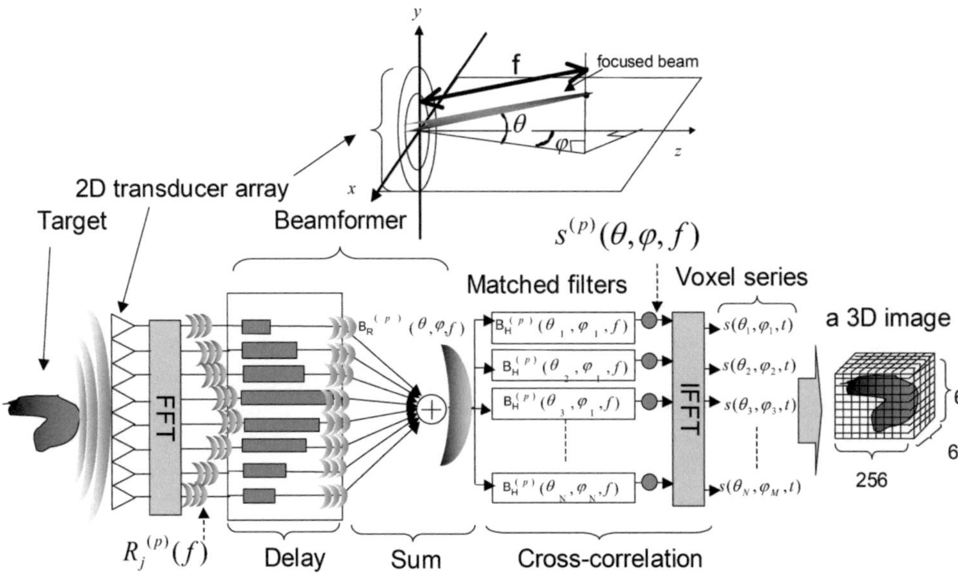

Fig. 5. Schematic representation of image reconstruction algorithm.

are obtained from the delay for the transmitters, which are stored as filter coefficients. Next, the waveforms received by the receivers are transformed by the FFT to the frequency domain, and $R_j^{(p)}(f)$ for each receiver is input to the beamformer containing phase rotations ($e^{j2\pi f \tau_{\theta,\varphi,j}}$) of the receivers; subsequently, the received beamform $B_R^{(p)}(\theta,\varphi,f)$ focused in the direction (θ,φ) in the frequency domain is computed. Each beamform is represented as follows.

$$B_H^{(p)}(\theta,\varphi,f) = \sum_{i=0}^{N_T-1} H_i^{(p)}(f) e^{-j2\pi f \tau_{\theta,\varphi,i}} \tag{11}$$

$$B_R^{(p)}(\theta,\varphi,f) = \sum_{j=0}^{N_R-1} R_j^{(p)}(f) e^{j2\pi f \tau_{\theta,\varphi,j}} \tag{12}$$

iii. Cross-correlation is performed using the matched filters, and IFFT is carried out for $B_R^{(p)}(\theta,\varphi,f)$ and $B_H^{(p)}(\theta,\varphi,f)$. First, the matched filters perform the operation, which is expressed as follows.

$$s^{(p)}(\theta,\varphi,f) = B_R^{(p)}(\theta,\varphi,f) \cdot B_H^{(p)}(\theta,\varphi,f)^* \tag{13}$$

$$= \sum_j R_j^{(p)}(f) e^{j2\pi f \tau_{\theta,\varphi,j}} \cdot \sum_i H_i^{(p)}(f)^* e^{j2\pi f \tau_{\theta,\varphi,i}} \tag{14}$$

This operation is referred to as complex multiplication; $s^{(p)}(\theta,\varphi,f)$ denotes the output result from the matched filter to form a beamform in the direction (θ,φ) for the p-th ultrasound transmission and reception cycle.

iv. The IFFT of $s^{(p)}(\theta,\varphi,f)$ is performed and the cross-correlation is completed. Consequently, complex voxel series is reconstructed in the direction (θ,φ). The data samples output from the HW is 2048 [samples/line] × 2 (real/imaginary). The series is in the time domain, and it is scaled to the spatial domain.

$$s^{(p)}(\theta,\varphi,t) = \mathfrak{I}^{-1}\left\{s^{(p)}(\theta,\varphi,f)\right\} \tag{15}$$

v. The abovementioned sequence of operations is repeated for all the directions $(N_\theta \times N_\varphi = 64 \times 64)$ in the reconstruction space.

vi. Finally, the output voxels form a 3D image. The abovementioned operation is repeated for every shot of ultrasound.

5. Computational complexity for the algorithm

We estimate the computational complexity of the algorithm on the basis of the parameters shown in Table 1. The obtained result is shown in Fig. 6. Here, "op" is a unit of computational complexity that denotes the number of multiplications or additions. As shown in Fig. 6, the D&S operation accounts for approximately 80% of the overall operation. This is because this operation involves complex multiplication, as shown in equations (11) and (12); the operation must be performed for all the directions in the imaging space. Therefore, the parallel implementation of the D&S operation should be effective for high-speed operation.

Parameters	Values
Number of receivers [ch]	32
Number of transmitters [ch]	32
Observed data length for a channel (time domain) [samples/ch]	2048
Observed data length for a channel (frequency domain) [samples/ch]	512
Number of focus directions in the image reconstruction space [line]	64 × 64

Table 1. Parameters for estimating the number of operations.

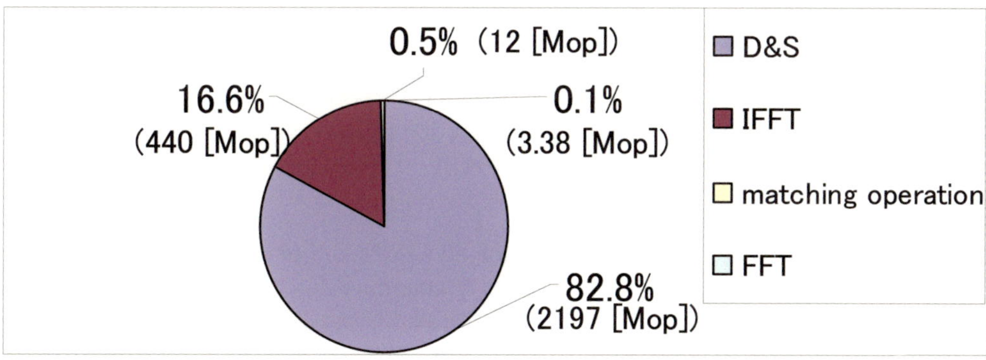

Fig. 6. Classification of operations.

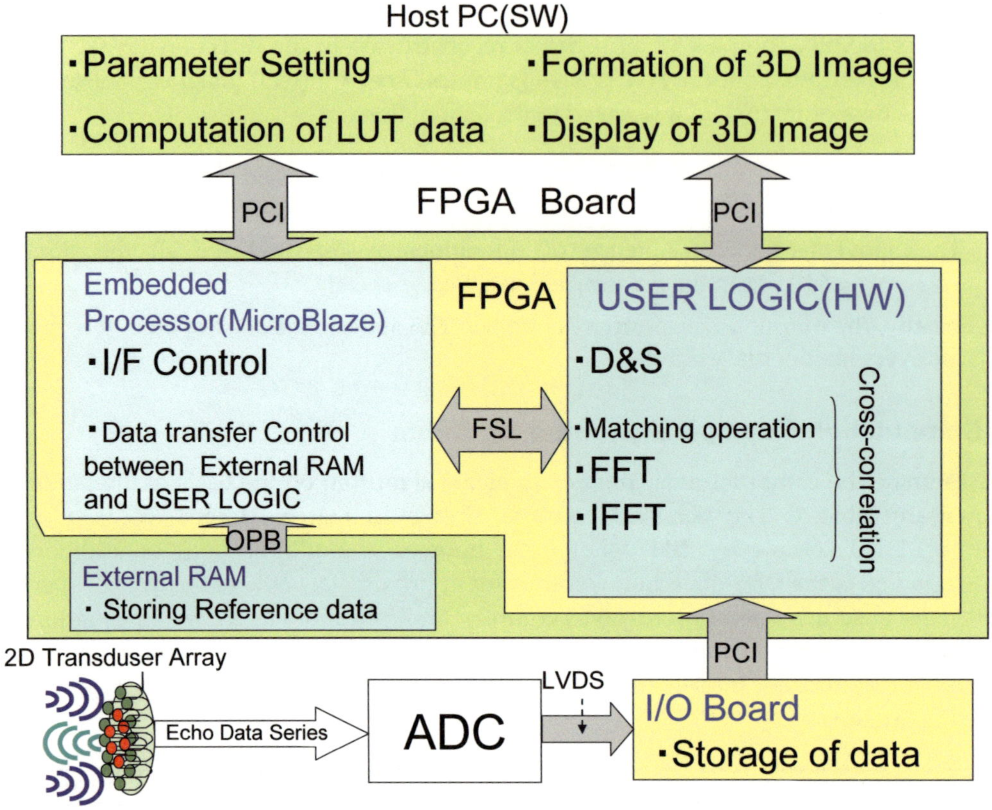

Fig. 7. Operational system.

6. Processing system

An outline of the processing system is described in this section. A schematic diagram of the system is shown in **Fig. 7**. The system consists of a host PC, the FPGA, an external RAM, ADCs, I/O boards, and a 2D transducer array. The function of each unit is as follows.

Host PC

Preprocessing and postprocessing operations are performed. In the former, the parameters required for the operation—reference waveforms and delay data—are determined. Subsequently, the obtained data are transferred to the FPGA board. In postprocessing, the host PC accepts the output of the FPGA and forms a 3D image, which is then displayed. The processing is repeated for every output of the FPGA.

FPGA

The use of FPGAs enables us to reconfigure the HW architecture when the specifications of the imaging system change. The FPGA consists of an embedded processor and user-defined logic (USER LOGIC). MicroBlaze (soft-core processor) is used as the embedded processor [10], and it performs I/F control of the PCI, fast simplex link (FSL) [10], and on-chip peripheral bus (OPB) [10]. In addition, it controls the data transfer between the host PC and USER LOGIC and between the external RAM and USER LOGIC. The delay data are stored in the internal RAM of the FPGA since the data size is a few hundred kilobytes. USER LOGIC is a dedicated operational unit that performs the D&S operation and cross-correlation. After USER LOGIC accepts the reference and delay data through the embedded processor, it performs the D&S operation and cross-correlation by using the echo data obtained from the I/O board. Further, the operated results are output to the host PC through the PCI.

External RAM

The reference waveforms for ultrasound transmissions are stored in the external RAM because the total size of the data for the operation is a few megabytes.

ADC (A/D Converter)

The echo data observed by the 2D transducer array are converted to 16 [bit/sample] digital data.

I/O Board

It temporarily stores the echo data obtained from the ADC. When USER LOGIC requests echo data for starting an operation, the I/O board transfers the required data.

2D Transducer Array

The 2D transducer array comprises 32 transmitters and 32 receivers.

7. HW design

The functional block diagram of USER LOGIC shown in Fig. 8 is developed in a manner similar to that shown in Fig. 9. H-data, T-data, and R-data in Fig. 9 denote the reference waveform data in the frequency domain, echo data in the frequency domain, and delay corresponding to each transmitter and receiver needed to perform D&S operation, respectively. The functions of the components included in USER LOGIC are as follows:

FFT

The echo data are transformed into the frequency domain.

H-data and T-data Look-up Table (LUT)

The H-data LUT contains H-data for one-shot image reconstruction [11], while the T-data LUT contains the T-data corresponding to the distance between the focuses in the image reconstruction space and the devices in the 2D transducer array.

D&S Beamformer

The D&S operation is performed with the H- and R-data for each channel. The T-data are read from the T-data LUT and the phase rotations are computed. Subsequently, the product of the phase rotation element and the waveform data is computed, and the products are then summed. Finally, the outputs of the reference and the received beamforms are generated.

Matching Operator

$s^{(p)}(\theta,\varphi,f)$ is obtained as the product of the outputs of the reference and the received beamform; this product is considered as a matching operation.

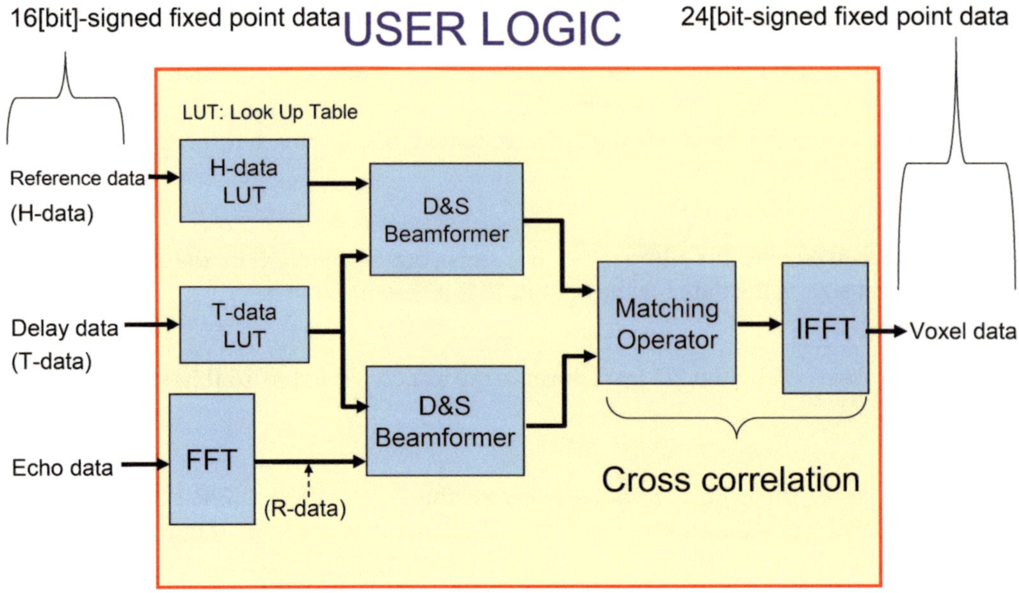

Fig. 8. Functional block diagram for HW design.

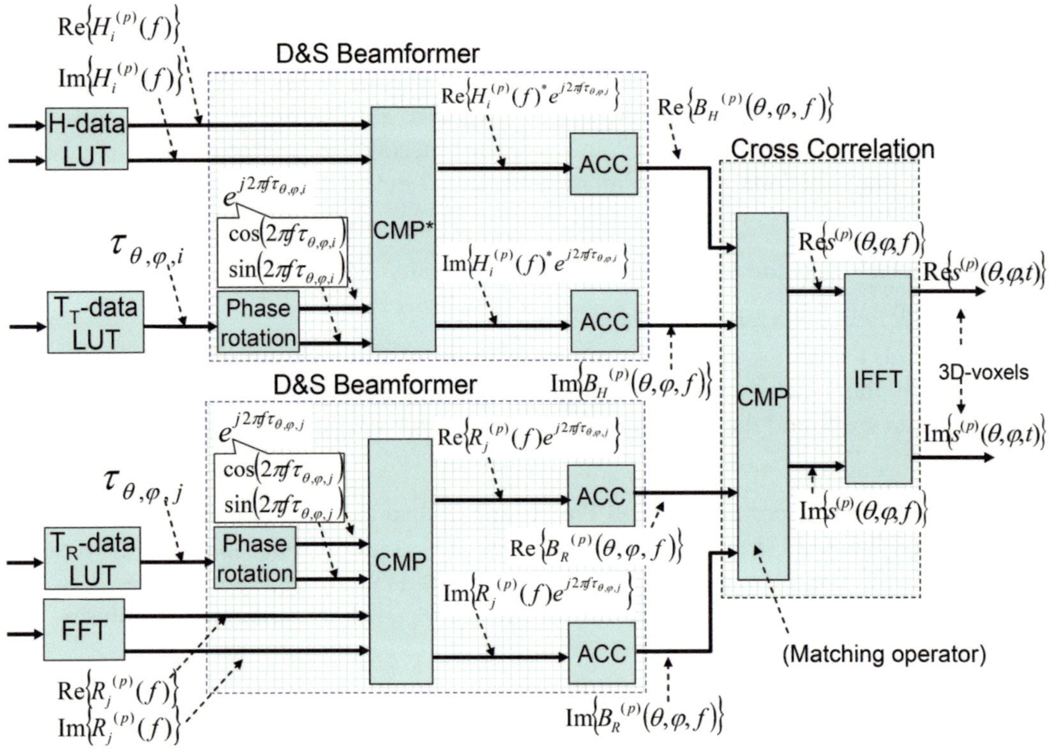

Fig. 9. Architecture mapping based on functional blocks.

IFFT

IFFT is performed for $s^{(p)}(\theta,\varphi,f)$ to complete the cross-correlation, and the complex voxel data $s^{(p)}(\theta,\varphi,t)$ are output.

Architecture mapping is presented in Fig. 9 for the HW design; the mapping is based on functional block diagram shown in Fig. 8. T_T- and T_R-data denote the delay corresponding to each transmitter and receiver, respectively. In addition, the figure includes the above equations to associate with the operational flow in the HW. We describe the function of each HW unit in detail.

The FFT and IFFT operators are realized by using Xilinx IP (Architecture type is Radix-2, pipelined, streaming I/O); the operations are performed for every one-channel data series and R-data (received data series in the frequency domain) are output as complex numbers.

The phase rotation unit (Fig. 10) [11] performs phase rotation using the T-data. The frequency f and delay τ are treated as discrete data. When the D&S operation begins, T-data from the RAM are input into the unit and an enable signal is asserted. This signal drives a counter that counts the number of frequencies. Sampled f_k and τ_l are input to the multiplier, and phase data $f_k \cdot \tau_l$ are output. The effective phase rotation angles are determined by the fractions of the phase data $f_k \cdot \tau_l$. Thus, fractional bits are used as effective data. The bits are then input to the sin/cos table ROM (Xilinx IP) to generate phase rotation. The table ROM outputs the sin and cos data corresponding to the ROM address; finally, the unit generates phase rotations.

CMP (Fig. 11) [11] and CAD (Fig. 12) [11] are the 18-bit multiplier and adder for the complex data, respectively. The units are composed of four multipliers and two adders; embedded multipliers are utilized to generate the multipliers. The CMPs in the D&S beamformer obtain the product of the waveform data and the phase rotation element. In fact, the CMP performs phase adjustment of the waveform data and the CMP used in the matching operator is utilized for the matching operation between the H-beam and the R-beam data in the frequency domain cross-correlation.

ACC (Fig. 13) [11] is the accumulator used to operate the beam data; it comprises an adder, two registers, a DMUX, and dual port RAM (Xilinx IP). The unit simultaneously performs addition and data write/read from the RAM for every clock cycle with a sample data output from the CMP in the D&S beamformer. The ACC repeats the operation for all the channel waveform data output from the CMP for the D&S operation and accumulates the results. Further, each beam data series is output by the switching of the DMUX when accumulation for all the channels is completed.

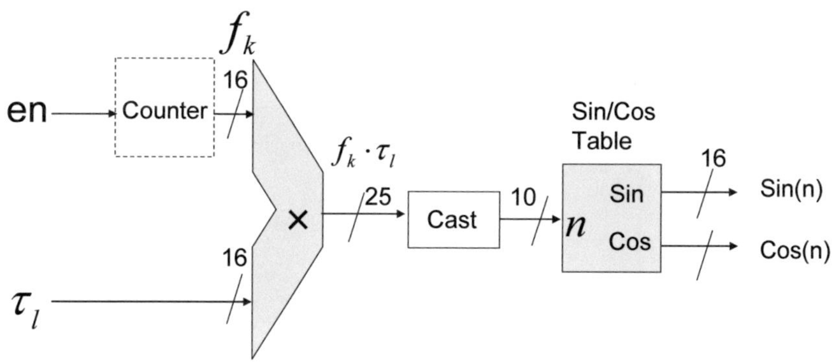

Fig. 10. Phase rotation unit.

$$(a_1 + jb_1)(a_2 + jb_2) = a_1a_2 - b_1b_2 + j(a_1b_2 + a_2b_1)$$

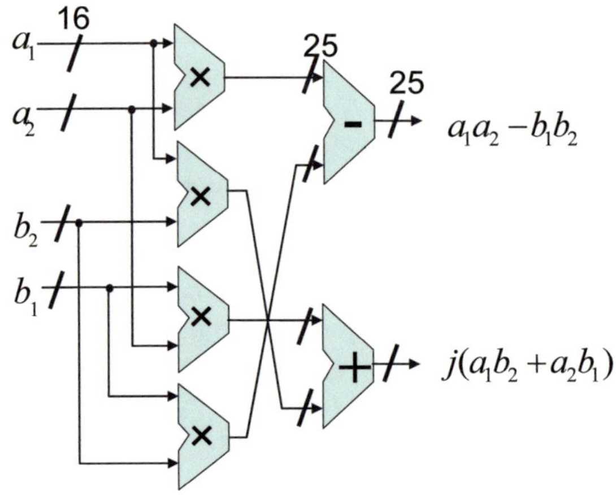

Fig. 11. Complex multiplier (CMP)

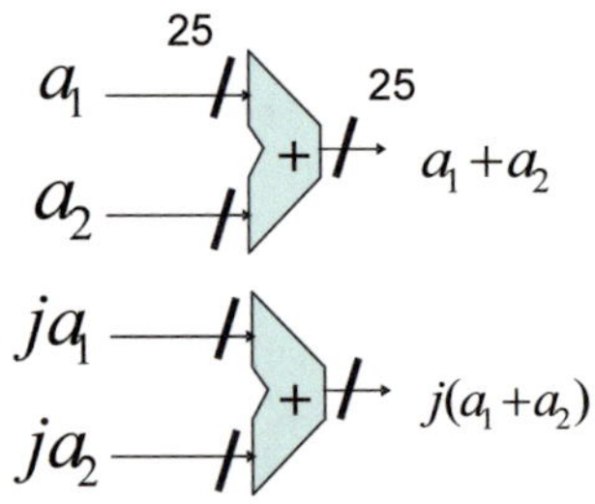

Fig. 12. Complex adder (CAD).

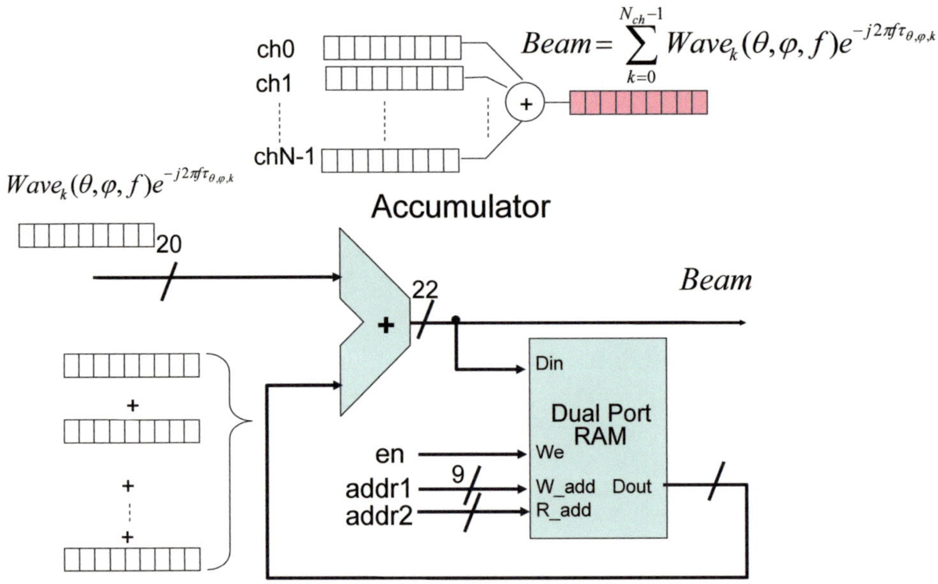

Fig. 13. Accumulator (ACC).

The architecture based on Fig. 6 corresponds to the use of the minimum number of functional units. In fact, the optimization placing multioperational units is not applied for the architecture to realize an efficient parallel operation. Here, we consider where the parallel operation is possible. Consequently, the parallel operation of the D&S operation is possible for optimization because the complex multiplication and accumulation can be performed for the waveform data of every channel. Fig. 14 shows refined architecture of the system shown in Fig. 9. The MicroBlaze MPU transfers the one-shot H-data series to the internal RAM whenever the HW completes a one-shot operation. The HW architecture is designed and simulated by using the design tools mentioned below. Further, VHDL is utilized for the HW design.

- Xilinx-ISE9.1i
- MathWorks – MATLAB/Simulink 2006a
- Xilinx – System Generator for DSP 9.1
- Mentor Graphics – ModelSimXEIII 6.0a

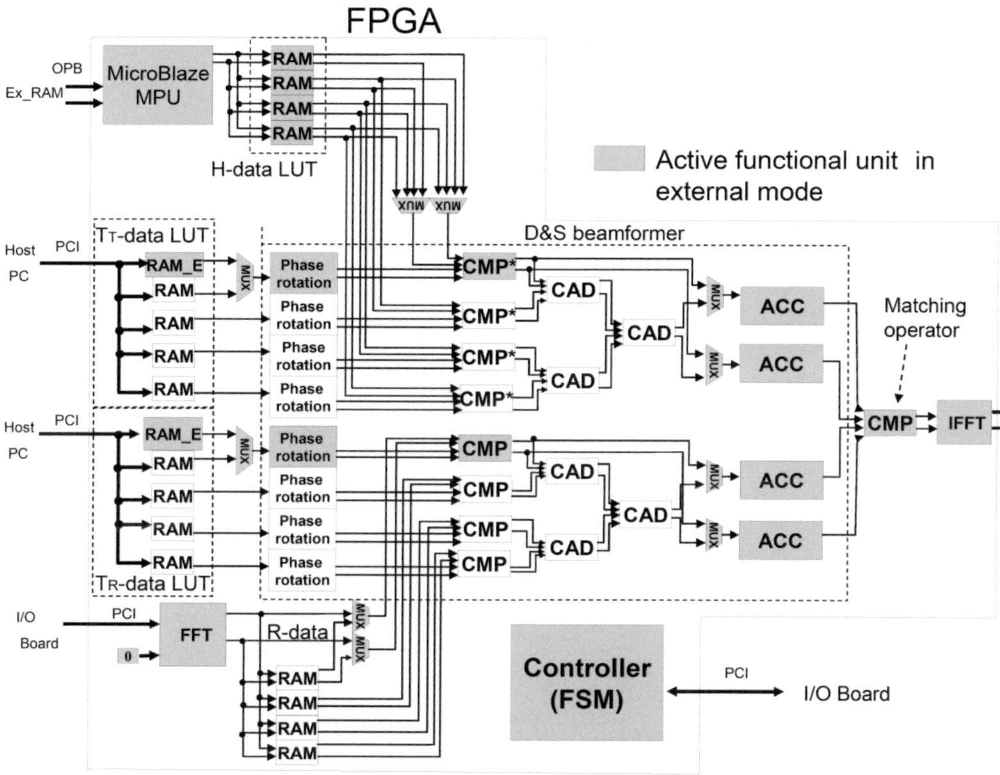

Fig. 14. Schematic diagram of HW.

8. Two operational modes

The HW operates in the following two modes.

External Mode

The HW begins the operation in this mode. A schematic diagram of this mode is shown in Fig. 15. The operation is performed in this mode when the echo data that are transferred from the I/O board are accepted by the FFT operator. This operator processes every 2048-point data (one-channel data length in the time domain), and the output is 512-point data in the frequency domain. RAM_Es are utilized when the HW operates in this mode only; the RAMs keep T-data (data size is 1 [line] × 32 [ch] words) to perform image reconstruction in a direction. The H-data is read from the RAM following the operational output of the FFT operator; the D&S operation and cross-correlation are performed.

The abovementioned operations are performed for every single channel's waveform data. If the operation in a particular direction is completed, then the operational mode is switched to the internal mode.

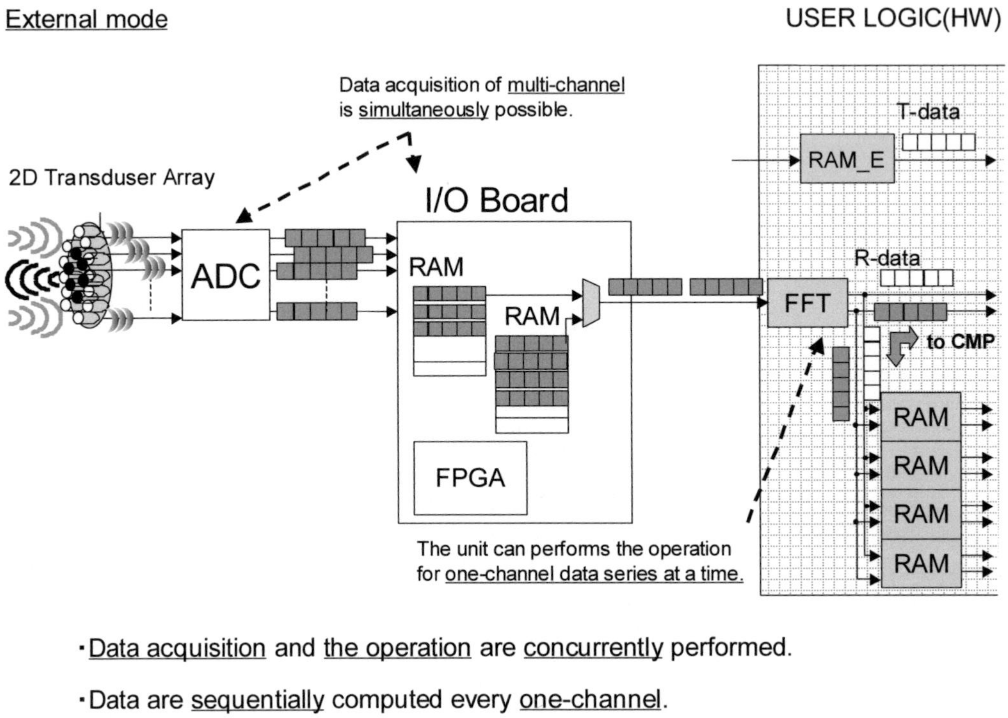

Fig. 15. Schematic diagram for the HW operation in external Mode.

Internal Mode

In the internal mode (Fig. 16), four-channel R- and H-data series are simultaneously read from each RAM; these data are performed in parallel. To perform the operation in parallel, all the functional units, except the front FFT operator and RAM_Es, become active and drive. A schematic diagram of this mode is shown in Fig. 12. The CADs are utilized to sum the waveform data output from the eight CMPs in the D&S beamformer; the summed data series is sent to the ACC as a partial beamform generated by delayed wave data from four channels. The operation of this mode is repeated for all the remaining directions ((64 × 64) - 1 [line]) in the image reconstruction space. When the HW is in this mode, the front FFT operator is in the inactive mode because the data acquisition is completed. However, if the operation in this mode is completed, MicroBlaze transfers the H-data from the external RAM to the internal RAM for the next shot operation. After that, the HW restarts the operation in the external mode.

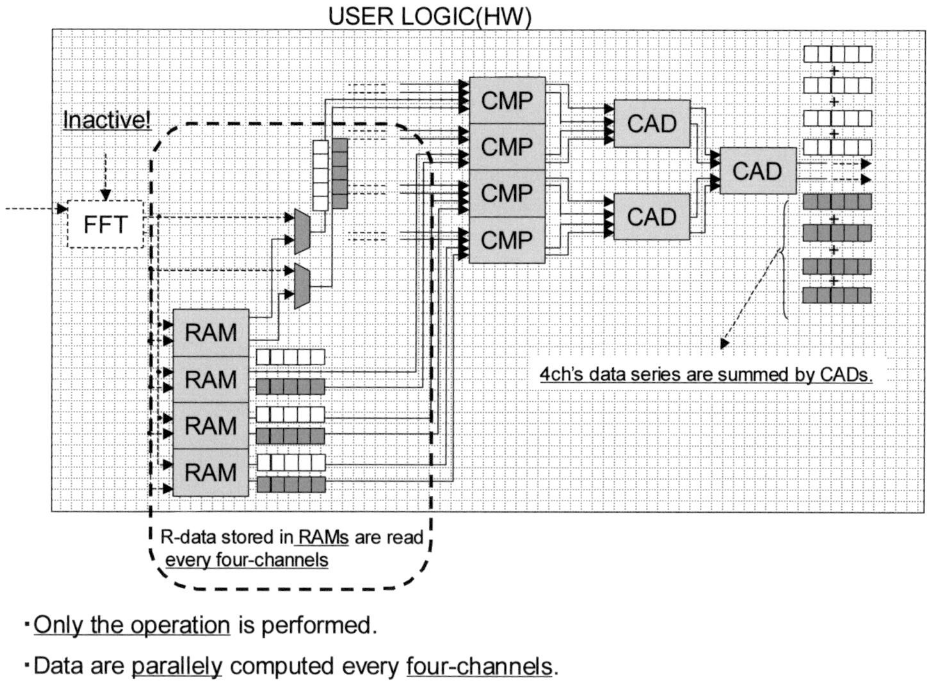

Fig. 16. Schematic diagram for the HW operation in internal mode

The state diagram for the operational flow in the HW is shown in **Fig. 17.** The HW performs the operation following this state transition and as the state transition is repeated.

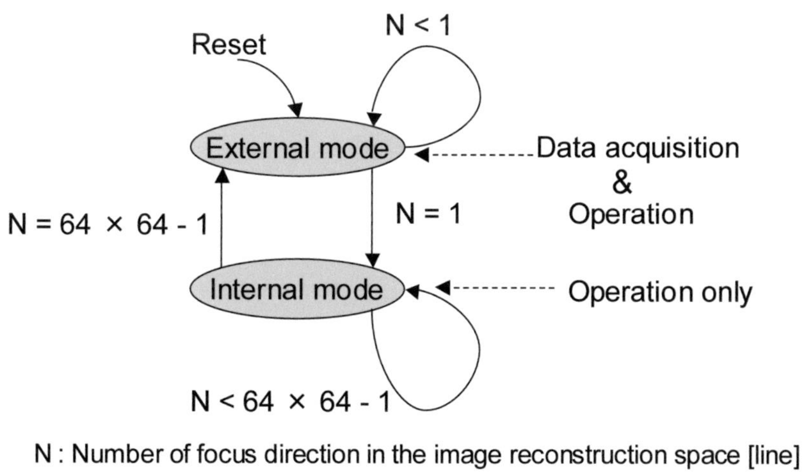

Fig. 17. State diagram for operational flow in the HW.

9. Synthesis result and performance evaluation

We synthesize the HW operation to implement it on an FPGA, and the scale and performance of the HW are evaluated. The target device is XCVFX100 of the Virtex-4 family.

Table 2 lists the device utilization summary for the resources required to implement the HW on the FPGA. Memory resources (FIFO16/RAMB16) are utilized more in comparison to other resources because a number of data with 64 × 64 [line] × 2 × 32 [ch] = 2^{18} words are required as the T-data for the D&S operation. Further, a number of data with 512 [word/ch] × 32 [ch] × 2 (real/imaginary part) = 2^{15} words are required to store the H- and R-data. DSP48s are utilized to construct FFT operators and CMPs; 60 DSP48s are utilized for FFT and IFFT operators; and 36 DSPs are utilized for CMPs.

Resource name	Used/Available	Utilization[%]
Slices	18541/42176	43.9
Slice Flip Flops	20928/84352	24.8
Four input LUTs	27098/84352	32.1
bonded IOBs	122/860	14.1
FIFO16/RAMB16s	350/376	93.0
GCLKs	1/32	3.1
DSP48s	96/160	60.0

Table 2. Device utilization summary for the HW on the FPGA.

With regard to the performance of the HW, the maximum frequency is approximately 137[MHz] (cycle time ≒ 7.3 [ns]).

Next, we evaluate the latency to reconstruct a 3D image. For this, we obtain the number of the operational clock cycles required for a 3D image; the latency is obtained from the number of clock cycles and the maximum frequency. Consequently, the latency for 3D images with a resolution of 64 × 64 × 256 voxels is approximately 170 [ms/frame], and the throughput is approximately 5.9 [frame/s]. When this result is compared with the latency of SW processing (approximately 40 [sec/frame]), the processing speed of HW is approximately 236 times faster than that of SW.

10. Critical path analysis and improvement

Next, we search critical (longest) path and then improve the path by modifying the architecture to the designed HW to raise clock frequency and processing performance. First, the HW is divided into some rough functional units. Then we search each path delay by synthesizing every the divided units. Consequently, there is the critical path on D&S beamformers from the synthesis report.

We search the path in detail again, we specify that the critical path exists on sin/cos table in phase rotation unit (Fig. 19). There is the path delay between input port for multiplier and output for sin/cos table.

So, we modify the implementation type of the table. As the table was implemented utilizing FPGA logic blocks in previous architecture, we change the implementation type utilizing Block RAM which is memory resources in FPGA (Fig. 20). Because FPGA logic block is treated as a combinational block, output signals from the table must be generated passing through plural stage's the logic block passes. Thus, the pass delay becomes longer in proportion to the stages. On the other hand, a table utilizing Block RAM generates by memory access only. Consequently, the pass delay becomes shorter than case of FPGA logic type, the critical path of the HW can be improved.

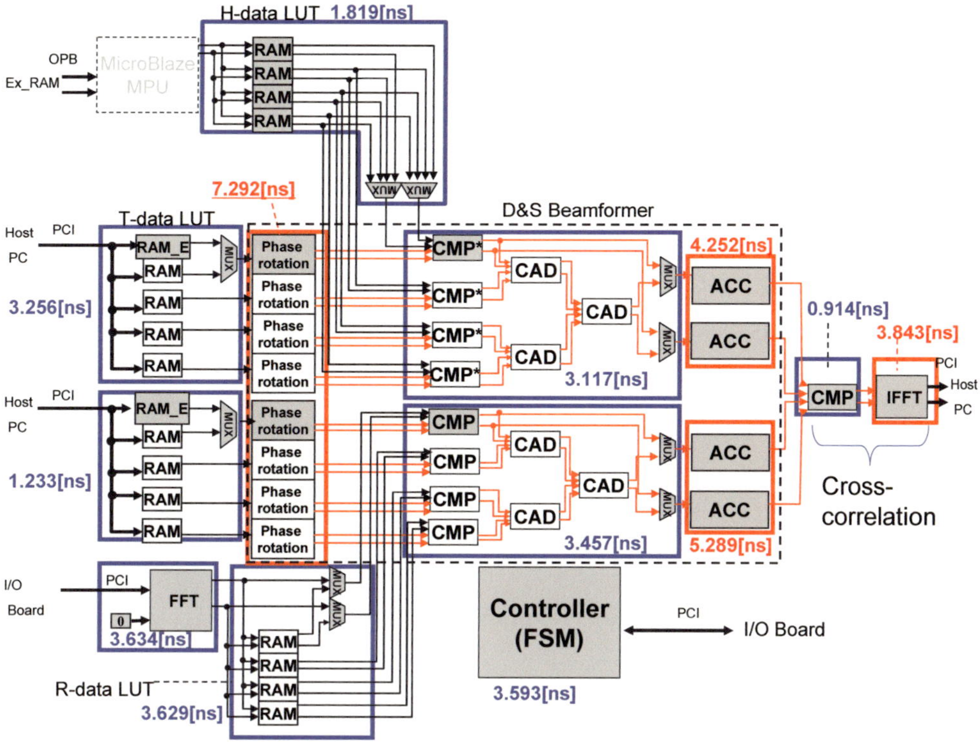

Fig. 18. Path delay for each units.

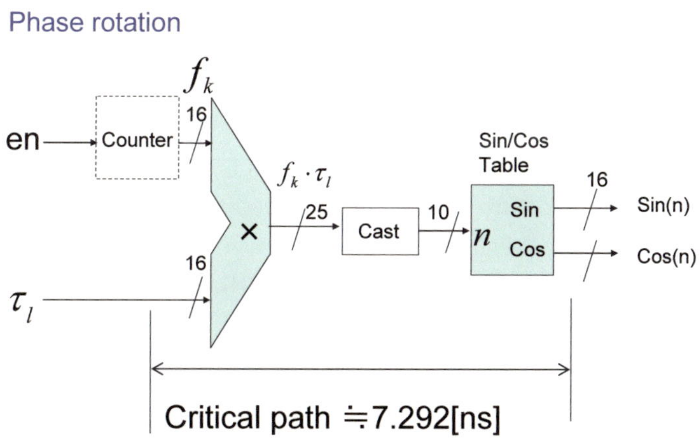

Fig. 19. Critical path in Phase rotation unit.

Subsequently, the next critical path exists on Dual port RAM in ACC of left hand in Fig. 21. In the same way, we modify the implementation type. The Dual port RAM was implanted by Block RAM. As alternative architecture, we implement the ACC utilizing shift register containing enable signal because ACC performs the operation by directly utilizing input data while abovementioned phase rotation unit's operation indirectly is performed by table access. Subsequently, some registers are inserted between CMP in cross-correlation and IFFT core, critical path on the data path is improved.

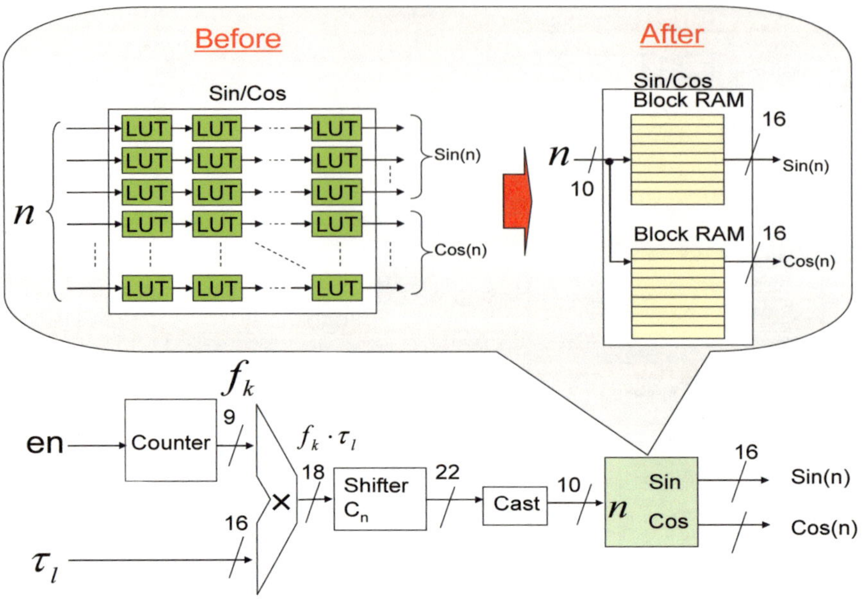

Fig. 20. Modifying sin/cos table based on FPGA structure.

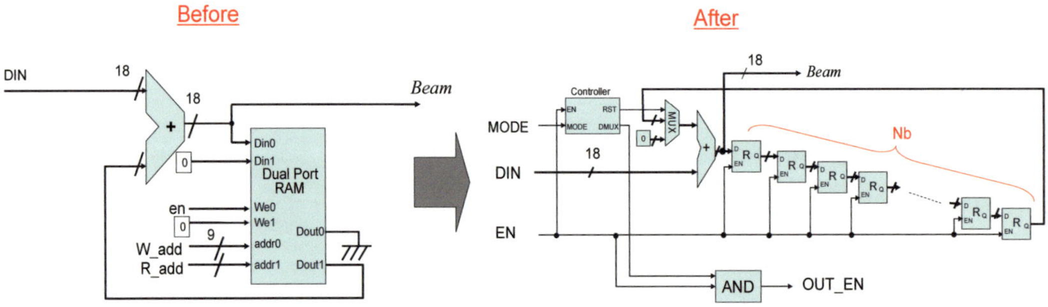

Fig. 21. Modification of architecture based on FPGA resources for ACC.

11. Synthesis result and performance evaluation after architecture improvement

Next, we synthesize the modified HW. Synthesis results are shown into TABLE 3.
Consequently, FPGA logic blocks (Slices and Slice Flip Flops) are utilized in great quantities, HW scale became larger. Because architecture of ACC is improved from Dual port RAM to FPGA logic blocks, a large amount of the logic blocks are comsumed.
Next, we evaluate performance after architecture improvement. Performance comparison is shown in Fig. 22.
Consequently, the maximum frequency is approximately 200 [MHz] (path delay ≒ 5[ns]), the path delay is approximately 32% shorter than previous version. In performance (processing speed) evaluation, the latency is approximately 116 [ms/frame], and the throughput is approximately 8.6 [frame/s].
The modified HW processing is approximately 1.5 times faster than the previous HW, and the processing speed is approximately 350 times faster than above the SW processing.

Resource name	Used/Available	Utilization[%]
Slices	34245 /42176	81.1
Slice Flip Flops	60280 /84352	71.4
Four input LUTs	18035 /84352	21.3
bonded IOBs	122/860	14.1
FIFO16/RAMB16s	376/376	100.0
GCLKs	1/32	3.1
DSP48s	96/160	60.0

Table 3. Device utilization summary for the HW after architecture improvement

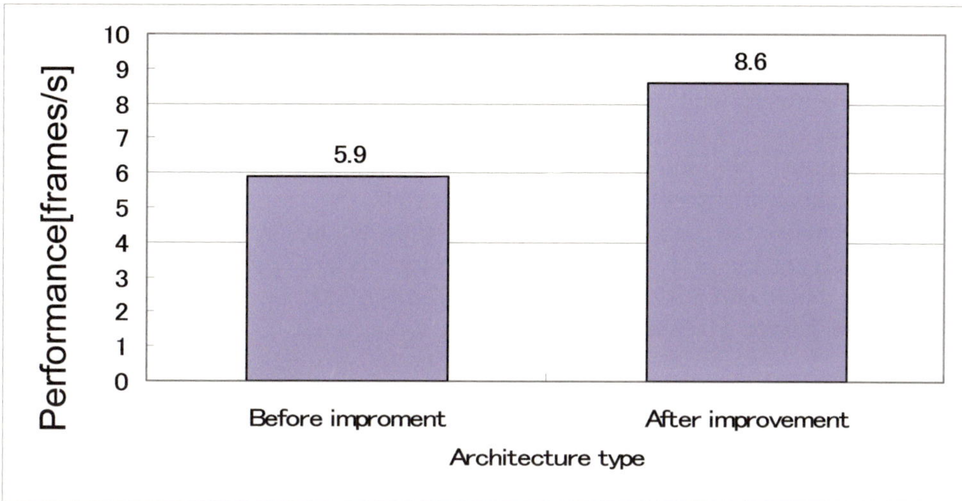

Fig. 22. Performance comparison.

12. Conclusion

In this study, we examined HW implementation on FPGA to realize efficient high-speed computation and lower cost with 3D ultrasound imaging.

Image reconstruction is performed in frequency domain to reduce computational complexity of cross-correlation, designed HW contains tens of complex multipliers and FFT/IFFT units. Also we implemented some operational pipelines to realize parallel D&S which includes the most computational complexity in the operation. By performing the operation in frequency domain, the HW can be obtain high parallelism for HW implementation on FPGA including limited resources.

Moreover the HW drives switching two operational modes according to action of the imaging system to allow efficient operation.

Consequently, the HW's processing speed is approximately 240 times faster than the SW processing. Also, we tried critical path analysis and improvement of the HW, the architecture modification based on FPGA resources was tried. Consequently. The modified HW's processing speed was approximately 1.5 times faster than previous version and 350 times faster than SW processing, respectively.

From the results in this study, we showed an effectiveness to design higher performance HW for FPGA utilizing cleverly its structure.

13. References

[1] Y. Tamura and T. Akatsuka: "A Multiple Shots 3alized Modulating Signals", Acoustical Imaging, 20, pD Holographic Sonar Using a Set of Orthogon, pp737–743, 1993.

[2] Y. Tamura, C. Ishihara, N. Okada, N. Ishii, M. Sato, T. Aoki, T. Hisamoto, and H. Yanagida : "High-Speed 3D Imaging System Using Coded Wavefront Generated by Walsh Function Modulated Signals", Proc. of IEEE UFFC, pp1666–1669 , 2002.

[3] C. Patterson, B. Martin, S. Ellingson, J. Simonetti, and S. Cutchin :"FPGA Cluster Computing in the ETA Radio Telescope", pp25–32, Proceedings of the 2007 International Conference on Field Programmable Technology, ICFPT 2007, Kokurakita, Kitakyushu, Japan, December 2007.

[4] Kentaro Sano, Oliver Pell, Wayne Luk, and Satoru Yamamoto, "FPGA-based Streaming Computation for Lattice Boltzmann Method", pp233–236, Proceedings of the 2007 International Conference on Field Programmable Technology, ICFPT 2007, Kokurakita, Kitakyushu, Japan, December 2007.

[5] Yoshihisa Tanaka, Susumu Kuroyanagi, and Akira Iwata, "A Technique for Hardware Implementation of Neural Networks using FPGA", pp175–182, IEICE technical report. Neurocomputing Vol.100, No.688, March 2001.

[6] K. Satoh, M. Miura, Y. Tamura, H. Yanagida, T. Yamasaki, C. Ishihara, and N. Okada, "Algorithms of 3-dimensional beamforming for synthetic aperture imaging system using pulses coded with Walsh functions", Proc. of IEEE-UFFC Ultrasound Symposium, pp1405–1408, Montreal, Canada, August 2004.

[7] Steven W. Smith, "Digital Signal Processing: A Practical Guide for Engineers and Scientists - chapter9 Applications of the DFT", pp180–184, Newnes, September 2002.

[8] F. Bertora, P. Pellegretti, and A. Questa, "An Alternative Frequency Domain Beam forming", IEEE-UFFC Ultrasound Symposium, pp1749–1752, Montreal Canada, August 2004.

[9] Paul Graham and Brent Nelson, "FPGAs and DSPs for Sonar Processing Inner Loop Computations", Technical Report CCL-1998-GN-1, Con_gurable Computating Laboratory, Electrical and Computer Engineering Department, Brigham Young University, 1998.

[10] Xilinx Co., "Embedded Magazine - The MicroBlaze v5.0 Soft-Processor Core: Optimized for Performance", pp18–21, Xcell Publications.

[11] K. Satoh, J. Tada, and Y. Tamura: "Image Reconstruction Operational Hardware for 3D Ultrasound Imaging", pp43–49, Journal of Society of Signal Processing Applications and Technology of Japan, December 2006.